LAW
QUESTIONS
& ANSWERS

EQUITY & TRUSTS

Questions and Answers Series

Series Editors   Margaret Wilkie and Rosalind Malcolm

Titles in the Series

'A' Level Law
Company Law
EC Law
Employment Law
Equity and Trusts
Family Law
Jurisprudence
Law of Contract
Law of Evidence
Law of Torts

Other titles in preparation

LAW Q&A
QUESTIONS & ANSWERS

EQUITY & TRUSTS

MARGARET WILKIE
Solicitor
Principal Lecturer in Law, University of Westminster

ROSALIND MALCOLM
Barrister
Lecturer in Law, University of Surrey

PETER LUXTON
Solicitor
Lecturer in Law, University of Sheffield

BLACKSTONE
PRESS LIMITED

First published in Great Britain 1994 by Blackstone Press Limited, 9-15 Aldine Street, London W12 8AW. Telephone: 081-740 1173

ISBN 1 85431 305 3

British Library Cataloguing in Publication Data
A CIP catalogue record for this book is available from the British Library

Typeset by Montage Studios Limited, Tonbridge, Kent
Printed by Bell & Bain Limited, Glasgow

Contents

Table of Cases   vii

Table of Statutes   xv

1   Introduction   1

2   The Nature of Equity and the Law of Trusts   4

3   The Three Certainties and Section 53 of the Law of Property Act 1925   20

4   Constitution of Trusts   32

5   Trusts, Powers and Discretionary Trusts   47

6   Charitable Trusts   60

7   Trusts of Imperfect Obligation   79

8   Implied and Resulting Trusts   88

9   Constructive Trusts   100

10   Administration of Trusts   131

11   Breach of Trusts   153

Contents

12 Equitable Doctrines   170

13 Equitable Remedies   179

14 Pick 'n' Mix Questions   198

Index   210

Table of Cases

A-G of the Bahamas v Royal Trust Co. [1986] 1 WLR 1001   71
A-G v Guardian Newspapers Ltd (No. 2) [1990] 1 AC 109   9, 187
A-G v Jacobs-Smith [1895] 2 QB 341, CA   33
Abrahams [1911] 1 Ch 108   147
Adams and the Kensington Vestry, re (1884) 27 ChD 394   23, 24
Agip (Africa) Ltd v Jackson [1989] 3 WLR 1367, [1990] Ch 265, [1991] Ch 547   120, 125,
   129, 130, 155, 157
Allen, re [1953] Ch 810, CA   51
Aluminium Industrie Vaassen BV v Romalpa Aluminium Ltd [1976] 1 WLR 676, CA
   156
American Cyanamid Co. v Ethicon Ltd [1975] AC 396   184, 188, 189, 190, 191, 192, 193
Anton Piller KG v Manufacturing Processes Ltd [1976] Ch 55   10, 182, 183, 188, 192
Ashburn Anstalt v W. J. Arnold & Co. [1988] 2 WLR 706, [1989] Ch 1   12
Astor's Settlement Trusts [1952] Ch 534   69, 81, 83, 85
Atkinson's Will Trusts, re [1978] 1 WLR 586   208
Babanaft International Co. SA v Bassatne [1990] Ch 13   189
Baden's Deed Trusts (No. 1), McPhail v Doulton [1971] AC 424   31, 57
Baden's Deed Trusts (No. 2), re [1973] Ch 9, CA   31, 50, 51
Baden, Delvaux and Lecuit v Societé General pour Favoriser le Development
   du Commerce et de L'Industrie en France SA [1983] BCLR 325   105, 123, 124, 125
   129, 130, 168
Balfour's Settlement, re [1938] Ch 928   54, 55
Bannister v Bannister [1948] 2 All ER 133, CA   104
Banque Belque Pour L'Etranger v Hambrouck [1921] 1 KB 321, CA   156
Barclays Bank Ltd v Quistclose Investments Ltd [1970] AC 567   27
Barlow's Will Trusts, re [1979] 1 WLR 278   31, 50, 51
Barnes v Addy (1874) 9 Ch App 244   105, 122, 127, 128
Bartlett v Barclays Bank Trust Co. Ltd [1980] Ch 515   133, 159, 161
Bateman's Will Trusts, re [1970] 1 WLR 1463   114, 208
Beaumont, re [1902] 1 Ch 889   46
Behnke v Bede Shipping Co. Ltd [1927] 1 KB 649   194
Bell's Indenture, re [1980] 1 WLR 1217   128
Belmont Finance Corporation Ltd v Williams Furniture Ltd [1979] Ch 250   124
Beloved Wilkes' Charity, re (1851) 3 Mac & G 440   133
Benjamin, re [1902] 1 Ch 723   151
Bentley v Craven (1853) 18 Beav 75   121
Best, re [1904] 2 Ch 354   71

Beswick v Beswick [1968] AC 58   39
Binions v Evans [1972] Ch 359, CA   12
Birch v Treasury Solicitor [1951] Ch 298   35, 45, 46
Birmingham v Renfrew (1937) 57 CLR 666   111, 115
Bishop of Oxford v Church Commissioners [1992] 1 WLR 1241   75, 76
Biscoe v Jackson (1887) 35 ChD 460   74
Blackwell v Blackwell [1929] AC 318, HL   116, 208
Blair v Duncan [1902] AC 37   71
Blyth v Fladgate [1891] 1 Ch 327   128
Boardman v Phipps [1967] 2 AC 46, HL   91, 104, 121
Bowman v Secular Society Ltd [1917] AC 406   64
Boyce v Boyce (1849) 16 Sim 476   25
Brier, re (1884) 26 ChD 238, CA   137, 203
Brooker, re [1926] WN 93   143
Brown v Burdett (1882) 21 ChD 667   85
Brumby v Milner [1976] 1 WLR 1096   44
Bucks Constabulary Friendly Society (No. 2) [1979] 1 WLR 936   98
Burns v Burns [1984] Ch 317   91, 104
Burrough v Philcox (1840) 5 My & Cr 72   58, 59
Burroughs-Fowler, re [1916] 2 Ch 251   55
Buttle v Saunders [1950] 2 All ER 193   75, 133
Caffoor v ITC [1961] AC 584, PC   67, 202
Cain v Moon [1896] 2 QB 283   44, 206
Calow v Calow [1928] Ch 710   175
Cannon v Hartley [1949] Ch 213   37, 201
Carl Zeiss Stiftung v Herbert Smith & Co (No. 2) [1969] 2 Ch 276   102, 128, 129
Carreras Rothmans Ltd v Freeman Mathews Treasure Ltd [1985] Ch 207   26
Carrington, re [1932] 1 Ch 1   175
Cavendish-Browne, re [1916] WN 341   38
Chamberlain, re (1976, unreported)   152
Chase Manhatten Bank NA v Israel-British Bank (London) Ltd [1981] Ch 105   156, 157
Chichester Diocesan Fund v Simpson [1944] AC 341   71
Chillingworth v Chambers [1896] 1 Ch 685, CA   160
City Equitable Fire Insurance Co. Ltd, re [1925] 1 Ch 407   137
Christ's Hospital v Grainger (1849) 1 Mac & G 460   70
Clarke, re (1901) 2 Ch 110   83
Clayton v Ashdown (1714) 2 Eq Ab 516   195
Clayton's Case (1816) 1 Mer 572   28, 97, 164, 166
Cleaver re [1981] 1 WLR 939   111
Clore's Settlement Trusts [1966] 1 WLR 955   145
Cohen v Roche [1927] 1 KB 169   194, 195
Cole, re [1958] Ch 877   70
Cole, re [1964] Ch 175   37
Coleman, re (1888) 39 ChD 443   54
Columbia Picture Industries Inc v Robinson [1987] Ch 38   181, 184
Comiskey v Bowring-Hanbury [1905] AC 84   21, 23, 24
Compton, re [1945] Ch 123, CA   67, 68, 201
Cook, re [1948] Ch 212   176
Cook's Settlement Trusts, re [1965] Ch 902   33, 38, 39, 201
Cooke v Head [1972] 1 WLR 518, CA   11, 103
Cooper, re [1939] Ch 811   118
Cottam, re [1955] 1 WLR 1299   74
Coulthurst, re [1951] Ch 661, CA   67
Cowan v Scargill [1985] Ch 270   75
Cowan de Groot Properties Ltd v Eagle Trust plc [1992] 4 All ER 700   105, 125, 129

Cowcher v Cowcher [1972] 1 WLR 425   10, 103
Craven's Estate, re [1937] Ch 423   45
Cross v Lloyd-Greame (1909) 102 LT 163   66
Cunnack v Edwards [1896] 2 Ch 679   97, 98
Davenport v Bishopp (1843) 2 Y & C Ch Cas 451   34
Davis v Richards & Wallington Ltd [1990] 1 WLR 1511   98
De Carteret, re [1933] Ch 103   66
De Francesco v Barnum (1890) 45 ChD 430   186
Dean, re (1889) 41 ChD 552   82
Denley's Trust Deed, re [1968] 1 Ch 373   83, 87
Densham Re [1975] 1 WLR 1519   109
Derby & Co. Ltd v Weldon (No. 3 and No. 4) (1989) 139 NLJ 11   11
Detmold, re (1889) 40 ChD 585   55
Dillwyn v Llewelyn (1862) 4 De DF & J 517   12, 35
Dimes v Scott (1828) 4 Russ 195   160
Dingle v Turner [1972] AC 601   67
Diplock, re [1951] AC 251, HL   129
Diplock, re [1948] Ch 465, CA   42, 153, 155, 157, 158, 162, 163, 164, 168, 169
Drummond, re [1914] 2 Ch 90   74
Dudman, re [1925] 1 Ch 553   45
Duffield v Elwes (1827) 1 Bli NS 497   46
Dupree's Deed Trusts, re [1945] Ch 16   63, 66
Eagle Trust plc v SBC Securities Ltd [1992] 4 All ER 488   125, 130
Earl of Chesterfield's Trusts, re (1883) 24 ChD 643   142, 144
Earl of Oxford's case (1615) 1 Rep Ch 1   17
Elias v Mitchell [1972] Ch 632   172
Emanuel v Emanuel [1982] 1 WLR 669   182
EMI Ltd v Pandit [1975] 1 WLR 302   182
Endacott, re [1960] Ch 232, CA   49, 81
Estate of Monica Dale (deceased), re (1993) *The Times*, 16 February   111, 115
Eves v Eves [1975] 1 WLR 1338, CA   9, 11, 91, 104, 105, 107
EVTR Ltd, re [1987] BCLC 646   28
Falconer v Falconer [1970] 1 WLR 1333, CA   108
Faraker, re [1912] 2 Ch 488   73
Farley v Westminster Bank Ltd [1939] AC 430, HL   64
Fellowes & Son v Fisher [1976] QB 122   191
Fletcher v Fletcher (1844) 4 Hare 67   34, 39, 201
Fletcher v Green (1864) 33 Beav 426   160
Flight v Bolland (1824) 4 Russ 298   195
Foord, re [1922] 2 Ch 519   95
Fowkes v Pascoe (1875) 10 Ch App 343   93
Fry, re [1946] Ch 312   41
Fry v Tapson (1884) 28 ChD   137
Gardner (No. 2), re [1923] 2 Ch 230   114, 117
Gartside v IRC [1968] AC 553   58
Gee, re [1948] Ch 284   120
George, re (1877) 5 ChD 837   147
General Accident Fire and Life Assurance Corporation Ltd v IRC [1963] 1 WLR 1207
   54, 55
Gestetner's Settlement, re [1953] Ch 672   57, 59, 135
Gibbard's Will Trusts [1967] 1 WLR 42   50
Gillingham Bus Disaster Fund, re [1958] Ch 300, [1959] Ch 62, CA   77, 97
Gilmour v Coates [1949] AC 426, HL   68
Gissing v Gissing [1971] AC 886, HL   91, 103, 104, 106, 107
GKN Bolts & Nuts Ltd (Automotive Division) Birmingham Works Sports and Social Club,
   re [1982] 1 WLR 774   98

Golay's Will Trust, re [1965] 1 WLR 969   24, 208
Goldschmidt, re [1957] 1 WLR 524   74
Gonin, re [1979] Ch 16   42
Gooch, re (1890) 62 LT 384   94
Good's Will Trusts, re [1950] 2 All ER 653   74
Gordon's Will Trusts, re [1978] 2 WLR 755, [1978] Ch 145   177
Goswell's Trusts [1915] 2 Ch 106   172
Grant v Edwards [1986] Ch 638   92, 108
Grant's Will Trusts, re [1980] 1 WLR 360   83, 86
Grey v IRC [1960] AC 1   38
Grimthorpe [1908] 2 Ch 675   172
Guild v IRC [1992] 2 WLR 397, [1992] 2 All ER 10, [1992] AC 310   62, 63, 67
Guinness plc v Saunders [1990] 1 All ER 652, [1990] 2 AC 663   121
Gulbenkian's Settlements, re [1968] Ch 126, CA   50
Gulbenkian's Settlements [1970] AC 508, HL   57, 205
Gulbenkian's Settlement Trusts (No. 2), re [1970] 1 Ch 408   50
Hagger, re [1930] 2 Ch 190   111
Haines, re, The Times, 7 November 1952   82
Hallett's Estate, re (1880) 13 ChD 696   156, 166, 167
Hamilton, re [1895] 2 Ch 370   23
Hay's Settlement Trusts, re [1982] 1 WLR 202   57, 206
Hetherington, re, Gibbs v McDonnell [1990] Ch 1   68
Hillier, re [1954] 1 WLR 700   77
Hobourn Air Raid Distress Fund, re [1946] Ch 194   96
Hodgson v Marks [1971] Ch 892   94
Holder v Holder [1968] Ch 353, CA   43
Holt v Heatherfield Trust Ltd [1942] 2 KB 1   42
Holt's Settlement, re [1969] 1 Ch 100   14
Howard, re, The Times, 30 October 1908   82
Howe v Earl of Dartmouth (1802) 7 Ves 137   15, 142, 143, 144, 145, 173
Hubbard v Pit [1976] QB 142   191
Huguenin v Baseley (1807) 14 Ves 273   117-118
Hussey v Palmer [1972] 1 WLR 1286, CA   11, 91, 102, 103, 108
Hytrac Conveyors Ltd v Conveyors International Ltd [1983] 1 WLR 44   184
Inwards v Baker [1965] 2 QB 29, CA   112
IRC v Baddeley [1955] AC 572, HL   67
IRC v Broadway Cottages Trust [1955] Ch 20, CA   50
IRC v City of Glasgow Police Athletic Association [1953] AC 380   62
IRC v Educational Grants Association Ltd [1967] Ch 993, CA   67, 202
IRC v McMullen [1981] AC 1   62, 63
IRC v Temperance Council (1926) 136 LT 27   65
Isaacs, re [1894] 3 Ch 506   175
Ives (ER) Investment Ltd v High [1967] 2 QB 379   113
J. T. Stratford & Son Ltd v Lindley [1965] AC 269   190
Jaffa v Taylor Galleries (unreported, 1991)   37
James, re [1935] Ch 449   42
Jefferys v Jefferys (1841) Cr & Ph 138   34
Jeune v Queens Cross Properties Ltd [1974] Ch 97   196
Jones v Lipman [1962] 1 WLR 832   195
Jones v Lock (1865) LR 1 Ch App 25   30, 204
Karak Rubber Co. Ltd v Burden (No. 2) [1972] 1 WLR 602   123, 124, 125
Kay's Settlement, re [1939] Ch 329   34, 38, 39, 201
Kayford Ltd, re [1975] 1 WLR 279   26, 27
Keech v Sandford (1726) Sel Cas Ch 61   104, 120

Keen, re [1937] Ch 236, CA   114, 208
Kelly, re [1932] IR 255   82
Klug v Klug [1918] 2 Ch 67   134
Knight v Knight (1840) 3 Beav 148   23
Knocker v Youle [1986] 1 WLR 934   150
Koeppler's WT, re [1986] Ch 423   65, 82
Koettgen's Will Trusts, re [1954] Ch 252   67, 201, 202
Kolb's Will Trusts, re [1962] Ch 531   24, 140, 141
Lacey, ex parte (1802) 6 Ves 625   121
Lambe v Eames (1871) 6 Ch App 597   23, 207
Lawes v Bennett (1785) 1 Cox Eq Cas 167   13, 15, 173, 175
Leahy v A-G (NW) [1959] AC 457   83
Leaper, re [1916] 1 Ch 579   46
Learoyd v Whiteley (1887) 12 App Cas 727, HL   133
Lechmere v Earl of Carlisle (1733) 3 P Wms 211   171
Leek, re [1969] 1 Ch 563, CA   50
Lepton's Charity, re [1972] Ch 276   73
Lillingston, re [1952] 2 All ER 184   45
Lipinski's Will Trusts, re [1976] Ch 235   83, 85, 87
Lipkin Gorman v Karpnale [1991] 3 WLR 10, [1991] 2 AC 548   154, 156, 162, 164, 168
Lipkin Gorman v Karpnale (1986) NLJ 659   124
Lister & Co. v Stubbs (1890) 45 ChD 1   155
Llewellin, re [1949] Ch 225   120
Lloyd's Bank Ltd v Rosset [1991] AC 107   11, 104, 107
Lock International plc v Beswick [1989] 1 WLR 1268   182, 183
Londonderry's Settlement, re [1965] Ch 918, CA   134
London Wine Co. (Shippers) Ltd, re (1975) 126 NLJ 977   28
Lord Dudley and Ward v Lady Dudley (1705) Prec Ch 241   19
Lucking's Will Trusts, re [1968] 1 WLR 866   138, 160, 203
Lumley v Wagner (1852) 1 De G M & G 604   187
Lysaght, re [1966] 1 Ch 191   74
Lyus v Prowsa Developments Ltd [1982] 1 WLR 1044   104
Macadam, re [1946] Ch 73   104, 120
Maddock, re [1902] 2 Ch 220   117
Mallott v Wilson [1903] 2 Ch 494   42
Manisty's Settlement, re [1974] Ch 17   51, 205
Mara v Browne [1896] 1 Ch 199   128
Mareva Compañía Naviera SA v International Bulkcarriers SA [1975] 2 Lloyd's
    Rep 509   11, 188, 192
Mariette, re [1915] 2 Ch 284   62
Mascall v Mascall (1985) 49 P & CR 119   42
Mason v Farbrother [1983] 2 All ER 1078   141
Mayo, re [1943] Ch 302   70
McCormick v Grogan (1869) LR 4 HL 82   116
McGeorge [1963] Ch 544   148
McGovern v A-G [1982] Ch 321   64
McPhail v Doulton [1971] AC 424   31, 49, 50, 51, 57, 135, 202, 205
Mills, re [1930] 1 Ch 654   57
Mills v Shields [1948] IR 367   45
Milroy v Lord (1862) 4 De GF & J 264   30, 33, 37, 38, 41, 200
Ministry of Health v Simpson [1951] AC 251, HL   164, 168
Moncrieff's Settlement Trusts, re [1962] 1 WLR 1344   150
Montagu's Settlement Trusts, re [1987] 1 Ch 264   123, 124, 127, 128, 129
Morice v Bishop of Durham (1804) 9 Ves 399, (1805) 10 Ves 522   69, 71, 81, 84

Moss, re [1949] 1 All ER 495   82
Mussoorie Bank Ltd v Raynor (1882) 7 App Cas 321   22, 207
Mustapha, re (1891) 8 TLR 160   45
National Anti-Vivisection Society v IRC [1948] AC 31, HL   64, 66
Neville Estates Ltd v Madden [1962] Ch 832   68, 83, 86
Niyazi's Will Trusts, re [1978] 1 WLR 910   74
Nottage, re [1895] 2 Ch 649, CA   62
NWL Ltd v Woods [1979] 1 WLR 1294   189, 192
Oatway, re [1903] 2 Ch 356   167
Oldham, re [1925] Ch 75   110
Oppenheim v Tobacco Securities Trust Co. Ltd [1951] AC 297   67
O'Rourke v Darbishire [1920] AC 581, HL   134
Ottaway v Norman [1972] Ch 698   114, 115
Oughtred v IRC [1960] AC 206, HL   14
Pascoe v Turner [1979] 1 WLR 431   35, 112
Patel v Ali [1984] Ch 283   195
Paul v Constance [1977] 1 WLR 527   27, 204
Paul v Paul (1882) 20 ChD 742   34
Pauling's Settlement Trusts, re [1964] Ch 303, CA   145, 159
Pemsel's Case [1891] AC 531   62, 63, 64, 66, 74, 77, 81, 201
Pilkington v IRC [1964] AC 612, HL   145
Pinion, re [1965] Ch 85, CA   66
Plumptre, re [1910] 1 Ch 609   33, 38, 42, 200
Polly Peck International plc v Nadir (No. 2) [1992] 4 All ER 764, CA   130
Posner v Scott-Lewis [1987] Ch 25   196, 197
Price v Strange [1978] Ch 337   195
Printers, re [1899] 2 Ch 184   97
Protheroe v Protheroe [1968] 1 WLR 519, CA   120
Pryce, re [1917] 1 Ch 234   38, 39, 201
Pusey v Pusey (1684) 1 Vern 273   194, 195
R v District Auditor, ex parte West Yorkshire County Council (1986) 26 RVR 24   51, 205
Ralli's Will Trusts, re [1964] Ch 288   35, 36, 37, 42
Raine, re [1929] 1 Ch 716   146
Rank Film Distributors Ltd v Video Information Centre [1982] AC 380   184
Reading v A-G [1951] AC 507, HL   104, 120
Recher's Will Trusts, re [1972] Ch 526   84, 86, 87, 97, 98
Rees, re [1950] Ch 204, CA   43
Regal (Hastings) v Gulliver [1942] 1 All ER 378, HL   121
Resch, re [1969] 1 AC 514   77
Richards v Delbridge (1874) LR 18 Eq 11   204
Richardson v Chapman (1760) 7 Bro PC 318   135
Richardson's Will Trusts, re [1958] Ch 504   54
Rochefoucauld v Bousted [1897] 1 Ch 196   104
Rose, re [1952] Ch 499, CA   38, 40, 41, 42, 200
Ryan v Mutual Tontine Westminster Chambers Association [1893] 1 Ch 116   196
Salt v Cooper (1880) 16 ChD 544   8
Sanders' Will Trusts, re [1954] Ch 265   74
Saulnier v Anderson (1987) 43 DLR (4th) 19   45
Saunders v Vautier (1841) 10 LJ Ch 354, (1841) 4 Beav 115   58, 134
Scawin v Scawin (1841) 1 Y & CCC 65   93
Scarisbrick, re [1944] Ch 229   68
Scott Ltd v Scott's Trustees [1959] AC 763   41
Seager v Copydex Ltd [1967] 1 WLR 923   8
Seager v Copydex Ltd (No. 2) [1969] 1 WLR 809   188

Seale's Marriage Settlement, re [1961] Ch 574   151
Selangor United Rubber Estates Ltd v Cradock (Bankrupt) (No. 3) [1968] 1 WLR 1555
    105, 123, 124, 125, 127
Sen v Headley [1991] 2 All ER 636, [1991] Ch 425   44, 46, 206
Sharpe, re [1980] 1 WLR 219   12
Sick and Funeral Society of St John's Sunday School, Golcar, re [1973] Ch 51   98
Simson, re [1946] Ch 299   64
Sinclair v Brougham [1914] AC 398, HL   155, 156, 162, 167
Smith v Cooke [1891] AC 297   95
Smith v Inner London Education Authority [1978] 1 All ER 411   192
Snowden (deceased) re [1979] Ch 528   115
Speight v Gaunt (1883) 9 App Cas 1   132, 133, 137, 203
Sprange v Barnard (1789) 2 Bro CC 585   31, 114
Springette v Defoe (1992) 24 HLR 552, CA   107
St Andrews Allotment Association, re [1969] 1 WLR 229   97, 98
Stead, re [1900] 1 Ch 237   117, 118
Steel v Wellcome Custodian Trustees Ltd [1988] 1 WLR 167   141
Steele's Will Trusts, re [1948] Ch 603   23
Stephens, re (1892) 8 TLR 792   62, 72
Stevenson v Wilson 1907 SC 445   41
Stewart, re [1908] 2 Ch 251   43
Stimpson, re [1931] 2 Ch 77   144
Strong v Bird (1874) LR 18 Eq 315   34, 42, 43
Suffert's Settlement, re [1961] Ch 1   150
Sutton, re (1885) 28 ChD 464   71
Sweeting (deceased), re [1988] 1 All ER 1016   15, 173, 175
Tate Access Floors Inc. v Boswell [1991] Ch 512   184
Taylor v Plumer (1815) 3 M & S 562   154
Thornton v Howe (1862) 31 Beav 14   66, 68
Tilley's Will Trusts [1967] Ch 1179   167
Tinsley v Milligan (1993) The Times, 28 June   7
Trollope, re [1927] 1 Ch 596   143
Trustees of the British Museum v A-G [1984] 1 WLR 418   141
Tyler, re [1967] 1 WLR 1269   43
Ulverston, re [1956] Ch 622   77
Universal Thermosensors Ltd v Hibben & Others [1992] 1 WLR 840, [1992] 3 All ER 257
    11, 182, 184, 188
United Scientific Holdings Ltd v Burnley Borough Council [1978] AC 904   6
Van den Bergh's Will Trusts [1943] 1 All ER 935   178
Vandervell v IRC [1967] 2 AC 291, HL   42, 90
Vandervell's Trusts (No. 2) re [1974] Ch 269   90, 93, 204
Vickery, re [1931] 1 Ch 572   136, 137, 138, 160, 202, 203
Vinogradoff, re [1935] WN 68   89, 93
Wakeham v Mackenzie [1968] 1 WLR 1175   112
Walsh v Lonsdale (1882) 20 ChD 9   7, 14
Warburton v Warburton (1702) 4 Bro PC 1   135
Warner Bros Pictures Inc. v Nelson [1937] 1 KB 209   187
Warren v Gurney [1944] 2 All ER 472, CA   93
Warren v Mendy [1989] 1 WLR 853   187
Waterman's Will Trusts, re [1952] 2 All ER 1054   133
Watson, re [1973] 1 WLR 1472   66, 68
Wedgwood, re [1915] 1 Ch 113   64, 82
Weeding v Weeding (1861) 1 J & M 424   173
Weekes' Settlement, re [1897] 1 Ch 289   59

Weston, re [1969] 1 Ch 223   151
West Sussex Constabulary's Widows, Children and Benevolent Fund Trusts, re
    [1971] Ch 1   97, 98
Whiteley, re [1910] 1 Ch 608   70
Whitwood Chemical Co. v Hardman [1891] 2 Ch 416   187
Wilkes v Allington [1931] 2 Ch 104   45
Williams-Ashman v Price and Williams [1942] 1 Ch 219   123, 127
Williams & Glyn's Bank Ltd v Boland [1981] AC 487, HL   13, 14, 172
Wilson, re [1913] 1 Ch 314   70, 74
Windeatt's Will Trusts, re [1969] 1 WLR 692   152
Wittke, re [1944] Ch 166   53, 55
Wolverhampton Corporation v Emmons [1901] 1 KB 515, CA   196
Woodhams, re [1981] 1 WLR 493   74
Wright v Morgan [1926] AC 788   121
Young, re [1951] Ch 344   114, 117

Table of Statutes

Chancery Amendment Act 1858   7, 18
Charities Act 1960   72, 73, 77
Charities Act 1985   73
Charities Act 1993   75
   s. 13   72, 73, 74
   s. 13(a)   72
   s. 13(a)(ii)   73
   s. 13(b)   72, 73
   s. 13(c)   72
   s. 13(d)   73
   s. 13(e)(i)   72
   s. 13(e)(ii)   72
   s. 13(e)(iii)   73
   s. 13(2)   73
   s. 14   75, 77
   s. 14(1)   77, 78
   s. 14(3)   78
   s. 14(4)   78
   s. 14(5)   78
   s. 74   73
   s. 74(2)(c)   73
   s. 74(5)   73
Common Law Procedure Act 1854   18
   s. 79   7
Companies Act 1948   124
Companies Act 1985   124

Employment Protection Act 1975   191
Executors Act 1830   23, 207

Judicature Act 1873   6, 7, 18
Judicature Act 1875   7, 18

Land Charges Act 1972   8

Land Registration Act 1925   8, 104, 172
   s. 54(1)   172
   s. 70(1)(g)   14, 172
Landlord and Tenant Act 1985, s. 17   197
Law of Property Act 1925   145
   s. 28(2)   143, 144, 173
   s. 33   48
   s. 34   174-5, 176
   s. 40   104, 112
   s. 41   6
   s. 52   206
   s. 53   27
   s. 53(1)   89
   s. 53(1)(b)   29, 91
   s. 53(1)(c)   38, 98
   s. 53(2)   14, 89
   s. 60(3)   94
   s. 175   147, 148
Law of Property (Miscellaneous
   Provisions) Act 1989   112
   s. 2   14
Limitation Act 1980, s. 21(3)   159

Matrimonial Causes Act 1973   54, 106
Matrimonial Proceedings and Property
   Act 1970, s. 37   106-7

Recreational Charities Act 1958   61, 63

Sale of Goods Act 1979, s. 52   194
Settled Land Act 1925   144, 145
   s. 73   143
Suicide Act 1961   45

Supreme Court Act 1981   180
  s. 37   193
  s. 37(3)   188

Trade Union and Labour Relations Act
  1974   180
  s. 16   186
  s. 17(1)   189
  s. 17(2)   189, 191, 192
Trustee Act 1925   147
  s. 9   160
  s. 23(1)   136, 137, 202
  s. 30   159, 160, 202, 203
  s. 30(1)   137-8
  s. 31   146, 147, 148
  s. 31(1)   147, 148
  s. 31(1)(ii)   148
  s. 31(2)   147
  s. 31(3)   146
  s. 32   53, 139, 142, 144, 145
  s. 33   53, 54, 55
  s. 33(1)(i)   54

Trustees Act 1925 — *continued*
  s. 61   133, 137, 159
  s. 69(2)   147
Trustee Act 1957   140
Trustee Investments Act 1961
  138,140, 143
  s. 15   140
  s. 2(3)   139
  s. 2(3)(a)   139
  s. 2(3)(b)   139-40
  s. 3   140
  s. 3(1)   140
  s. 6(1)   140
  s. 6(1)(a)   140
  s. 6(1)(b)   140

Variation of Trusts Act 1958   149, 151
  s. 1   140, 149
  s. 1(1)(a)-(d)   149-50, 151

Wills Act 1837   104, 116, 117, 208
  s. 9   116

1 Introduction

This book has been written by three lecturers with many years' experience of researching and teaching equity and trusts on different law degree courses at various universities. It is an attempt to give guidance to students on what is expected in the answer to typical questions on the topic (and also, in some instances, on what is superfluous and irrelevant!). We have, in places, pointed out what might distinguish a good answer (class 2(i) or better) from one of a lower quality.

We are acutely aware that many institutions are now adopting assessed coursework as part of their total mark for a subject at the end of the year. Where we feel that the topic is one which might lend itself to this type of coursework, we have included, in the introduction to the question, references to academic articles and further cases which would assist in a deeper study of the area. Very often, assessed coursework will stipulate a maximum limit on the number of words you should write. If this is the case, then you should keep within such limits. This may well require careful planning and balancing of the material in your answer, part of the exercise being to test your ability to write clearly and concisely.

Although the material in all equity and trusts courses will have a large part in common, individual lecturers may accord parts of the subject more extensive treatment. It would be a foolish student indeed who did not heed the emphasis given by his or her lecturer to any particular parts of the course. If your lecturer has, for instance, written a book on charities, it is likely to be a subject dear to the heart and one which will be taught and examined.

Many of the questions on equity and trusts are likely to be problem questions. In dealing with a problem-type examination paper in particular, it is wise to spend a good few minutes at the beginning carefully reading the questions. Ignore the student next to you with a scratchy pen who turns over the first page of the answer book while you are still thinking. There is nothing more deflating than realising, on an examination post mortem, that there was a question on the paper in which you could have done well . . . much better than one you did attempt!

Equally important for essay and problem questions is to spend a few minutes, before you actually embark on writing your answer, in jotting down a rough plan of what should be included. This should be brief — perhaps just a few key words or case names, which you can then expand to a paragraph in your answer. You will have been intelligent enough to calculate the time available for each question (after allowing time for reading the paper thoroughly at the beginning) and you should then keep to your plan: avoid writing excessively on a point which interests you to the detriment of other parts of the question. It is a common experience for examiners to find that the first two or three pages of some examination scripts contain nothing of relevance at all. We suspect those are the scripts of candidates who start writing from the first moment, without allowing prior pause for thought.

There are a few other obvious techniques which will endear you to your examiner. Leave the margins on your answer book clear — they are for your examiners' use and not yours. Start each question on a new page and number not only the question clearly, but also the different parts of it. Leave a line between each part. Illegible writing is a handicap in life, but especially so in the examination room. It may not in itself lose you marks, but it will irritate your examiner. Also, an examiner whose attention is directed to deciphering a barely legible script is less likely to be able to follow the argument you are putting forward, which could possibly result in lost marks. Spelling has been called a low form of cunning, but it is important and if it is not your forte, it is worth working on it. This is especially so with legal terms and judges' names. If you do not wish to give the impression you have never opened a law book in your life, you should try to avoid crass errors. (Candidates attempting charity answers, please note: the judge who laid down the four heads of charity was Lord Macnaghten — there is no 'u' in the name and the 'n' is not capital.)

If you suffer from dyslexia, or have an impairment which might affect your ability to write, you might consider it a good idea to mention it to your tutor in advance of your examination. Most institutions are willing to make allowances for this. Some, for example, are prepared to give extra time at the examination, or extra facilities such as the provision of an amanuensis.

The most important point of all is to be sure to ANSWER THE QUESTION YOU ARE ASKED rather than the question you would like to have been asked (perhaps because you revised it in detail the night before). You are unlikely to get marks for irrelevant material and you risk trying the patience of your examiner, which may be wearing thin by the hundred and first script — which just happens to be yours. Avoid writing a treatise on the law on the subject raised by the question — seldom do questions say, 'Write all you know about . . .' Above all, assume that all legalities relating to the problem are in order, unless the question specifically suggests otherwise: do not look a gift horse in the mouth. For example, it is not necessary to set out the requirements for a valid will or a valid trust if the question simply states that a will or a trust was made with no indication of any flaws.

Good reading, and good luck!

2   The Nature of Equity and the Law of Trusts

INTRODUCTION

The topics covered by this chapter are, by their very nature, bound to be broad and discursive. If you took the opportunity at the beginning of your course (or even during the preceding summer vacation) to undertake some of the general reading recommended by your lecturer, you will reap your reward here. Success in answering these questions depends on a broad reading of the available literature and an historical, even philosophical, approach. You may largely ignore the minutiae of the law reports in favour of a jurisprudential understanding of the development of equity and its doctrinal bases.

The relevant literature includes: Maitland, F. W., *Equity*, 2nd edn, Cambridge University Press, 1936; Holdsworth, W., *History of English Law*, 7th edn, London: Sweet & Maxwell; Snell, E., *Principles of Equity*, 29th edn, London: Sweet & Maxwell 1991; Pollock, F., *Jurisprudence and Legal Essays*, London: Macmillan, 1961; Ashburner, *Principles of Equity*, 1st edn, 1902.

Check your own reading list for additional material recommended by your lecturer.

The chapter contains four essay questions. The usual principles apply in tackling such questions in exam conditions: draw up a plan in rough and stick to it; do not ramble; make a series of points; write a conclusion.

However, there is a difference in answering essay questions of this type and some of the essay questions covered in the rest of the book. Essays that require discussion of substantive law do, at least, start with something on which to hang your hat. An essay, for example, on the development of the *Anton Piller* order, or on the constructive trust, requires an analysis of a sequence of case law. If you know half a dozen cases on the point, then the art is to angle them at the question. Different essay titles on the same area of substantive law usually require the same case law but with a different nose! Essay questions on highly theoretical subjects do require a different style. They require a factual base and plenty of examples of the points you are making, but for high marks they need a touch of original thinking. Even if your thinking is not original, they require a thoughtful intellectual analysis of other people's thinking. If you have not thought about the issues raised by these questions before you enter the examination room, then you are not going to achieve high marks on these questions. If you have the makings of a highly practical lawyer, then select a problem question!

It is quite likely that these topics could crop up as assessed essay questions. If so, then a long session in the library is the starting point. Conduct your preparation for the essay as if you were undertaking a piece of research. Survey the literature noting carefully your sources. Then think over your arguments. Do you agree with X that there has been a fusion of law and equity or do you agree with Y that there has not? Why do you agree or disagree? Do you see both sides of the argument? Argue the case with your friends then write it up while the adrenaline is flowing.

QUESTION 1

The innate conservatism of English lawyers may have made them slow to recognise that by the Judicature Act 1873 the two systems of substantive and adjectival law formerly administered by courts of law and courts of equity . . . were fused. As at the confluence of the Rhone and the Saone, it may be possible for a short distance to discern the source from which each part of the combined stream came, but there comes a point at which this ceases to be possible. If Professor Ashburner's fluvial metaphor is to be retained at all, the confluent streams of law and equity have surely mingled now. (Lord Diplock in *United Scientific Holdings Ltd* v *Burnley Borough Council* [1978] AC 904).

Discuss.

Commentary

It is interesting to note that there are several statements from judges of the highest seniority which concur with the statement of Lord Diplock quoted above, at least to the extent that they consider that this issue is redundant and the combined effect of the systems should be considered. See, for example, Lord Evershed, (1948) JSPTL 180, Lord Denning, (1952) CLP 1, and in *Landmarks in the Law* (Butterworths, 1984). Academic writers seem, in general, to take a different view. So, the question is provocative, even controversial. Do not hesitate to write your answer in a similar vein if you have strong views.

Suggested Answer

The statement by Lord Diplock was accepted unanimously by the judges in the House of Lords. The case concerned the timing of the service of notices triggering rent review clauses. The notice to trigger a rent review had been served late by the landlord and the question arose as to whether time was of the essence. The Law of Property Act 1925, s. 41 provides that 'stipulations in a contract, as to time or otherwise, which according to rules of equity are not deemed to be or to have become of the essence of the contract, are also construed and have effect at law in accordance with the same rules'. The section clearly states that a rule of equity is to be adopted within the body of legal rules. Lord Diplock proclaimed that the systems had, quite simply, become fused and that no distinction was to be drawn between law and equity.

This view is at the most extreme, yet, it is one apparently shared by other eminent judges. Lord Denning in 'Landmarks in the Law' states that 'the fusion is complete'. Sir George Jessel MR in *Walsh* v *Lonsdale* (1882) 21 ChD 9, one of the first cases on this issue to be heard subsequent to the Judicature Acts 1873 — 1875, said 'there are not two estates as there were formerly, one estate at common law by reason of the payment of rent from year to year, and an estate at equity under the agreement. There is only one court, and the equity rules prevail in it'. In *Tinsley* v *Milligan, The Times*, 28 June 1993, Lord Browne-Wilkinson said that English law was now single law which was made up of legal and equitable interests and a person owning either type of estate had a right of property amounting to a right in rem not merely a right in personam.

The difficulty originates from the early development of equity as a separate system to the common law. The common law courts emerged in the centuries following the Norman conquest. Intervention by the Lord Chancellor gradually developed into a separate body of law, known as equity, which had, by the fifteenth century, become well established. The Chancellor's jurisdiction was exercised through what became the Court of Chancery. The two systems were sometimes in conflict. Parties seeking common law relief would need to seek the jurisdiction of the common law courts. If they wanted equitable relief they would go to the Court of Chancery. This might occur during the course of the same litigation. The common law courts only had limited jurisdiction to grant equitable relief. The Common Law Procedure Act 1854, s. 79, gave the common law courts a limited power of granting injunctions; the Chancery Amendment Act 1858 gave power to the Court of Chancery to award damages instead of (or in addition to) injunctions or specific performance.

The problem became acute in the nineteenth century and a series of Parliamentary reports led eventually to the Judicature Acts 1873 and 1875. These Acts amalgamated the superior courts into one Supreme Court of Judicature. The Courts of Queen's Bench, Exchequer and Common Pleas and the Court of Chancery, the Court of Exchequer Chamber and the Court of Appeal in Chancery, were all replaced by the Supreme Court. The Supreme Court consisted of the Court of Appeal and the High Court which originally had five divisions (subsequently reduced to three). The Supreme Court could administer both rules of common law and equity. Thus, there is no question as to the fusion of the courts. The two distinct sets of courts fused on 1 November 1875. Sir George Jessel MR, who, as Solicitor-General, was the government officer largely responsible for the Judicature Acts, said in *Salt* v *Cooper* (1880) 16 ChD 544, that the main object of the Acts was not the fusion of law and equity, but the vesting in one tribunal of the administration of law and equity in all actions coming before that tribunal.

Yet it is difficult to pursue Lord Diplock's dictum further to the point of saying that the substantive rules of law and equity are themselves indistinguishable. In trusts there is a distinction between legal and equitable interests and the right to trace property in equity depends on the existence of a fiduciary relationship. In property law the equitable doctrine of part performance was only enforceable by an equitable remedy. In unregistered land, legal and equitable interests are distinguishable in that legal interests bind the whole world with the exception of equity's darling (the bona fide purchaser of a legal estate for value without notice). The Land Charges Act 1972 makes a number of equitable interests registrable and indeed has the effect of determining that such interests which are not registered are void. Nevertheless, a group of equitable interests still fall outside the ambit of the statute and are subject to the equitable doctrine of notice. Equitable interests behind a trust, pre-1925 equitable easements and restrictive covenants fall into this category.

The right to damages in a common law action cannot be challenged on the grounds that the plaintiff did not come to court with 'clean hands': a defence which would be available to a claim in equity. The claim to an equitable remedy lies, conversely, at the discretion of the judge. In these examples, the distinction between equity and the common law remains important.

It is possible to cite examples, however, where the distinction has become irrelevant. In registered land, the categories of registered, minor and overriding interests imposed by the Land Registration Act 1925 cut across the distinction between legal and equitable interests. Statute has rendered the distinction redundant.

In general, legal rights and remedies remain distinct from equitable ones. Some overlap does, however, occur, for example, an injunction, an equitable remedy, can be sought for an anticipatory breach of contract, or to stop a nuisance, both common law actions. In *Seager* v *Copydex Ltd* [1967] 1 WLR 923, CA, an action was brought for breach of confidence in respect of confidential information revealed by the defendants about a carpet grip. Such an action is equitable and normally the equitable remedies of injunction and account are available. However, an injunction would have been ineffective and the judge awarded damages. It would seem, therefore, that a common law remedy is available for an equitable action for breach of confidence. This was recently affirmed in the Spycatcher case, *A-G* v *Guardian Newspapers Ltd (No. 2)* [1990] 1 AC 109 at p. 286 by Lord Goff.

Thus, the systems are administered in the same courts, but in general the distinction remains relevant although some overlaps do occur.

QUESTION 2

Equity is not past the age of child bearing. (per Lord Denning MR, *Eves* v *Eves* [1975] 1 WLR 1338, CA).

Discuss.

Commentary

This question may sometimes appear as an assessed essay. Confronted in the examination room, it may seem daunting. What should be included? Clearly the source of the quotation should be considered. In context, it is being used to justify a new development in equity; in the particular case cited, the new model constructive trust. It would be justifiable to limit the answer to this particular topic, but, on the other hand, it could be broadened to include all the new developments over recent years in the field of equity. To select one or the other approach cannot be wrong. However, as in many situations, in attempting to produce the answer the examiner wants, you should consider the approach in lectures. Did the lecturer use this as a general theme throughout the course? This might indicate the wide ranging approach. Or was particular attention paid to the novelty of the new model constructive trust?

If the question is set as coursework there is a greater argument for adopting the broad approach. There is scope for a powerful dissertation. In the examination room it may be safer to adopt the narrow approach rather than attempt to be too ambitious. It could, of course, be a gift of a question if you know a little about everything, rather than a lot about a limited subject.

The answer suggested here takes the broad approach.

Suggested Answer

When equity originally developed as a gloss to the common law it was innovative; it developed new remedies and recognised new rights where the common law failed to act. The efficacy of equity was largely due to its ability to adapt and innovate, yet inevitably, this development itself became regulated in a similar way to the development of the common law. There are maxims of equity which dictate the outcome of disputes. Although the judge has a discretion in the granting of an equitable remedy, that discretion is exercised according to settled principles. Thus, it might be said that equity can develop no further; the rules of precedent predetermine the outcome.

Yet, this is belied by a number of new developments in equity, for example, the recognition of restrictive covenants, the expansion of remedies, the development of doctrines such as proprietary estoppel, the enhanced status of contractual licences and, as referred to in the quotation from the judgment of Lord Denning MR, the new model constructive trust, are all illustrations of developments in equity.

There is an attempt, however, to justify these new developments, which are all examples of judicial creativity, by precedent. As Bagnall J said in *Cowcher* v *Cowcher* [1972] 1 WLR 425 at p. 430: 'This does not mean that equity is past childbearing; simply that its progeny must be legitimate — by precedent out of principle. It is well that this should be so; otherwise no lawyer could safely advise on his client's title and every quarrel would lead to a law-suit'.

Equity developed the remedies of the injunction, specific performance, account, rectification and rescission. The injunction has, of late, been a growth area. The *Anton Piller* order (named after the case *Anton Piller KG* v *Manufacturing Processes Ltd* [1976] Ch 55), reflects the growth of new technology and the need to protect ownership rights in that property. Intellectual property such as video and audio tapes and computer programs can easily be destroyed before an action for breach of copyright can be brought. Confidential information relating to industrial processes can disappear leaving a plaintiff with no means of proof. The *Anton Piller* order developed to allow a plaintiff to enter a defendant's premises to search for and seize such property where there was a clear risk that such property would be destroyed prior to action. As an area of equitable creativity, it is still being refined by the judges with the latest case of

Universal Thermosensors Ltd v *Hibben & Others* [1992] 1 WLR 840, laying down a series of guidelines for the exercise of such a draconian order.

The *Mareva* injunction is another example of a refined application of an established remedy developed in the case of *Mareva Compania Naviera SA of Panama* v *International Bulk Carriers SA* [1975] 2 Lloyd's Rep 509. While an action may succeed, if it is impossible to enforce a judgment because there are no assets, then the judgment is worthless. In international disputes, assets may be transferred abroad to make the judgment debt impossible, or at least, very difficult, to follow. Recognising this dilemma, the judges in the *Mareva* case were prepared to grant an order freezing the defendant's assets. Recent cases have now demonstrated that the courts are prepared to make this order available world-wide in certain circumstances (see, for example, *Derby & Co. Ltd* v *Weldon (No. 3 and No. 4)* (1989) 139 NLJ 11).

Equity initially recognised the trust. This was one of the original developments of equity. However, the protection granted to equitable owners behind a trust has recently developed significantly with the new model constructive trust, the contractual licence and the doctrine of proprietary estoppel.

The constructive trust of a new model developed largely due to the creative activity of Lord Denning MR. In *Hussey* v *Palmer* [1972] 1 WLR 1286, CA, Lord Denning described the constructive trust as one 'imposed by law wherever justice and good conscience require it'. Cases such as *Eves* v *Eves* [1975] 1 WLR 1338, CA, where the woman was given an equitable interest in the property representing her contribution in terms of heavy work, and *Cooke* v *Head* [1972] 1 WLR 518, CA, a similar case, took this development further. However, it may be that this development has halted since the retirement of Lord Denning. Several cases, including *Lloyd's Bank* v *Rosset* [1991] 1 AC 107, have re-established earlier principles in this field relating to the existence of a common intention that an equitable interest should arise, and the existence of a direct financial contribution. These principles which are more akin to those relating to the establishment of a resulting trust.

The new model constructive trust has been most alive in the field of licences. At common law, a contractual licence was controlled by the doctrine of privity of contract, and failed to provide protection against a third party. Equitable remedies have been made available to prevent a licensor breaking a contractual licence and to enable a licence to bind third parties. It has been accepted that certain licences may create an equitable proprietary interest by way of a constructive trust or proprietary estoppel. In *Binions* v *Evans* [1972] Ch 359, CA, it was held by Lord Denning MR that purchasers were bound by a contractual licence between the former owners and Mrs Evans, an occupant. A constructive trust was imposed in her favour as the purchasers had bought expressly subject to Mrs Evans interest and had, for that reason, paid a reduced price. Also in *Re Sharpe* [1980] 1 WLR 219, a constructive trust was imposed on a trustee in bankruptcy in respect of an interest acquired by an aunt who lent money to her nephew for a house purchase on the understanding that she could live there for the rest of her life.

The fluidity of these developing areas is again shown in recent case law which appears to hold back from a development which may have pushed the frontiers too far. Obiter dicta by the Court of Appeal in *Ashburn Anstalt* v *W. J. Arnold & Co.* [1989] Ch 1, suggests that a licence will only give rise to a constructive trust where the conscience of a third party is affected. It will be imposed where their conduct so warrants. Judicial creativity in equitable fields is thus made subject to refinements by judges in later cases.

Proprietary estoppel is another example of an equitable doctrine which has seen significant developments in the interests of justice since its establishment in the leading case of *Dillwyn* v *Llewelyn* (1862) 4 De GF & J 517. The doctrine is based on encouragement and acquiescence whereby equity was prepared to intervene and adjust the rights of the parties. Again, it is a development which stands outside the system of property rights and their registration established by Parliament.

So, although there may be setbacks in the development of new doctrines when later judges seek to rationalise and consolidate new principles, nevertheless it is clear that equity maintains its traditions.

QUESTION 3

Explain and discuss the maxim, 'equity looks upon that as done which ought to be done'. To what extent (if any) does this maxim operate to impose a trust on any person?

Commentary

This discussion question requires an examination of the various applications of the maxim. It touches upon a number of different fields. For a more detailed discussion of the doctrine of conversion in the context of trusts of land, perhaps in the context of an assessed essay, reference might be made to the Law Commission Working Paper No. 94 (1985), Trusts of Land. On the application of the doctrine in the context of *Williams & Glyn's Bank Ltd v Boland* [1981] AC 487, HL, see Stuart Anderson (1984) 100 LQR 86.

Some aspects of this are esoteric, for example, the rule in *Lawes v Bennett* (1785) 1 Cox 167. Many lecturers do not cover this rule in their courses. If that is the case, then you may not be expected to deal with it in a question of this sort. The guidance on the suggested content of this answer offered here must be tempered by what you have been expected to cover in your syllabus.

Suggested Answer

The maxims of equity operate as guidelines for the exercise of judicial discretion. Although equity did not acquire the rigidity of the common law, it did develop a body of principles. An equitable remedy is available at the discretion of the judge. The judge is assisted in the exercise of this discretion by these principles. They provide, for example, that for plaintiffs to be granted equitable remedies, they must come to court with clean hands; they must have behaved equitably and must not have delayed in seeking the intervention of equity. These principles, known as maxims, do not operate as binding precedent but provide a basis for the development of equity. Some of them have, however, formed the basis for certain rules which are binding. There are 12 maxims in addition to some general principles.

The maxim 'equity looks upon that as done which ought to be done' demonstrates the principle that, where there is a specifically enforceable obligation, equity will enforce it as though the obligation had been carried out. The common law is rigid in that, if the proper formality has not been carried out (for example, the execution of a deed for the transfer of an interest in land) then it will not recognise the interest. Equity is prepared, nonetheless, to enforce the obligation as though all due formalities are present.

For example, a contract for the sale of land is specifically enforceable if it has been effected in accordance with the rules laid down in the Law of Property (Miscellaneous Provisions) Act 1989, s. 2. It constitutes an estate contract which creates an equitable interest in favour of the purchaser. It is binding on third parties with the exception of a bona fide purchaser for value of a legal estate without notice of the equitable interest. Notice is provided by registration. A limited trust arises whereby the vendor holds the property on trust to convey to the purchaser. The trust is considered to be a constructive trust.

It is arguable, on the authority of *Oughtred* v *IRC* [1960] AC 206, HL, and *Re Holt's Settlement* [1969] 1 Ch 100, that, once an agreement has been entered into which is specifically enforceable, then the equitable interest passes without the need for formalities, as provided by the Law of Property Act 1925, s. 53(2).

The trust is limited in that the purchaser is not entitled to income from the land prior to completion, nor is the vendor obliged to convey until the purchase price is paid. The trust arises from the fact that the contract is specifically enforceable in equity.

Similarly, a contract for a lease, provided it complies with the contractual requirements, is enforceable in equity under the rule in *Walsh* v *Lonsdale* (1882) 20 ChD 9. Although the due formality of a deed required at law has not been complied with, equity sees as done that which ought to be done, and enforces the contract for the lease.

The maxim underlies the doctrine of conversion. This doctrine states that where there is a trust for sale of land, equity assumes that the sale has already taken place. This means, therefore, that such interests are deemed to have been converted into personalty already, even if the land has not been sold. Since many trusts for sale arise where couples purchase a home for their joint occupation, this means that their interests are frequently held in this manner long before the property is sold. The problem was considered in *Williams & Glyn's Bank Ltd* v *Boland* [1981] AC 487, HL. Mrs Boland was deemed to have an interest behind a trust for sale. The contest arose between her equitable interest and the interest of the bank, the bona fide purchaser. If Mrs Boland had an interest in land then she would have an overriding interest under the Land Registration Act 1925, s. 70(1)(g). However, if her interest had already been converted into personalty, she would not have an overriding interest. It was held, however, that the purpose of the doctrine was to simplify conveyancing in cases where the intention was to sell the land immediately. The doctrine should not be extended beyond that to a case where it was clearly a fiction.

It has, in fact, been proposed by the Law Commission (Working Paper No. 94 (1985), *Trusts of Land*), that trusts for the sale of land should be replaced by trusts with the power of sale. This would mean that the interest behind the trust would be an interest in land until the power was exercised.

A more obscure application of the doctrine is the rule in *Lawes* v *Bennett* (1785) 1 Cox 167, which applies to the exercise of an option. If a leaseholder is granted an option to purchase the freehold and the freeholder dies before the option is exercised, then the disposition of the rents pending the exercise of the option, and the eventual purchase price, must be determined. The rents will go to the person entitled to the freehold. This would be either a residuary or a specific devisee. The proceeds of sale, however, which are payable when (and if) the option is exercised, pass to the residuary legatee as conversion into personalty is deemed to have taken place.

The maxim was applied to conditional contracts in the more recent case of *Re Sweeting (deceased)* [1988] 1 All ER 1016. A contract for the sale of land, subject to conditions, was not completed until after death. It was held that the proceeds of sale went to the residuary legatee as the interest had already been converted into personalty.

The maxim also underlies the rule in *Howe* v *Earl of Dartmouth* (1802) 7 Ves 137, which relates to the duty to convert wasting assets. The rule is limited in that it only applies to residuary personalty settled by will in favour of persons with successive interests. The duty is that, where there are hazardous, wasting or reversionary assets they must be converted. So, for example, a lease for less than 60 years is a wasting asset. It will produce an income for the life tenant but will have a diminishing capital value for the remaindermen. Such an asset must be sold and reinvested into authorised investments. Likewise, a reversionary interest will not benefit a tenant for life although it will benefit the remainderman. It, too, must be sold and reinvested.

So, the maxim applies to a variety of cases where equity is prepared to act as though the common law requirements had been fully complied with or to convert property where it is equitable to do so.

QUESTION 4

What is equity?

Commentary

This question requires an historical and jurisprudential analysis of the meaning and position of equity in the legal system.

It is important to use examples to avoid an undirected discussion. The approach suggested here is to deal with the historical side first, using this as a vehicle for a discussion of the contribution which equity has made to the legal system.

Suggested Answer

Equity to the layman means fairness and justice, but in the legal context its meaning is much more strictly defined. There are rules of equity; it must obey the rules of precedent as does the common law, and its development may appear equally inflexible and rigid.

Yet, because of its historical development and the reasons underlying this, there does remain an element of discretion and the potential for judges to retain some flexibility in the determination of disputes.

Equity developed as a result of the inflexibility of the common law; it 'wiped away the tears of the common law' in the words of one American jurist. When the common law developed the strictures of the writ system through the twelfth and the thirteenth centuries and failed to develop further remedies, individuals aggrieved by the failure of the common law to remedy their apparent injustice petitioned the King and Council. The King was the fountain of justice and if his judges failed to provide a remedy, then the solution was to petition the King directly. The King, preoccupied with affairs of state, handed these petitions to his chief minister, the Chancellor. The Chancellor was head of the Chancery, amongst other state departments. The Chancery was the office which issued writs and, therefore, when the courts failed to provide a remedy, it was appropriate to seek the assistance of the head of the court system. Originally the Chancellor was usually an ecclesiastic. The last non-lawyer was Lord Shaftesbury who retired in 1672. Receiving citizens' petitions, the Chancellor adjudicated them, not according to the common law, but according to principles of fairness and justice; thus developed equity.

Early on, each individual Chancellor developed personal systems of justice giving rise to the criticism that equity had been as long as the Chancellor's foot. The Lord Chancellor did indeed sit alone in his court of equity, or Chancery, as it became known. It was not until 1813 that a Vice-Chancellor was appointed to deal with the volume of work. Equity began to emerge as a clear set of principles, rather than a personal jurisdiction of the Chancellor, during the Chancellorship of Lord Nottingham in 1673. By the end of Lord Eldon's Chancellorship in 1827 equity was established as a precise jurisdiction.

But the development of a parallel yet separate system of dispute resolution was inevitably bound to create a conflict. An individual aggrieved by a failure of the common law to remedy a gross injustice would apply to the court of equity. The Chancellor, if the case warranted it, would grant a remedy preventing the common law court from enforcing their order.

The catharsis occurred in the *Earl of Oxford's case* (1615) 1 Rep Ch 1 where the court of common law ordered the payment of a debt. The debt had already been paid, but the deed giving rise to the obligation had not been cancelled. The court of equity was prepared to grant an order preventing this and rectifying the deed.

The clash was eventually resolved in favour of equity; where there is a conflict, equity prevails. This rule is now enshrined in the Supreme Court Act, s. 49.

A series of maxims underlies the operation of equity, establishing a series of principles. For example: 'equity looks upon that as done which ought to be done'; 'he who comes to equity must come with clean hands'; 'equity will not allow a statute to be used as a cloak for fraud', are all examples of the maxims.

The remedies developed by equity, such as injunctions and specific performance, are, unlike the common law remedy of damages, subject to the discretion of the judge. Thus a judge may decide that, although a breach of contract has been established, the conduct of the plaintiff is such that an equitable remedy should not be granted. In addition, if damages are an adequate remedy, then there is no need to substitute an equitable remedy.

In substantive law, equity has frequently reflected the reality of transactions between private citizens. It recognised the trust when the common law had refused to acknowledge the existence of a beneficiary and provide remedies for breach of trust against a defaulting trustee. The concept of the trust has been the vehicle for much creative activity on the part of the courts of equity. The trust has developed from an express agreement between parties to situations where the conduct of parties has led the courts to imply the existence of a trust.

So, equity remains a separate system of rules operating independently of the common law. Until the late nineteenth century it operated in a separate set of courts. So, a plaintiff seeking both legal and equitable remedies would be obliged to pursue an action in separate courts. Much delay and expense ensued. The position was eventually resolved in the Judicature Acts 1873 and 1875 which established a system of courts in which both the rules of equity and common law could be administered. The position had already been ameliorated to some degree by the Common Law Procedure Act 1854, which gave the common law courts power to grant equitable remedies, and the Chancery Amendment Act 1858 (Lord Cairns' Act), which gave the Court of Chancery power to award damages in addition to, or in substitution for, an injunction or a decree of specific performance. A plaintiff can, therefore seek both damages and an injunction in the same court.

The equitable jurisdiction is, in fact, a personal jurisdiction operating against the conscience of the individual, whereas the common law jurisdiction operates against real property. Thus, an order from a court of equity preventing a legal order being enforced operates against the conscience of the defendant. In theory, therefore, there is no clash between the jurisdictions. In practice, there is a significant constraint on the common law jurisdiction.

The historical distinction does remain, however, in the existence of separate divisions of the High Court, viz, the Chancery Division (which deals primarily with matters which involve equitable rights and remedies) and the Queen's Bench Division (which deals primarily with matters involving rights and remedies at common law).

So, equity represents a later development of law, laying an additional layer of rules over the existing common law which, in the majority of cases, provides an adequate remedy: 'Equity, therefore, does not destroy the law, nor create it, but assists it' (per Sir Nathan Wright LJ in *Lord Dudley and Ward* v *Lady Dudley* (1705) Pr Ch 241 at p. 244).

3 The Three Certainties and Section 53 of the Law of Property Act 1925

INTRODUCTION

Questions on certainties are usually problem-type questions. Frequently all three of the certainties — intention, subject-matter and objects — will be included in one question. The classic form of a question in this area involves a will with a series of gifts, each of which raises a separate issue on certainty; the testator will have just died and you will be asked to advise the executors.

The question may be confined to certainty within trusts. However, you may be expected to make a comparison with the rules for certainty for powers, particularly if the question concerns certainty of objects also (see question 3(c)). If you intend to answer a question on certainty therefore, you should also know the distinction between trusts and powers.

A wide knowledge of case law is essential for answering these problems. Frequently, parts of the question may appear to be based directly on one case. Avoid the temptation to start your answer with a reference to the case. Establish the general principle, apply it to the particular problem, and then support it with a reference to the particular case.

Sometimes there is a trap in these apparently straightforward questions. If the question seems to fit very obviously into a particular precedent, look out for a later precedent which may distinguish it. See question 1(a) for an example of this. Apart from this possibility, these problem questions are usually plain sailing if you know the basic principles and some of the cases. It is more important to remember the wording used in a case than the name. If you find names difficult to memorise, you can always write: 'In a decided case . . .'.

When dealing with different parts of the question avoid repeating yourself. If you have dealt with certainty of intention in part (a), for example, then do not run through the points again for part (b). The examiner would not want more than a brief reference to the point if it occurred in a different form in part (b) and would not give you marks for regurgitating the same law again. Part (b) will invariably involve a different issue, perhaps another certainty, and you should deal with this at more length. If you think both parts are on certainty of intention and nothing else, then you are probably in trouble and should choose another question.

Problem questions are relatively easy to devise and discussion questions are quite rare in this field — unless your examiners happen to be gifted creative writers. We have therefore included three problem-type questions in this chapter. Any essay question which your examiner devised is likely to be straightforward and you could use the material in these problem questions for it.

Generally, these problem questions are gifts to the reasonably well prepared examinee. No such person should get less than a 2(ii) on such a question. Conversely, it is quite difficult to get a first. You would really need to impress the examiner with a detailed knowledge of the cases, perhaps even referring to distinguishing judgments (as in question 1(a) with the reference to *Comiskey* v *Bowring-Hanbury* [1905] AC 84).

Not infrequently, examiners have been known to include certainty in 'pick 'n' mix'-type questions. Tread warily! Certainty could be mixed in with questions on topics such as construction of trusts, charities or trusts of imperfect obligation. For an example, see question 2 in chapter 4.

QUESTION 1

Lucien, who died recently, left a will appointing Bill and Ben his executors and trustees. The will contained the following dispositions:

(a)   'My freehold house to my wife Harriet absolutely in full confidence that she will hold it for either my daughter Tessa or my son James as she sees fit.'

(b)   'The income from my blue-chip shares to my trustees Bill and Ben from which they must ensure that my old Uncle Tom has a reasonable standard of living.'

(c)   'Three of my Van Gogh paintings to my trustees to hold one of them in trust for my sister Pearl, whichever she may choose, and the other two in trust for my sister Jewel.' Pearl died before the testator.

Advise Bill and Ben as to the validity of these dispositions.

Would your answer in (c) differ if Pearl had survived the testator but died before choosing?

Commentary

This question is an example of how two parts of a question, (a) and (b), may both include different examples of uncertainty as to words or intention. You should therefore state the general law on this subject fairly fully in your answer to (a), but merely refer to it briefly and apply it in your answer to (b).

Both parts (b) and (c) include uncertainties as to subject-matter, and again any general statement of law on this should be made under (b) and avoid repetition of this under (c).

It may be appropriate to mention some cases briefly in (a) and discuss them further in (b) and (c), but make sure that they are relevant ones, e.g., *Mussoorie Bank Ltd* v *Raynor* (1882) 7 App Cas 321, where the words 'feeling confident that she will act justly to our children in distributing the same' were held not to create a trust. However, as well as looking for an understanding of the requirement of certainty of intention, the examiner will be looking for a proper application of the law to the problem set and not a general discussion of cases which are dissimilar. Remember that there are three parts to the question and you should not spend an undue amount of time on one part at the expense of the other parts.

Suggested Answer

(a)   In *Knight* v *Knight* (1840) 3 Beav 148, Lord Langdale MR said that three certainties were required to establish a valid trust, namely, certainty of words (or intention), subject-matter and objects. The question to consider here is whether the words used are sufficiently obligatory to impose a trust. Until the Executors' Act 1830, courts were very ready to find a trust, as property to which a trust was not attached would remain in the hands of the executors. The Executors' Act 1830 changed this, however, and from then on the courts were less willing to find a trust where words which could be construed as merely precatory were used. *Lambe* v *Eames* (1871) 6 Ch App 597 is generally regarded as the turning-point, where the court refused to construe merely precatory words as creating a trust. In *Re Steele's Will Trusts* [1948] Ch 603 it was said that the exception to this would be where a testator had used identical wording to that previously held to create a trust. This case has been criticised, however, for replacing a search for the author's intention with a mechanical application of legal rules; furthermore it ignores the fact that the meaning of words can change over time.

There are two conflicting cases where words used were similar to those found here. In *Re Adams and the Kensington Vestry* (1884) 27 ChD 394 a gift 'to the absolute use of my wife . . . in full confidence that she will do what is right as to the disposal thereof between my children' was held not to impose any trust upon the wife but was construed by the court to be an absolute gift to her. In *Comiskey* v *Bowring-Hanbury* [1905] AC 84, however, the House of Lords considered a bequest to the testator's wife of 'the whole of my real and personal estate absolutely in full confidence that she will make use of it as I should have made myself and that at her death she will devise it to such one or more of my nieces as she may think fit and in default to my nieces equally' and held it to be an absolute gift subject to an executory gift over, as there was a clear intent that the nieces should benefit in any event.

In *Re Hamilton* [1895] 2 Ch 370 it was said by Lindley LJ that each disposition must be construed on its own merits. The disposition in this problem appears to be nearer to *Re Adams and the Kensington Vestry* than to *Comiskey* v *Bowring-Hanbury* on the ground that there is no gift over in default. Nevertheless it may be possible to distinguish the disposition in (a) from *Re Adams and the Kensington Vestry* on the specificity of the ultimate beneficiaries — in which case it could be construed as imposing a trust.

If there is a trust, it is a discretionary trust for either Tessa or James, and there is therefore no uncertainty of objects. If the words are held not to impose a trust, then the disposition operates as an absolute gift to Harriet.

(b)   For a trust to be valid, the subject-matter must also be certain. This includes both the property and the beneficial interests which the beneficiaries are to take. If either of these is uncertain, the trust will fail. In this case, it is possible that both are uncertain.

In *Re Kolb's Will Trusts* [1962] Ch 531 it was said that a reference to stocks and shares 'in the blue-chip category' was insufficiently certain because the term 'blue chip', whilst used to indicate a very good share, has no precise meaning. If so, the trust will fail for uncertainty of subject-matter, which means that all Lucien's shares (and the income therefrom) not otherwise validly and specifically bequeathed, will form part of Lucien's residuary estate. If, however, the reference to blue-chip shares is held sufficiently certain it becomes necessary to consider other parts of this disposition.

The wording 'they must ensure' might well be sufficiently obligatory to impose a trust on the income in the hands of the trustees, as it indicates that the trustees were not intended to enjoy the whole of the income beneficially. It would appear, however, that they are not to use the whole of the income of Uncle Tom. Sufficient income for a reasonable standard of living might appear to be uncertain, but in *Re Golay's Will Trusts* [1965] 1 WLR 969 it was held that 'a reasonable income' was capable of being quantified objectively in relation to a person's lifestyle. Presumably, therefore, a sufficient income relating to Uncle Tom's lifestyle could be ascertained.

(c)   The problem in this part of the question is again to determine the subject-matter of the trust. The interests of Pearl and Jewel are uncertain until Pearl has made her choice; death means that no choice can now be made.

In *Boyce* v *Boyce* (1849) 16 Sim 476, a testator left three houses in his will, 'one to Maria, which she may choose; the others to Charlotte'. Maria predeceased the testator, and the trust for Charlotte, which was dependent upon Maria's choice, was held to fail for certainty of subject-matter. Pearl having predeceased the testator, it is impossible to determine which paintings should be held in trust for Jewel. All three paintings will therefore fall into residue. In the absence of a residuary gift, they will pass, as on intestacy, to Lucien's next of kin.

If Pearl had survived the testator but died before making a choice, although prima facie there is still an uncertainty of subject-matter, it is possible that this would enable the circumstances to be distinguished from *Boyce* v *Boyce*. The *Boyce* v *Boyce* situation has an element of ademption about it as the testator is presumed to know that Pearl has predeceased him and is therefore unable to make a choice. However, if the testator has no reason to suppose that Pearl will not choose, and dies in the belief that he has set up a valid trust, it might be possible for equity to intervene, although it is not clear how. The maxim 'Equity is equality' would not reflect the testator's intentions.

[handwritten margin note: failure of a specific legacy]

One tenuous argument might be that Lucien intended to make Pearl a trustee of the power of selection, i.e., that it is a trust power to select. This would mean that the maxim 'Equity will not allow a trust to fail for want of a trustee' could be applied, and someone else (or even the court) could make the choice. On the wording of the disposition, however, there seems little to favour such a construction.

QUESTION 2

Clockwise Ltd is a mail-order company selling a particularly popular line of talking alarm clocks. It received numerous orders with accompanying cheques but, because of difficulties with the suppliers of certain components, was unable to dispatch the orders. On the advice of the company's accountants, the cheques were paid into a separate bank account which the bank was instructed to call the 'Customers' Trust Deposit Account'. Due to an error of the bank clerk, the account was called instead 'Clockwise No. 2 Account'.

Clockwise Ltd also wished to purchase some new machinery, and one of its business associates, Ticktock plc, agreed to lend the company the sum of £10,000 solely for this purpose. This money was paid into another separate account called 'Clockwise No. 3 Account'. Clockwise Ltd signed an agreement for the purchase of the machine and paid a deposit of £3,000 from this account, leaving in it £7,000.

Unfortunately, the problems with Clockwise's suppliers became more acute and Clockwise Ltd has now gone into liquidation. The bank (which is owed money by the company) and the liquidator are claiming the moneys in the No. 2 and No. 3 accounts.

(a)   Advise the bank and the liquidator.

(b)   Would your answer differ if the monies paid by the customers, and lent by Ticktock plc had, by an error of Clockwise Ltd, been paid instead into Clockwise Ltd's general trading account?

Commentary

This question on certainties is based on a number of commercial cases where the existence of a trust has been pleaded successfully to prevent money paid to a company for a particular purpose being available for distribution generally to its creditors. The cases have been criticised in academic articles (see, for example, Goodhart and Jones, 'The Infiltration of Equitable Doctrine into English Commercial Law' (1980) 43 MLR 489 and P. J. Millett, 'The Quistclose Trust: Who Can Enforce It? (1985) 101 LQR 266). They are, however, defensible on the practical grounds that if potential customers or lenders who are helping a company to survive are not allowed to protect their property, they will not be prepared to deal with the company at all. In *Re Kayford Ltd* [1975] 1 WLR 279, where Megarry J found that a trust had been created, he made the point in his judgment that, although it was quite proper for the mail order company to have done what it did with money received from members of the public, he was not so sure that the same considerations should apply to commercial creditors. The distinction has not been drawn in subsequent cases, however, where the courts have found trusts in favour of commercial creditors also (see *Carreras Rothmans Ltd* v *Freeman Matthews Treasure Ltd* [1985] Ch 207).

Suggested Answer

(a)   One of the three certainties essential to establish a valid trust is the certainty of words or intention. Words are not themselves necessary:

the person in whom the property is vested may manifest a clear intention to create a trust by actions.

In *Paul* v *Constance* [1977] 1 WLR 527 a man said on several occasions that funds in a deposit account in his name belonged both to himself and his mistress. Section 53 of the Law of Property Act 1925 does not require any formality for the creation of a trust of personalty, and these oral statements were held to be sufficient to create a trust for his mistress of half of the money in the account.

In *Re Kayford Ltd* [1975] 1 WLR 279, a mail order company, which was experiencing financial difficulties, paid cheques received from customers into a separate dormant account which only at a later date was called 'Customers' Trust Deposit Account'. Megarry J held that this appellation was a sufficient manifestation of intention to create a trust of the moneys therein for the customers. Being a trust of personalty, no written formalities were required by the Law of Property Act 1925, s. 53, for its creation. The moneys having been kept separately meant that there was certainty of subject-matter; the objects of the trust (the customers) were also certain.

Although in the question the account into which the moneys have been paid does not bear the name 'Trust Account', the fact of segregation of the money received from the customers may be sufficient evidence of certainty of intention to create a trust. As the money has been kept separately there is also certainty of subject-matter; the beneficiaries are the customers. The money would not therefore be available to the banker or the liquidator.

Similarly, where property is handed over for a particular purpose only, this may be sufficient to impress it with a trust for that purpose. In *Barclays Bank Ltd* v *Quistclose Investments Ltd* [1970] AC 567, Quistclose lent some £200,000 to Rolls Razor Ltd (which was in financial difficulties) for the sole purpose of paying a dividend on its ordinary shares. The money was paid into a separate bank account. Rolls Razor went into liquidation before the dividend was paid. It was held that the money was not available for distribution by the liquidator to the general creditors of the company. It had from the start been impressed with a trust for a particular purpose (the payment of a dividend) and had therefore never belonged to Rolls Razor beneficially. When the trust failed because the liquidation prevented the payment of the dividend, the money was held on a resulting trust for Quistclose.

Applying these principles to the question, it would seem that the money paid by Clockwise Ltd into a separate account for the purpose of purchasing machinery would similarly be impressed with a trust for that purpose, and again would not be available to the bank or the liquidator.

Does the fact that part of this money has already been appropriated for the purpose affect the trust as to the remainder? In *Re EVTR Ltd* [1987] BCLC 646, money lent for the purchase of a machine was paid to the borrower company's solicitors. When the borrower company went into liquidation, it had already paid part of the money to the suppliers under a contract of purchase. The Court of Appeal found no reason to distinguish between the resulting trust, which would have arisen if the purpose for which the money was paid had failed initially, and the failure of the purpose only subsequently. Money returned by the suppliers was held to go on a resulting trust for the lender. In the question it is likely that the £7,000 still held by Clockwise Ltd, and any money repayable to them from the £3,000 deposit paid, will go on a resulting trust for Ticktock plc.

(b)   What if the monies in either case are paid into Clockwise Ltd's general trading account by error? In such circumstances, although the necessary intention to create a trust might be there, it would almost certainly be impossible to find a trust. In the case of the customers' cheques, presumably if a trust were intended, it would affect only funds paid into the designated account. Payment into a different account would therefore prevent the trust being constituted. In the case of Ticktock's money, although the money would be impressed with a trust from the start, there would be the practical problem that money paid into the general trading account might, in accordance with the rule in *Clayton's case* (i.e., *Devaynes* v *Noble, Clayton's case* (1816) 1 Mer 572) have been spent.

In *Re London Wine Co. (Shippers) Ltd* (1975) 126 NLJ 977 a purported allocation of a portion of the wine in a cellar was held insufficient to confer a property interest, since no bottles had been set apart for the purpose.

QUESTION 3

Consider whether a trust has been created in the following circumstances:

(a)   Eliza orally declared herself a trustee of her house, Dunroamin, for her son Percy. She subsequently wrote a letter to Percy informing him that she had done so.

(b)   Oliver, on visiting his only niece, Alison, aged 10, handed her an emerald ring which had belonged to her grandmother. As he handed it over, Oliver told Alison that she was to have the ring. When Oliver left, he took the ring with him, and when he died shortly afterwards, it was found among his effects.

(c)   Simon, who died recently, made a will leaving, *inter alia*, 'the residue of my estate to my dear wife Sarah trusting that she will dispose of whatever she does not want between such of my relatives and friends as she shall select'.

Commentary

This is a certainty question mixed with other areas of trust law. In (a) all three certainties are satisfied, but you are required to consider whether the necessary formalities for the creation of a trust of land have been complied with. Part (b) raises the question of the constitution of a trust and the difference between a trust and a gift. Part (c) raises doubts about all three certainties, but also requires a knowledge of the test for certainty of objects for discretionary trust and powers, and some of the cases on this. In part (c) you will probably consider certainty of words and subject-matter first. If you come to the conclusion that the trust would fail on either or both of these, do not of course be deterred from discussing certainty of objects also. The examiner will undoubtedly be looking for a discussion of all three certainties.

Suggested Answer

(a)   The three certainties for a trust are satisfied, but the Law of Property Act 1925, s. 53(1)(b), requires that 'a declaration of trust respecting any land or any interest therein must be manifested and proved by some writing signed by some person who is able to declare such trust or by his will'. Although the oral declaration of trust by Eliza is therefore ineffective, the subsequent letter testifying to the oral declaration would be sufficient for the purpose of s. 53. The section does not require that the trust should be created in writing, but merely that its creation should be evidenced in writing.

(b)   If Oliver had declared himself to be a trustee of Alison's ring, this would have been effective as it is possible to create a trust of personalty by words alone. As the ring is still in his possession, he would have held it as trustee and the trust would have been fully constituted. His words would have had the effect of severing the beneficial ownership in the ring, thereby creating the duality of ownership essential to a trust.

However, Turner LJ stated in *Milroy* v *Lord* (1862) 4 De GF & J 264 at p. 274 that the court will not allow a purported gift which is ineffective because there is no delivery of the subject-matter to take effect as a trust. In *Jones* v *Lock* (1865) LR 1 Ch App 25, a father put a cheque into the hand of his nine-month-old son saying, 'I give this to baby for himself'. When he later died and the cheque was found among his effects, it was held that there had been no effective gift; nor had any effective trust of the cheque been created.

If Oliver's words on handing over the ring to Alison indicate an intention to make a present gift, the gift is thereby perfected and his taking back the ring cannot recall such gift. In such circumstances, he would, at most, be a bailee of the ring for Alison.

On the other hand, Oliver's words on handing over the ring might indicate merely an intention to make a gift of it in the future. In these circumstances, Alison has merely custody or bailment of the ring, and Oliver is free to take it back (which he does).

If Oliver had made it clear when he left that he was taking the ring with him for safe-keeping but he regarded it as belonging to Alison, this might have been sufficient intent to create a trust of it for Alison with himself as trustee, or else merely a bailment with himself as bailee. However, there is no evidence to support such interpretation, and it is therefore probable that there will be an ineffective gift and an ineffective trust.

(c)   First, it might be argued that the word 'trusting' in this context is a more colloquial expression than the legal words 'on trust for', implying merely reliance upon Sarah's integrity rather than imposing an obligation on her. If this is argued successfully, then the words are precatory in nature and fail to satisfy the certainty of words necessary to create a trust.

Secondly, 'the residue of my estate' is sufficiently capable of ascertainment to form the subject-matter of a trust (the residue being the remainder of a person's estate not specifically disposed of). Nevertheless there is uncertainty of subject-matter here because the share which the friends and relatives are to receive ('whatever she does not want') is necessarily uncertain. In *Sprange* v *Barnard* (1789) 2 Bro CC 585, a gift to the testatrix's husband with a provision that 'at his death, the remaining part of what is left, that he does not want for his own wants and use' was divided between the testatrix's brother and sisters, failed as a trust for uncertainty of subject-matter.

The third certainty, that of objects, also has to be considered here. If the requirements of certainty of words and subject-matter were satisfied, there might still be a problem with regard to certainty of objects. This would be a discretionary trust and the test for certainty of objects is that laid down by the House of Lords in *McPhail* v *Doulton* [1971] AC 424, namely, can it be said of any given postulant that they are, or are not, within the scope of the discretion? When the Court of Appeal considered the application of this test to the word 'relatives' in *Re Baden's Deed Trusts (No. 2)* [1973] Ch 9, the Court of Appeal decided that the expression 'relatives' was conceptually certain enough to satisfy the test, although the judges had differing reasons for deciding this. We therefore have high judicial authority that the word 'relatives' is conceptually certain.

In *Re Barlow's Will Trusts* [1979] 1 WLR 278, the testatrix directed that 'any friends of mine' might buy a painting from her collection at a reduced price. This was not valid, but only because the court interpreted this as a series of provisions to apply conditionally to anyone who was able to satisfy the trustees that he or she was a friend. The test for certainty of objects of conditional gifts is, however, more relaxed than that applicable to certainty of objects of discretionary trusts. Had the provision been construed as a discretionary trust (or fiduciary power) to select amongst the testator's friends, it would not have satisfied the test in *McPhail* v *Doulton*. If part (c) involves a discretionary trust, the disposition might well fail the *McPhail* v *Doulton* test for conceptual certainty.

4 Constitution of Trusts

INTRODUCTION

Constitution of trusts is a fascinating area of equity which has produced a welter of academic discussion in articles and elsewhere: it is therefore a popular topic with examiners. Since, moreover, it naturally falls within the earlier part of a course on trusts, it is one which the student should have plenty of time to absorb. This is generally a good area in which hard-working students can gain high marks. Since constitution of trusts is an aspect of the creation of trusts, this topic may well be combined in an examination question with one or more of the three certainties and with formalities. But watch out for other combinations!

QUESTION 1

Equity will not assist a volunteer.

Explain and discuss.

Commentary

Superficially this may appear a simple question, but there is considerable opportunity for a student prepared to draw on their knowledge and understanding of different parts of the subject. The area is vast, but the secret is in selecting the material which most directly addresses the question. Note carefully that you are required not merely to explain the maxim, but to discuss it.

Suggested Answer

The quotation is one of the maxims of equity. It is a pithy way of stating that, where a trust is incompletely constituted or a gift is imperfectly made, equity will not give its remedy of specific performance to an intended beneficiary who is a volunteer, or to the intended donee. In the context of gifts, the maxim is often expressed in the form 'equity will not perfect an imperfect gift': see *Milroy* v *Lord* (1862) 4 De GF & J 264. A volunteer is a person who has not furnished consideration for the creation of the trust. Consideration in equity consists of both common law consideration (money or money's worth) and (in certain instances) marriage. It is clear that a covenant (although it may be enforceable at common law) does not comprise consideration in equity.

If marriage is to constitute consideration, the trust must be made either before and in consideration of a particular marriage, or (if made after the marriage) in pursuance of an ante-nuptial agreement to make such a trust. Furthermore, only certain persons within a marriage settlement are treated by equity as providing consideration: these are the spouses to the marriage and their issue. Issue of a former marriage and illegitimate children will prima facie fall outside the marriage consideration: *Re Cook's Settlement Trusts* [1965] Ch 902. But they may come within it if their interests are so closely intertwined with those of the issue of the marriage in question that they cannot be separated: *A-G* v *Jacobs-Smith* [1895] 2 QB 341, CA. Next-of-kin are outside the marriage consideration: *Re Plumptre* [1910] 1 Ch 609.

The quotation needs to be treated with care, as equity will protect a beneficiary's interest under a completely constituted trust even if that beneficiary is a volunteer (as in *Paul* v *Paul* (1882) 20 Ch D 742, where the settlor, having completely constituted the trust, was not permitted to reclaim the property on the ground that the beneficiaries were volunteers). The maxim also means that where a trust is completely constituted in regard to certain items of property, but incompletely constituted in regard to other items, volunteer beneficiaries cannot compel the settlor to transfer the latter into the trust: *Jefferys* v *Jefferys* (1841) Cr & Ph 138. However, if some of the would-be beneficiaries under an incompletely constituted trust have provided consideration for its creation, they may obtain specific performance. The consequence will be that the trust becomes completely constituted, thus also benefiting the volunteers, who could not have sued personally: *Davenport* v *Bishopp* (1843) 2 Y & C Ch Cas 451.

In certain instances it appears that equity goes further than merely not assisting a volunteer, and will frustrate an action brought at common law to aid a volunteer. Thus, the court has directed covenantees of a voluntary covenant not to sue the covenantor for damages at common law since this would give the volunteers indirectly what they are not entitled to obtain directly: *Re Kay's Settlement* [1939] Ch 329. In principle, however, such an action should be denied the covenantees only when they hold the benefit of the covenant on a resulting trust for the covenantor. An action by them ought to be available if the covenant is itself the subject-matter of the express trust, as it was in *Fletcher* v *Fletcher* (1844) 4 Hare 67. In such a case the trust is completely constituted vis-à-vis the covenant, even though it is incompletely constituted as regards the property to which such covenant relates. Thus, although equity will not give specific performance vis-à-vis such property, it will not frustrate an action brought by the trustee-covenantees for damages for breach of covenant at common law. Indeed, in such circumstances, equity will (if necessary) compel the covenantee to lend his name to an action at common law against the covenantor.

Equity recognises three so-called exceptions to the maxim that it will not assist a volunteer. The first is the rule in *Strong* v *Bird* (1874) LR 18 Eq 315 whereby, if the intended donee of an *inter vivos* gift becomes the executor, or even the administrator, of the intending donor upon the latter's death, the legal title passes to him. This, together with a continuing intention to make a gift on the deceased's part, perfects the gift. Arguably, however, this is not so much an exception to the maxim as an illustration of the means by which a gift can be perfected. This principle has been extended to trusts: *Re Ralli's Will Trusts* [1964] Ch 288.

The second exception is *donationes mortis causa*. Equity's assistance is not needed (and therefore the maxim is inapplicable) if the subject-matter of the trust is transferred to the intended donee during the donor's lifetime, albeit subject to the usual conditions to which such gifts are subject. If, however, the intended donee's title remains imperfect at the donor's death, equity's assistance will be required, and this constitutes a genuine exception to the maxim. This will be the case, for instance, if the subject matter of the *donatio mortis causa* is a chose in action, and the donor hands over merely the indicia of title: *Birch* v *Treasury Solicitor* [1951] Ch 298.

A third exception is proprietary estoppel. If A encourages, or even acquiesces in B's acting to his detriment in the belief that he has rights in the property of A, equity may protect B should A act inconsistently with such rights. This is the principle which can be traced back to *Dillwyn* v *Llewelyn* (1862) 4 De DF & J 517. A modern (and perhaps startling) instance is *Pascoe* v *Turner* [1979] 1 WLR 431, where the Court of Appeal held that the equity raised by the estoppel could be satisfied only by a conveyance of the fee simple. Equity was there assisting a volunteer, but it is unclear whether the remedy in such a case is always commensurate with the extent of the promise: i.e., whether proprietary estoppel is here a means by which imperfect gifts are rendered perfect (see Moriaty (1984) 100 LQR 376, Dewar (1986) 49 MLR 741, and Thompson [1986] Conv 406).

QUESTION 2

On the marriage of Guinevere to Lancelot in 1987, Guinevere covenanted by deed with Abbott and Burger, the trustees of the marriage settlement, to bring into the settlement:

(a)   an antique loom which she owned;

(b)   her beneficial interest under the Shallott Trust;

(c)   any property which she might thereafter acquire.

Under the terms of the marriage settlement, the property subject to it was to be held in trust for Guinevere and Lancelot for their joint lives, then for the survivor for life, the remainder in trust for the children and remoter issue of the marriage, and subject thereto for the respective next of kin of Guinevere and Lancelot.

Several times after this, Guinevere showed Abbott and Burger the loom when they visited Lancelot and herself at home. In 1988 Guinevere orally directed the trustees of the Shallott Trust to hold her interest thereunder in trust for Abbott and Burger. In 1989 Guinevere's father died; he bequeathed to her his shares in Camelot Ltd.

Last year Guinevere and Lancelot both died in a boating accident. There were no children of the marriage. The shares in Camelot Ltd were still standing in Guinevere's name at the time of her death. By her will, Guinevere appointed Eleanor her executrix and left all her property to charity.

Advise Mariana, Guinevere's sole surviving relative.

Commentary

This is a typical sort of examination question on volunteers and incompletely constituted trusts. The area of law is complex and involves apparently conflicting decisions upon which a variety of academic views has been expressed.

You should note carefully the dates specified, since any action for damages for breach of covenant will become statute-barred 12 years after the right of action arises. In the case of after-acquired property, time starts to run only when the property is acquired. Even if statute-barring were to apply, however, you would still need to consider whether the covenant had been the subject-matter of the trust because, if it had been, the trustees would be personally liable in damages to the beneficiary for breach of trust in failing to bring the action in time. The damages would be equal to the value of the items covenanted to be settled.

You should check who is appointed executor or administrator. If the person happens to be one of the trustees, the trust may be completely constituted under the principle in _Re Ralli's Will Trusts_ [1964] Ch 288. In this question, we are told that Guinevere's executrix is Eleanor, so _Re_

Ralli cannot apply. We are not, however, told who became the personal representatives of Guinevere's father's will. If either Abbott or Burger (or both) filled this position, the trust would become completely constituted under this principle in respect of the shares.

It is always difficult to advise students to what extent they need to consider matters whose relevance turns on facts which are not stated. In the present question a mention of a possible *Re Ralli* scenario in regard to the shares would be impressive. You must, however, cover the salient points, and issues which are peripheral to the facts of the problem should not be allowed to squeeze out the more important (and therefore more mark-earning!) issues.

Another point to watch out for is *Cannon v Hartley* [1949] Ch 213. If Mariana had herself been one of the covenantees of the marriage settlement, then this case is good authority for the principle that she can sue and recover substantial damages in respect of her loss.

Suggested Answer

If the trusts of the marriage settlement are fully constituted as regards each item of property, Mariana will be a beneficiary under a fully constituted trust. Initially, therefore, it must be decided whether the marriage settlement is completely constituted. The method of creation of trust which Guinevere chose was to transfer property to trustees. For the constitution of a trust by such method, there must be both a valid declaration of trust and an effective transfer of the property to the trustees: see *Milroy v Lord* (1862) 4 De GF & J 264, per Turner LJ. The terms of the marriage settlement are a clear declaration of trust. As regards transfer, however, it is necessary to take each item of property in turn.

(a) The loom is a chattel, which is transferred either by delivery or deed. Delivery requires a physical handing over; merely showing the loom to Abbott and Burger does not comprise a delivery: *Re Cole* [1964] Ch 175. It should be noted however that, as tenant for life, Guinevere would be expected to retain possession of the loom even after it had been brought into the trust. In such a case, it is possible that, with the agreement of the trustees, legal title could pass to them without the need for physical delivery to them: cf *Jaffa v Taylor Galleries* (unreported, 1991). In that event, Guinevere would thereafter be holding the loom merely as bailee.

(b)   Such a direction comprises a disposition of a subsisting equitable interest for the purposes of the Law of Property Act 1925, s. 53(1)(c): see *Grey* v *IRC* [1960] AC 1. It must therefore be in writing signed by the disponor or his agent. Since Guinevere's direction was merely oral, the purported assignment is void.

(c)   Shares in a company are transferred by entry in the company's register of members, and this has not occurred. There is, moreover, nothing to suggest that Guinevere did everything she needed to do to make a perfect gift in equity according to the principle of *Re Rose* [1952] Ch 499, CA.

Can Mariana require Eleanor (as executrix) to transfer the items to Abbott and Burger? Where a trust is incompletely constituted, equity will assist a would-be beneficiary only if that person has provided consideration, which means either money or money's worth or marriage. There is no evidence that Mariana provided money or money's worth. Moreover, although the question involves a marriage settlement, it is clear that only the spouses themselves and their issue are within the marriage consideration: next of kin fall outside it: *Re Plumptre* [1910] 1 Ch 609; *Re Cook's Settlement Trusts* [1965] Ch 902. A person who has not provided consideration is known as a volunteer, and equity will not assist a volunteer: *Milroy* v *Lord* (1862) 4 De GF & J 264.

If the property has not been transferred, there are further possible arguments upon which Mariana might rely. First, could not Abbott and Burger simply sue Eleanor as executrix of Guinevere's estate for breach of the covenant to transfer and thereby recover damages to be held in trust for Mariana? The cases reveal that the courts do not favour this approach. In *Re Pryce* [1917] 1 Ch 234, the court refused to direct the trustees to sue; and in *Re Kay* [1939] Ch 329 the court went further and directed them not to sue. Professor Elliott subsequently argued that if trustees do not ask the court but simply go ahead and sue, they will recover substantial damages which they will hold in trust for the volunteers: Elliott (1960) 76 LQR 100. However, his authorities (notably *Re Cavendish-Browne* [1916] WN 341) are not weighty and, even if the action were to succeed, the covenantees (who suffer no personal loss) might recover nominal damages only. To allow the covenantees a discretion whether to sue might encourage bribery: see Rickett (1979) 32 CLP 1. Moreover, *Re Cook* has more recently confirmed the earlier judicial view.

Secondly, could not Abbott and Burger seek specific performance? In *Beswick* v *Beswick* [1968] AC 58 the House of Lords was prepared to allow an order for specific performance (which benefited a third party) where damages were an inadequate remedy for the contracting party. That principle cannot apply here, however, because the equitable remedy is available only where, as in *Beswick*, consideration has been supplied. In the present case there is none: a covenant is not consideration in equity.

Thirdly, it might be argued that there is already a completely constituted trust, i.e., of the covenant, a chose in action, which vested in the trustees in 1987. If so, Abbott and Burger must sue for damages for breach of covenant.

The cases are not easy to reconcile. In *Fletcher* v *Fletcher* (1844) 4 Hare 67, Wigram V-C held that a covenant to settle a sum of money on persons who were volunteers was itself the subject matter of the trust: equity's aid to perfect the trust was therefore not required. This idea was however rejected in *Re Pryce* and *Re Kay*. It was suggested by Buckley J in *Re Cook* that whilst there might be a valid trust of the benefit of a covenant which relates to property in existence and within the ownership of the covenantor at the time of execution of the covenant, there can be no trust of a covenant to transfer other types of property. On this view, the covenant in the present case could not generate a trust in respect of the after-acquired property, namely the shares, but it could in respect of the loom and the interest under the Shallott Trust. Some critics of Buckley J's distinction contend that the requirement that the subject-matter be in existence and owned by the settlor at the date of the covenant is always satisfied, since such subject-matter is the covenant itself: see Meagher and Lehane (1976) 92 LQR 427.

Hanbury & Martin (*Modern Equity*, 14th edn, London: Sweet & Maxwell, 1993, p. 135) suggest that a significant factor is the intention to create a trust. When *Fletcher* v *Fletcher* was decided the courts were more willing to find an intention to create a trust of a chose in action than they are today. Arguably, there is little point in entering into a covenant under which only volunteers can benefit unless the covenant itself is intended to be held in trust. Since Guinevere's settlement was intended to be a marriage settlement, it was envisaged that there might be persons within the marriage consideration. This further weakens the argument based on a trust of a chose in action.

On the authorities as they stand, it would appear that Mariana might be able to establish her position as a beneficiary of a trust of a chose in action in respect of the loom and the interest under the Shallott Trust, but not in respect of the shares.

QUESTION 3

In 1990, Acute handed his share certificate in respect of his shareholding in Diacritical Ltd to Cedilla, together with a share transfer form which Acute had completed in favour of Cedilla. As he handed these documents over, Acute instructed Cedilla to hold the shares in trust for Acute's nephew, Grave. Cedilla agreed. Shortly after, Cedilla attempted to obtain registration of the shares in her own name, but was defeated by the exercise by the directors of Diacritical Ltd of a power contained in the company's articles to refuse registration.

In 1991, Acute received back the share certificate from Cedilla. He handed it to his cousin, Umlaut, informing him that the shares were a gift to him.

Last month, Acute died with the shares still standing in his name. In his will he appointed Umlaut his executor and gave all his property to Cedilla.

Discuss who is entitled to the shares.

Commentary

This is a complex question, both because the relevant law itself is difficult, and also because you need to sort out in your mind the priorities of several claimants — never the easiest thing in the examination room. There is a lot to write so you will need to be economical with the facts of the cases. Cases should be cited to support legal principle; facts can be given sparingly in order to distinguish one case from another. See, for instance, the treatment in the suggested answer of the authorities which support, or which appear to conflict with, the principle of *Re Rose* [1952] Ch 499, CA. If you have a good understanding and keep a clear head, this is the sort of question where you could score very heavily.

Suggested Answer

Grave is beneficially entitled to the shares if he can establish that he is a beneficiary under a fully constituted trust of them. A trust is completely constituted only if there is compliance with the requirements laid down in *Milroy* v *Lord* (1862) 4 De GF & J 264. Where, as here, the settlor seeks to confer the benefit of property on a person by vesting it in a trustee, two things must be done. First, there must be a clear declaration by the settlor of the terms of the trust. Here, the instructions to Cedilla suffice. Secondly, the settlor must do all he can to vest the property in the intended trustee. The legal title to the shares will not pass to Cedilla unless and until the company registers Cedilla's name in its register of members. Since this has not been done, the legal title to the shares has not passed. The share transfer may nevertheless be perfect in equity if, in accordance with *Milroy* v *Lord*, the settlor has done everything necessary to be done by him to transfer the shares. In *Re Rose* [1952] Ch 499, the Court of Appeal held that a gift of shares was perfect in equity as soon as the donor had put the donee into the position of being able to take steps to complete the transfer: i.e., when the donor had handed to the donee the share certificate and executed share transfer form.

On this basis, the trust in favour of Grave would have been completely constituted from the date in 1990 when these documents were delivered to Cedilla. If so, from that date, Acute would have held the legal title to the shares in trust for Cedilla, who would herself have held the equitable interest thereunder on a sub-trust for Grave. This makes Cedilla a trustee of a completely constituted trust for Grave. She is therefore under a duty to ensure that the trust property is safeguarded — by taking steps to bring in the legal title to the shares (as she did attempt to do), and (if necessary) by compelling Acute to transfer to her any dividends he receives in respect of that holding.

The transfers in *Re Rose* were registered, but there is nothing in the case to suggest a different result where registration is refused. The principle in *Re Rose* has been attacked for thus saddling an intended donor with an unintended and potentially permanent trusteeship: see McKay (1976) 40 Conv (NS) 139. This objection carries some force; moreover a permanent trusteeship in this context contrasts sharply with a contract for the sale of shares where (if the company refuses to register the purchaser) the vendor cannot be fixed with a permanent trusteeship: see *Stevenson* v *Wilson* 1907 SC 445, considered (without criticism) by the House of Lords in *Scott Ltd* v *Scott's Trustees* [1959] AC 763.

A case difficult to reconcile with *Re Rose* is *Re Fry* [1946] Ch 312; but that case may be considered, perhaps, to turn on the effect of relevant

Defence Regulations. Apart from that decision, the principle of *Re Rose* is consistent with a range of authorities: see, particularly, *Mallott* v *Wilson* [1903] 2 Ch 494 and *Mascall* v *Mascall* (1985) 49 P & CR 119. The principle was assumed correct by the House of Lords in *Vandervell* v *IRC* [1967] 2 AC 291, HL and it also operates in the case of equitable assignments of legal choses in action: *Holt* v *Heatherfield Trust Ltd* [1942] 2 KB 1.

If *Re Rose* applies, Grave is a beneficiary under a trust of the shares, and is entitled to the dividends which Diacritical Ltd will continue to pay to Acute (and, after Acute's death, to Acute's personal representative). On this basis, the purported gift of the shares to Umlaut, even if ultimately perfected (as discussed below) is later in time, and is therefore subject to the rights of Grave. Similarly, Acute cannot by his will give to Cedilla property which he does not own beneficially. Thus the gift of all his property to Cedilla does not include the shares.

If, however, a court were to distinguish or overrule *Re Rose* and hold that the trust was incompletely constituted, then, unless Grave had provided consideration for the creation of the trust, he could not (as a volunteer) gain the assistance of equity: *Re Plumptre* [1910] 1 Ch 609. Since, however, Acute gave all his property in his will to Cedilla, the intended trustee of the shares, it is arguable that the trust in favour of Grave is completely constituted on Acute's death, since Cedilla then has a right as beneficiary under the will to see that the property is properly distributed: *Re Diplock* [1948] Ch 465, CA. She will ultimately obtain the legal title to the shares when the executor, Umlaut, transfers the shares into her name. It makes no difference that the legal title comes to Cedilla, the intended trustee, in a different capacity: *Re Ralli's Will Trusts* [1964] Ch 288.

There is, however, one further twist: Umlaut's appointment as executor. If it can be shown that Acute had a continuing intention to give the shares to Umlaut from 1991 until his death, the imperfect gift to Umlaut might be perfected under what is known as the rule in *Strong* v *Bird* (1874) LR 18 Eq 315 (i.e., by the acquisition by Umlaut of the legal title to the shares as executor). In principle, this would seem to postpone the equity of the beneficiaries under the will to that of the executor. It was upon this basis that Walton J in *Re Gonin* [1979] Ch 16 objected to the decision in *Re James* [1935] Ch 449, which had extended the rule to administrators. This objection may carry less weight where the intended donee becomes executor, since such appointment results from the testator's own voluntary act. The objection may not be entirely overcome, however, since an executor does stand in a fiduciary relationship to the beneficiaries under the will, and to permit him to have a prior claim seems to fly in the face of normal equitable principles designed to prevent a conflict of interest: cf *Holder* v *Holder* [1968] Ch 353, CA. Nevertheless, the application of the rule to executors is well-established: *Re Stewart* [1908] 2 Ch 251. Umlaut will therefore be permitted to bring evidence outside the will that Acute intended to give him the shares. Since such evidence derives from the intended donee, however, it will need to be treated with caution: cf cases involving secret trusts: *Re Rees* [1950] Ch 204, CA, and *Re Tyler* [1967] 1 WLR 1269.

If, therefore, the intended trust in favour of Grave was not perfected in 1990, Umlaut may be able to satisfy the court that he is entitled to the shares under the rule in *Strong* v *Bird* in priority to both Cedilla and Grave.

QUESTION 4

Three months ago, Lear, a keen rambler, caught a chill after spending a stormy winter's night wandering lost on the moors. He was taken to hospital suffering from pneumonia. When his eldest daughter, Goneril, visited him, he handed her the key to a deed box which was in his study at home. Lear told Goneril that he did not expect to live much longer and that, if anything were to happen to him, Goneril was to have the contents of the box.

Shortly after, when Lear's middle daughter, Regan, was by his bedside, Lear handed to her the Land Certificate relating to his country cottage in Gloucestershire, which he owned in fee simple. He advised Regan that, if he did not pull through, Regan was to have the cottage.

Last month, during a visit by his youngest daughter, Cordelia, Lear wrote a cheque for £10,000 in her favour. He informed her that this was to be her share of his property on his death.

Last week Lear, who remained seriously ill in hospital, deliberately took an overdose of sleeping pills, from which he died.

Goneril has now opened the deed box, and finds that it contains the keys and vehicle registration document to Lear's car, and a bank pass book relating to Lear's deposit account with the Serpent's Tooth Bank plc. It is discovered that, a couple of weeks before his death, Lear had leased the country cottage to Edmund for a term of 21 years. In his will, Lear gave all his property to charity.

Advise Lear's daughters.

Commentary

Those with little or no Latin should note that *donatio* is a noun meaning gift, so one can refer either to a '*donatio mortis causa*', or to a gift '*mortis causa*'. The plural is *donationes mortis causa*. Succour may be sought from remarks of Lord Simon of Glaisdale in *Brumby* v *Milner* [1976] 1 WLR 1096, a tax case, where his Lordship deprecated the unnecessary use by lawyers of Latin terms. In the present case, however, the English equivalent is slightly more of a mouthful, and the Latin reminds us of the Roman Law origins of this principle, which finds its modern counterpart in the Civil Law.

Suggested Answer

Lear evidently intended the gifts to the daughters to take effect only in the event of his death. Such gifts would normally be testamentary in nature and valid only if made in accordance with the Wills Act 1837 (as amended). Such formalities are absent here. Nevertheless, Lear's daughters will be able to take the property concerned if they can establish a valid *donatio mortis causa* in respect of each item.

To constitute a gift *mortis causa*, three elements must be satisfied. These have been affirmed by the courts many times (e.g., in *Cain* v *Moon* [1896] 2 QB 283, and, most recently, in *Sen* v *Headley* [1991] Ch 425).

First, the gift must be intended to be conditional upon death, so that it is not perfect until death, before which time it can be revoked by the donor. The gift must also be intended to be automatically revoked in the event of the donor's survival. Such conditions will be readily inferred where the gift is made in contemplation of death, which appears to be the case here.

Secondly, the gift must be made in contemplation of death, which must be more than a contemplation that the donor, like all living things, must some day die. This requirement is met where the donor is suffering from a life-threatening illness (*Saulnier* v *Anderson* (1987) 43 DLR (4th) 19) and seems therefore to be met in the instant case. However, in *Re Dudman* [1925] 1 Ch 553, it was held that a *donatio mortis causa* made in contemplation of suicide (at that time a crime) was not valid. Suicide is no longer a crime (Suicide Act 1961) and the present position is unclear. Such a purported *donatio* might still be invalid today on the ground that the requisite contemplation of death imports an element of uncertainty as to whether and when death will ensue. Such uncertainty is absent if the donor has the intention of taking his own life. In the problem, however, at the time he made the *donationes mortis causa*, Lear may have contemplated death by pneumonia, not by suicide. In *Wilkes* v *Allington* [1931] 2 Ch 104, it was held that it does not matter if death occurs from a disease other than that contemplated. A *donatio* might therefore not be invalidated if death occurs by suicide not contemplated at the time the *donatio* was made: see *Mills* v *Shields* [1948] IR 367.

Thirdly, the donor must part with dominion over the subject-matter of the *donatio*. Delivery to the intended donee of the only key to a locked receptacle which contains the subject-matter suffices, even if the subject-matter could have been handed over: *Re Mustapha* (1891) 8 TLR 160. It has, however, been stated *obiter* that there is no sufficient parting with dominion if the donor retains a duplicate key: *Re Craven's Estate* [1937] Ch 423. The statement in the question that 'the key' was handed over to Goneril implies that it was the only key, in which case this requirement is satisfied. Moreover, it does not matter if the box itself contains another key which opens a further box: *Re Lillingston* [1952] 2 All ER 184.

On this principle, since the deed box contains the key to Lear's car, it would appear that (unless Lear retained a duplicate key) a valid *donatio* has been made of the car. Although the passing of dominion over a chattel is usually effected by physical delivery, delivery of the key both enables Goneril to take possession of the car and (together with the delivery of the vehicle registration document, which evidences Lear's ownership) effectively puts it out of Lear's power to deal with it.

Parting with dominion over a chose in action requires the donor to part with the essential evidence or *indicia* of title: *Birch* v *Treasury Solicitor* [1951] Ch 298. There, the Court of Appeal held (*inter alia*) that a *donatio mortis causa* of a chose in action represented by a deposit pass book to Barclay's Bank was effected by delivery to the donee of the pass book. In such instances, equity will perfect the imperfect gift by treating the deceased's personal representatives as trustees of the chose in action for the donee: *Duffield* v *Elwes* (1827) 1 Bli NS 497. This principle would therefore apply to Lear's deposit account with the Serpent's Tooth Bank plc.

Lear's country cottage is land and, until recently, it was doubted, on the basis of dicta in *Duffield* v *Elwes*, whether land could ever be the subject-matter of a *donatio mortis causa*. In *Sen* v *Headley* [1991] Ch 425, however, the Court of Appeal held that it could. There was no difference in substance between the principle applicable to choses in action established in *Birch* v *Treasury Solicitor* and the parting with dominion over land by the delivery of the title deeds. Although the doctrine of *donationes mortis causa* is anomalous, it was preferable to avoid creating anomalies of anomalies. *Sen* v *Headley* concerned unregistered land, but the same principle would appear to apply to the delivery of the Land Certificate in registered land.

Although Lear has parted with dominion over the Land Certificate, whether he has parted with dominion over the cottage itself is less clear. He did after all subsequently lease it out. Such a situation was hypothesised in *Sen* v *Headley* by the Court of Appeal, which opined that a retention by the donor of a power to deal with the subject-matter did not invariably preclude a parting with dominion. It was a matter of fact in each case. Although the donor in *Sen* v *Headley* retained a key to the premises, the donee had her own set and was in *de facto* control. The problem does not state how many sets of keys there are, nor who has possession of them. If Regan has the only set of keys to the cottage, that might, in accordance with *Sen* v *Headley*, be a sufficient parting with dominion by Lear. Nevertheless, the legal principle is obscure. Mummery J at first instance could not see how the equitable interest of the donee, which arises only on the death of the donor, can be binding upon a tenant of a lease granted during the donor's lifetime. The Court of Appeal does not seem to provide a satisfactory answer to this.

It is well-established that delivery of the donor's own cheque to the intended donee cannot constitute a valid *donatio mortis causa*: *Re Beaumont* [1902] 1 Ch 889, *Re Leaper* [1916] 1 Ch 579. A cheque is merely a revocable order to a banker to pay a sum of money. The position may be otherwise if the cheque is presented and the donor's account credited during the donor's lifetime or before the bank has been informed of his death. Subject to these qualifications, Cordelia can derive no benefit from the cheque, which is mere waste paper.

5 Trusts, Powers and Discretionary Trusts

INTRODUCTION

A thorough understanding of the distinction between trusts and powers is essential. The different types of trusts — fixed and discretionary trusts (sometimes known as trust powers) — have significantly different rules affecting their validity. There is also the distinction to be grasped between mere powers and fiduciary powers.

The question may call for an analysis of the distinction between a discretionary trust and a power. They can look very similar and their purpose may also be identical. A testator may wish to allow the possibility of a group benefiting from a gift but may intend a more sophisticated approach than an equal division. Some trusted person or some professional person may be given the task of selecting beneficiaries from the group according to need. Yet, the effect of the difference for the potential recipients of the gift is critical. Depending on the construction of the gift, they may acquire some rights or they may acquire none. They may be able to force a distribution, or at least a consideration of the distribution, or they may be utterly helpless in the hands of an indolent 'donee'. Needless to say, it is not always easy to determine into which category the gift falls. The cases are helpful but not always conclusive, hence the popularity of this topic as an exam question.

There may be a mere power or a fiduciary power. Take for example, the following gift: property to trustees to hold on trust for the children, subject to the widower's power to select which child should benefit, in default of such selection the trustees to divide equally unless they decide that one or more of the children should receive an unequal share. The widower has a mere personal power; the trustees, because they are trustees, have a fiduciary power. The distinction, and its consequences, need to be understood.

The validity of the gift may depend on its construction as a power, a fixed trust or a discretionary trust. The rules relating to certainty of objects, capriciousness and administrative workability vary according to the decision as to which concept the gift falls into. There is no correlation between the rules. For example, the rule for certainty of objects in powers and discretionary trusts is the same, but differs from the rule for fixed trusts. It is arguable, however, that the test for administrative workability differs between powers and discretionary trusts. Capriciousness may be yet another determinant of validity. Knowledge of the case law is crucial.

The other type of trust included in this chapter is the protective trust. Whole questions on the protective trust are not a certainty for every exam paper. This does not imply that, from the point of view of the examiner, these questions are too straightforward to provide good question material. There is conflicting case law and the effect of the Law of Property Act 1925, s. 33 to deal with.

QUESTION 1

Adam, who has just died, made the following dispositions in his will:

(a) £50,000 to my trustees on trust to apply the net income of the fund in making, at their absolute discretion, grants to or for the benefit of any of the employees or former employees of Abel & Sons, their spouses or dependants, or any others having a moral claim on me.

(b) £5,000 to my trustees to be invested and the income to be divided equally amongst my friends at the 'Paradise' public house, Edenton.

(c) The dividends from my shares to be applied by my trustees for the benefit of the middle classes of my home town, Edenton.

(d) The residue of my estate to my wife, Eve, absolutely, but I direct my trustees to allow such old friends of mine who wish to do so, to acquire any of my collection of stuffed reptiles at fifty per cent of market price.

Advise the trustees of the will as to the validity of these dispositions.

Commentary

There usually appears in examination papers a question on certainty of objects dealing with the ramifications of the House of Lords' decision in *McPhail* v *Doulton* [1971] AC 424. So, a careful preparation of the case law will repay the effort!

For a high mark, some discussion of the issues going beyond a simple application of the cases to the problem is desirable. Some further discussion of the issues of conceptual certainty, evidential certainty, ascertainability and administrative workability would be appropriate.

Suggested Answer

(a) A trust must be for ascertained or ascertainable beneficiaries: *Re Endacott* [1960] Ch 232, CA. The test to determine certainty of objects in a discretionary trust was decided by the House of Lords in *McPhail* v *Doulton* [1971] AC 424 ('can it be said with certainty that any given individual is or is not a member of the class?').

Since this decision, therefore, it is no longer necessary to prepare a complete list of objects of a discretionary trust as is still required in a fixed trust (*IRC* v *Broadway Cottages Trust* [1955] Ch 20, CA). The test for certainty of objects in a discretionary trust is now the same as for mere powers (*Re Gulbenkian's Settlement Trust (No. 2)* [1970] 1 Ch 408).

It is necessary, therefore, to apply the test to the terms of Adam's will and ask: can it be said with certainty whether any individual is or is not an employee or former employee of Abel & Sons, or their spouse or dependant, or any other having a moral claim on Abel?

In *Re Baden's Deed Trusts (No. 2)* [1973] Ch 9, CA, the terms 'relatives' and 'dependants' were subjected to the test. It was considered that the terms were conceptually certain and, therefore, sufficient to satisfy the test.

The term 'spouses' is clearly certain as a concept and this part of the gift would be valid.

However, the gift also includes a category of 'any others having a moral claim on me'. It was said in *McPhail* v *Doulton* that such an expression is conceptually uncertain.

It is not clear whether this would cause the whole gift to fail for uncertainty or whether the courts could sever the offending part, thereby saving the valid parts (*Re Leek* [1969] 1 Ch 563, CA; *Re Gulbenkian's Settlements* [1968] Ch 126 at 138, CA).

(b)   A gift to divide the income equally amongst my friends at the 'Paradise' is a fixed trust. The beneficiaries hold equitable interests under the trust in fixed shares. It is necessary to be able to draw up a list of all the beneficiaries in order for the division to be made. The older and stricter rule in *IRC* v *Broadway Cottages Trust* [1955] Ch 20, CA, applies. The expression 'friends' is not a term that is sufficiently certain for such a complete list to be drawn up. The expression 'old friends' was held to be certain in *Re Gibbard's Will Trusts* [1967] 1 WLR 42. But this case used the test of whether it could be shown that someone was in the class. This test is now defunct so the case is not good authority for this point. A gift to 'friends' was upheld in *Re Barlow's Will Trusts* [1979] 1 WLR 278, but this was a series of gifts with a condition precedent. The size of the gift to each recipient did not alter according to the numbers in the class, therefore it is not authority for certainty of the expression 'friends' in a fixed trust.

(c)   This gift constitutes a purported discretionary trust. It raises questions about certainty of objects and administrative workability.

First, the problem of certainty of objects is raised in respect of the definition of 'middle classes' (*McPhail* v *Doulton*). Again, it is necessary to decide whether such a concept is certain applying the test in *McPhail* v *Doulton*. Although it may be possible to say definitely whether some individuals are or are not members of the middle classes, there may be a number of people who cannot be classified in this way. There was a difference of approach amongst the judges in *Re Baden's Deed Trusts (No. 2)*.

Megaw LJ accepted that there may be a substantial number of persons about whom it could not be proved whether they are in or out. However, this may relate more to the question of evidential uncertainty. Conceptual certainty means that the class must be definable. Evidential certainty is the proof an applicant must supply to establish membership of the class. In the case of a gift to 'middle classes' it is difficult to define criteria for such a concept.

However, if the gift is valid, then the question of administrative workability arises. In *McPhail* v *Doulton* it was said that if the class was too wide, then the trust would be too difficult to administer. A discretionary trustee has duties to survey the class and this is impossible in a class of great width. This was the position in the case of *R* v *District Auditor, ex parte West Yorkshire County Council* (1986) 26 RVR 24, where a trust for the inhabitants of the county of West Yorkshire was held to be too wide and therefore void for administrative unworkability. If the trust could be construed as a power this rule would not apply: *Re Manisty's Settlement* [1974] Ch 17.

(d)   This gift must be distinguished from discretionary trusts. It is not a trust for a class but a gift to individuals who must first satisfy the condition that they are 'old friends'. Such a gift does not require conceptual certainty. The gift will be valid if only one person seeking to take can be identified as an 'old friend' (*Re Allen* [1953] Ch 810, CA). In *Re Barlow's Will Trusts* [1979] 1 WLR 278, the direction to sell a painting at a preferential price to 'any friends of mine who may wish to buy one' was held to be a valid gift. A friend was a social acquaintance of long standing and anyone who satisfied this condition precedent would take the gift.

On the basis of this authority, a gift to 'old friends' should, therefore, be valid.

QUESTION 2

In January 1970 Simon settled property on Tom and Tam 'on protective trusts' for Betty (who was then aged 20) until she should reach the age of 30 and, if no determining event had by then occurred, upon trust for Betty absolutely, if a determining event had occurred, then upon protective trust for Betty until she should attain the age of 40, but, if no determining event had by then occurred, upon trust for her absolutely, and subject thereto, to hold the property in trust for Betty for life with remainder to her children, Romulus and Remus.

In December 1979 Betty asked the trustees to pay her £50,000 for the purpose of setting up a feline beauty parlour. Although such amount exceeded the income of the trust, Tom and Tam duly paid the money. Later, having taken legal advice that this constituted a breach of trust, they sought to remedy the breach by withholding a part of Betty's income from the following year. Betty's beauty parlour was not a success. It subsequently went out of business and Betty went bankrupt. Tom and Tam continued to pay the fees at the local further education college where Betty was studying for a diploma in hairdressing and beauty.

In June 1987, Betty's husband petitioned for divorce on the ground of Betty's unreasonable behaviour. The divorce court awarded him custody of the children and ordered Betty to pay maintenance for the children, to be charged on Betty's interest under the settlement. Betty has refused to pay.

Advise Tom and Tam as to the following:

(a)   The legal effect of the aforementioned events on the settlement.

(b)   The nature of the interests of Betty, Romulus and Remus under the settlement, from 1970 onwards.

Would your advice differ if Betty, as opposed to Simon, had been the settlor?

Commentary

The facts in the question make it appear long and confusing. However, if you have revised protective trusts, this is the question for you as it is discrete. A rough plan setting out the sequence of events is desirable; a flow chart showing dates and ages might make it even clearer.

There is a number of points in the question, each supported by a case, so it is largely a matter of spotting them all. The more you spot, the higher the mark. A diagram of events might prevent you missing any.

The point on the matrimonial order raises two cases which are difficult to reconcile. Grasp the nettle and deal with the conflict, explaining which one is preferred and why. For further discussion on this point see (1963) 27 Conv NS517; F. R. Crane.

The reference to the note by R. E. Megarry in the Law Quarterly Review is not essential merely to pass, but demonstrates a breadth of reading which is essential for achieving a higher class.

Suggested Answer

(a)   The settlement creates a determinable interest in favour of Betty. This interest is stated to be subject to protective trusts and it is clear from the language of the gift that it is intended to be subject to the provisions contained in Trustee Act 1925, s. 33 (*Re Wittke* [1944] Ch 166).

The settlement does, in fact, create a series of protective trusts. The advantage of this is that, if a determining event occurs before Betty is 30, she gets a second chance before her interest is irrevocably reduced to a life interest. This application of the protective trust was recommended by R. E. Megarry as making the best possible use of the existing machinery ((1958) 74 LQR 184).

In December 1979 the trustees make an advance to Betty of £50,000 to set up a feline beauty parlour. Section 33(1) provides that '. . . an advance under any statutory or express power . . .' is not a determining event. An advance may, therefore, be made if there is an express power in the settlement or, if the life tenant consents, under the provisions in the Trustee Act 1925, s. 32. This section confers upon the trustees power to pay capital for the advancement or benefit of any persons entitled, even if (like Betty), they are entitled merely contingently to the capital. An advancement properly made, therefore, does not constitute a determining event. Setting up a beneficiary in business is an appropriate reason for an advance. However, whether the advance was lawfully made or not, the attempt by the trustees to impound Betty's income to make good the breach which they believed had occurred, is a determining event for the purposes of s. 33 (*Re Balfour's Settlement* [1938] Ch 928).

Betty's bankruptcy is a determining event and will bring into effect the discretionary trusts under s. 33(1)(i).

The trustees continue to pay Betty's college fees after the determining events. Once the determinable interest has come to an end, the discretionary trusts arise. The trustees are able to make payments at their absolute discretion to the principal beneficiary, his or her spouse and issue for their maintenance, support or other benefit. Betty, as the principal beneficiary, may, therefore, receive payments at the discretion of the trustees even though she has no proprietary interest in the trust. However, a difficulty arises where the principal beneficiary has been declared bankrupt. If she receives more than what is sufficient for her mere support, then the trustee in bankruptcy may impound any payments made to her. However, it would seem that where payments are made to a third party for services rendered to the principal beneficiary, the trustee in bankruptcy is unable to intercept such a payment (*Re Coleman* (1888) 39 ChD 443).

In June 1987 a court order is made charging Betty's interest with a maintenance order. This order is available to the Family Division of the High Court under the Matrimonial Causes Act 1973. There are conflicting cases on whether this is an event which will determine her protective interest. In *Re Richardson's Will Trusts* [1958] Ch 504, it was held that such an order caused a forfeiture. However, in *General Accident Fire and Life Assurance Corporation Ltd* v *IRC* [1963] 1 WLR 1207, part of the income was ordered to be paid to an ex-wife and this did not cause a forfeiture. The object of the protective trust is to protect the principal beneficiary from financial not personal disasters. *Re Richardson* was not referred to in the later case and commentators suggest that the *General Accident* case is to be preferred. In that event, the court order will not determine the interest.

    (b)   The nature of the interests of Betty, Romulus and Remus:

(i)   The settlement is created in January 1970. It is declared to be made on 'protective trusts'. This will be sufficient to incorporate the Trustee Act 1925, s. 33 (*Re Wittke* [1944] Ch 166).

Thus, Betty has a determinable interest in the property until she reaches 30 in 1980. Romulus and Remus will have interests under discretionary trusts if a determining event occurs during this period. It is determinable if Betty is deprived in any way of the whole or part of the income from the fund.

(ii)   In 1979, before the end of the first protected period, a determining event occurs when the trustees withhold her income. The discretionary trusts come into operation at this point and Betty, Romulus and Remus are potential beneficiaries of this trust. The second protected period begins in 1980.

(iii)   In 1987 the maintenance order is charged on income Betty is receiving under the settlement. If the *General Accident* case is followed there is no termination of Betty's interest. She, therefore, reaches the age of 40 in 1990 without a determining event occurring. At this point, therefore, the protective trust comes to an end and Betty takes the property absolutely.

If Betty were the settlor instead of Simon, this would affect the advice about the bankruptcy which occurred in 1979. A settlor may protect another person from the consequences of their bankruptcy. However, settlors may not protect their own property from bankruptcy in this way. In *Re Burroughs-Fowler* [1916] 2 Ch 251, the settlor settled property in trust for himself until a specified event should occur, whereupon the income should be paid to his wife. One of the events was bankruptcy, which did occur. It was held that the trustee in bankruptcy was entitled to the income.

This applies only to bankruptcy, and not to other determining events. So, there would be no difference in the advice in respect of the other events. In December 1979, when the bankruptcy occurs, Betty's interest has already determined as a result of the trustees' decision to withhold income (*Re Balfour's Settlement*). As the discretionary trusts have already arisen, the bankruptcy can have no effect (*Re Detmold* (1889) 40 ChD 585).

QUESTION 3

It is difficult in borderline cases to draw a dividing line between discretionary trusts and powers. . . . The division turns on the proper construction of the language of the instrument. The matter is made more difficult by reason of the fact that a discretionary trust may be 'exhaustive' or 'non-exhaustive'. (Hanbury and Martin, *Modern Equity*, 14th edn, London: Sweet & Maxwell, 1993.)

Discuss.

Commentary

This essay question requires a discussion of the distinction between discretionary trusts and powers with reference to relevant literature; see, for example, (1974) 37 MLR 643, (Y. Grbich), *Farwell on Powers* (3rd edn, 1916) and *Halsbury's Laws of England* (4th edn, vol. 36, p. 529 (London: Butterworths). In particular, such reference must be made where an essay of this type is set as an assessed essay.

A straightforward explanation of the difference and the importance of the distinction between discretionary trusts and powers is required. The essay could be grouped under different headings to clarify the different aspects of the problem; for example, the different position of the trustees/donees, and the potential recipients.

Suggested Answer

At first sight a discretionary trust and a power may achieve the same purpose. A gift is made which is available for a group of people. The actual recipients of the gift are left to the decision of a third party. The object of such a gift is not to benefit each member of the group equally regardless of their need, instead, a power of selection is given to a trusted third party. That person is to make the selection according to criteria fixed by the settlor or at their absolute discretion. If the settlor wished each member of the group to benefit, then this would have been achieved by creating a fixed gift in equal or other shares.

The person making the selection may be obliged to use up all the property in making a selection, as in an exhaustive trust, or there may be power to accumulate income and make no selection as in a non-exhaustive trust.

However, the distinction between discretionary trusts and powers does create fundamental distinctions between the duties of trustees and the donees of a power, and between the position of the ultimate beneficiaries under each.

Duty of Trustees under Discretionary Trusts

A trustee is under an imperative duty to perform the trust. If the trust is discretionary, the trustees are obliged to consider the exercise of their discretion. If they fail to exercise their discretion the court can order them to do so. If the trust is exhaustive, they must make an appointment even though the decision as to the recipient and the size of the distribution is at the trustees' discretion. The court will intervene and make an appointment if the trustees fail to act, or if the trustees predecease the testator — the trust will not fail for want of a trustee. If no appointment is made the property will normally be divided equally between the beneficiaries on the basis that equality is equity.

Duty of Donees of Power

There is an initial distinction to be drawn between fiduciary powers and mere powers. A fiduciary power is a power of appointment granted to a trustee or to a person in a fiduciary position (*Re Mills* [1930] 1 Ch 654). Because such persons are in a fiduciary position, this colours the manner of their exercise of the power. In *Re Hay's Settlement Trusts* [1982] 1 WLR 202, it was held that the donee of a fiduciary power must consider the exercise of the power and survey the potential beneficiaries from time to time. The court may intervene if the trustee fails to consider the exercise of the power or exercises it inappropriately.

However, even where there is a fiduciary power the donee is not required to draw up a complete list. In *Re Gestetner's Settlement* [1953] Ch 672, a power given to trustees, to distribute amongst a huge and fluctuating class consisting of employees of a number of companies, was considered valid, even though it was impossible to consider all the potential objects. The test for certainty of powers, as established in *Re Gulbenkian's Settlement* [1970] AC 508, is, in fact, the same for certainty of objects in a discretionary trust. This was confirmed in *Re Baden's Deed Trusts (No. 1), McPhail v Doulton* [1971] AC 424. The test is that it must be possible to say with certainty whether any given individual is or is not a member of the class.

A bare power does not impose on the donee any fiduciary duties. A donee of a power may exercise the power at will. If the power is not exercised, the court cannot compel the donee to exercise it or even to consider its exercise. If no appointment is made, the property reverts back to the settlor or the settlor's estate. If the donee predeceases the testator, then the power lapses.

Position of Beneficiaries under a Discretionary Trust

The beneficiaries under a fixed trust own the property in equity, and, if of full age and sound mind, can call for the trust to be extinguished and the property distributed (*Saunders* v *Vautier* (1841) 10 LJ Ch 354). Under a discretionary trust, no individual beneficiary owns a particular part of the trust property until an appointment has been made (*Gartside* v *IRC* [1968] AC 553). However, as a group, all the potential beneficiaries own the trust property and, as in a fixed trust, if adult and of sound mind, they can call for the trust to be brought to an end.

Position of Objects of a Power

The objects of a power have no interest in the property. They cannot call for a distribution to be made. They only acquire an interest once a distribution is made in their favour. They have no right to seek the intervention of the court if no appointment is made. If no appointment is made, therefore, unless there is a gift over, the property will revert on resulting trust to the settlor or the settlor's estate. The only occasion on which the objects can apply to court is to restrain the exercise of a power which is outside the terms of the instrument granting it.

Construction of Document to Distinguish between Power and Discretionary Trust

As indicated in the question, it may be extremely difficult to decide whether a power or a discretionary trust has been created. The language of the gift in a well drafted document should make it clear. Failing this, various methods have been adopted by the judiciary to clarify this question.

In *Burrough* v *Philcox* (1840) 5 My & Cr 72, property was left by the testator to his two children for their lives. The survivor was given a power to leave the property in her will 'amongst my nephews and nieces or their children, either all to one of them, or to as many of them as my surviving child should think proper'. The court decided that this was effective to create a trust. As no selection was made, the court would intervene and make the gift in equal shares amongst the beneficiaries. Had the conclusion been that the gift was a mere power, then the court would have been powerless to intervene and the property would have resulted back to the settlor's estate. Lord Cottenham in *Burrough* v *Philcox* said that where there is a general intention in favour of a class with a particular intention to select particular individuals from that class then, if the selection fails, the class will benefit as a whole. The significant factor is an intention to benefit the objects of the gift if no selection is made.

Such a general intention cannot be deduced where the settlor provides a gift over in default of appointment. This implicitly acknowledges that no selection might be made and there is no power to force a selection. A power, therefore, has been created (*Re Gestetner*). The reverse does not, unfortunately, always hold true. In *Re Weekes' Settlement* [1897] 1 Ch 289, it was held that there was no intention to create a trust even though there was no gift over.

So, the distinction is often hard to deduce in cases where the instrument is not clear. The distinction, nevertheless, is important in terms of the differing rights and duties of the trustees and donees and the potential objects of the trust or power.

6 Charitable Trusts

INTRODUCTION

In our experience the topic of charitable trusts is a favourite one for examiners and students alike. There are complexities in this area, however, and it can be difficult in borderline cases to decide whether a particular trust is charitable or not. Nevertheless, the law itself is probably more easily understood than in some other topics in equity and trusts. The examiners may devote an entire question to charitable trusts. On the other hand, a question on this area may be mixed with another topic. A favourite combination in practice involves a mixing with non-charitable purpose trusts.

QUESTION 1

Geoffrey, who died recently, left a will directing his executors and trustees to constitute his residuary estate a trust fund and to hold one third thereof upon trust for each of the following purposes:

(a) To provide sports equipment and prizes for snooker tournaments for university students.

(b) To assist the vicar and churchwardens of St. Peter's, Faversham, in parish works.

(c) To encourage the preservation of the world's rainforests.

Consider whether these dispositions are of a charitable nature.

Commentary

Since you are asked to advise as to the charitable nature of each disposition, it is unnecessary to consider whether any of them might be otherwise valid (e.g., as a trust of imperfect obligation). Had the question, however, demanded that you 'advise as to the validity' of the dispositions, a discussion of other means of upholding them would have been appropriate.

Do not waste time dealing with points which do not cause problems. There is no need, for instance, in part (b) of the present question, to write at length about whether the advancement of various esoteric beliefs might nevertheless be charitable.

If you are permitted to take statutes into the examination, you will not gain many marks for merely reciting what they contain. Reference to the Recreational Charities Act 1958 should, in such cases, refer to the relevant section and paragraphs, but quotations should be limited to the key words: e.g., in the answer to part (a) of the present question, to the issue of 'need'.

The answer does not conclude definitely as to whether any of the dispositions is charitable. This is because whether a particular purpose is charitable is a mixed question of law and fact. As a law student you are expected to know the law; but you cannot be decisive about matters of construction. For this reason, it is best merely to indicate what you consider the more likely construction and state the law relevant to it. You might, however, go on to consider the consequences which would flow from any other reasonable constructions.

Sport is likely to be a key issue for charity law in the 1990's. Note, for instance, the House of Lords' recent consideration of it in *Guild* v *IRC* [1992] AC 310. Sport is therefore likely to appear fairly regularly in examination questions. At the time of writing there is a question-mark over the charitable status of gun clubs: the Charity Commissioners have provisionally refused to register two new rifle clubs. Such clubs have been considered charitable on the basis of *Re Stephens* (1892) 8 TLR 792. The Hungerford Disaster may have prompted the Charity Commissioners to revise their views on this issue. For a spirited defence of the charitable status of rifle clubs, however, see Clarke, (1992-3) 1 *Charity Law and Practice Review* 137.

An article on the relationship between politics and charity, which would be useful reading in preparation for an essay on that topic (a perennial favourite with examiners), is Forder [1984] Conv 263.

Suggested Answer

To be charitable, each of the dispositions must promote a charitable purpose, it must contain a public benefit, and the purpose must be wholly and exclusively charitable. It is necessary to consider each disposition separately.

(a)   The promotion of sport is not itself a charitable purpose: *Re Nottage* [1895] 2 Ch 649, CA. It may, however, be charitable if it can be regarded as a means of furthering a purpose which is charitable. Thus, the provision of squash courts in a school was held charitable in *Re Mariette* [1915] 2 Ch 284, because the judge regarded the playing of sport as an integral part of the boys' education, and the advancement of education is a charitable purpose within the second head of charity laid down by Lord Macnaghten in *Pemsel's Case* [1891] AC 531. This principle might apply to university students, most of whom are no more than a few years above school age. It is, however, a matter of construction whether, in each case, the purpose is merely the promotion of sport (and so not charitable, as in *IRC* v *City of Glasgow Police Athletic Association* [1953] AC 380) or a means of furthering a charitable purpose. In *IRC* v *McMullen* [1981] AC

1, the House of Lords held that a trust to provide facilities for pupils at schools and universities to play football was charitable as being for the advancement of education. In that case, however, the trust deed stated that this was a means of improving their minds. Since no such words are expressed here, the provision of sports equipment will be charitable under the second head of *Pemsel's Case* only if the court is willing to infer that the testator intended the avowed purpose to be merely a means to a charitable end.

The provision of prizes for snooker tournaments may be charitable if the game is itself educational and available only to young persons. In *Re Dupree's Deed Trusts* [1945] Ch 16, a trust for an annual chess tournament for boys and young men up to the age of 21 was held to be charitable, the court accepting the evidence of a school teacher that chess is educational. The judge did, however, regard it as near the borderline; and snooker, though a game of physical skill, must surely be considered less intellectual than chess. On that basis, the provision of prizes for snooker tournaments in the question would not be charitable for the advancement of education.

This is not, however, the end of the matter. Under the Recreational Charities Act 1958 it is charitable to provide facilities for recreation or other leisure time occupation in the interests of social welfare. The requirement of social welfare is satisfied if the facilities are provided to improve the conditions of life for the persons for whom they are primarily intended, and either such persons have need of such facilities (for the reasons there specified, including youth) or the facilities are to be open to the members or female members of the public at large. Although the majority of the Court of Appeal in *IRC* v *McMullen* took the view that the requirement of need imported some element of deprivation, the House of Lords in *Guild* v *IRC* [1992] 2 All ER 10 held that this is not so. Assuming, therefore, that there is evidence of a need for such facilities and equipment at universities, both the purposes mentioned in (a) are likely to be held charitable. Unless both are held charitable, the trust will fail as not being wholly and exclusively charitable.

(b) As office-holders, the vicar and churchwardens promote a charitable purpose, regarding the advancement of religion, the third head of charity in *Pemsel's Case*. Therefore a gift to these persons described as such, without more, would be regarded as a good charitable gift for the advancement of religion. The problem here, however, is that a purpose is specified: namely, parish work. This means that the persons specified hold the property for such a purpose, and the charitable status of the gift depends upon whether a trust for parish work is wholly and exclusively charitable. In *Re Simson* [1946] Ch 299, a gift to a vicar 'for his work in the parish' was held charitable; whereas in *Farley* v *Westminster Bank Ltd* [1939] AC 430, HL, a gift to a vicar 'for parish work' was not. The difference was that in *Farley* the parish work was not limited to work which fell within the charitable scope of the vicar's office. It could, for example, include a civic reception for a footballer. It is, in each case, a matter of construction; but, unless the court can put a different construction on the present gift from that of the House of Lords in *Farley*, it will fail as not being wholly and exclusively charitable.

(c)   The preservation of the environment is accepted as a charitable purpose within the fourth head of Lord Macnaghten's classification in *Pemsel's Case*. The public benefit means a benefit to the public in the United Kingdom; but scientific evidence has revealed the importance of the rain forests to the world's climate, and suggests that they contain as yet undiscovered species of plants which may assist in the development of cures for human diseases. The preservation of the animals in the forests may also tend to moral improvement of the human race: *Re Wedgwood* [1915] 1 Ch 113. Thus, subject to the possible qualification which follows, even though no rainforests are in the United Kingdom, this trust would appear to satisfy the public benefit requirement and, therefore, to be charitable.

The qualification is that a trust will be denied charitable status if its purpose is considered to be political. A trust which aims to change the law is political because the court has no means of judging whether a proposed change in the law is or is not for the benefit of the public in the United Kingdom: *McGovern* v *A-G* [1982] Ch 321. In the *McGovern* case it was thought that there was a risk that the aims of the trust established by Amnesty International might prejudice this country's relations with countries overseas. An additional reason for the denial of charitable status to political trusts is that the Attorney-General might be required to enforce trusts whose purposes are against the interests of the state: *Bowman* v *Secular Society Ltd* [1917] AC 406; *National Anti-Vivisection Society* v *IRC* [1948] AC 31, HL. It might therefore be argued that the purpose specified in the problem could be carried out by seeking to change the law of the UK or of other countries, and this would make it a political purpose and so vitiate charitable status. It is, perhaps, the word 'encourage' which causes anxiety on this point.

Nevertheless, given the scientific evidence mentioned above, the court might well consider that any potential political element is merely ancillary to the charitable purpose: *IRC* v *Temperance Council* (1926) 136 LT 27. If this is the case, the trust will still be wholly and exclusively charitable. Charities are, after all, permitted a limited amount of political activity. They may, for instance, put forward a reasoned memorandum recommending changes in the law: see the Charity Commissioners' guidelines in their Reports for 1981 (paras 53-56) and 1986 (App A). The borderline, indeed, between education and propaganda is sometimes narrow: see *Re Koeppler* [1986] Ch 423. Only an unsympathetic judge, however, would be likely to deny charitable status to a trust for the purpose specified in the question.

QUESTION 2

To be charitable, a trust must promote a public benefit.

Discuss.

Commentary

In an essay question it is additionally important to have a structure in mind before you start writing, because such questions (unlike some problem questions) will not always suggest a structure to you. Examiners will be impressed by a well-structured and coherently argued essay. The basic structure to the following suggested answer is the distinction between the two senses in which public benefit is used. Note that, in the first sense, cases are drawn upon from those pertaining to the definition of charity. It is necessary to be selective, mentioning only those relevant to the answer. By preparing a preliminary structure, perhaps by way of a few rough notes, you will obtain a better idea of how much time (and therefore detail) you can afford to give to each aspect of the answer.

The question is short and therefore, perhaps, appealing. The danger with it is that the student may not spot everything which is asked. This is always a potential danger with very short questions. In our experience a large number of students will fail to deal with both aspects of public benefit, but not those who study this suggested answer!

Suggested Answer

This statement is generally correct. The concept of public benefit in the law of charity is used in two different senses.

First, it can mean that the purpose itself must be of public benefit. The absence of public benefit in this sense, when required, means that the trust cannot be for a charitable purpose. In the context of Lord Macnaghten's fourth head of charity in *Pemsel's Case* [1891] AC 531, 'other purposes beneficial to the community', this requirement is self-evident. Similarly, a trust cannot be charitable as being for the advancement of education (the second head) unless public benefit is established. Under both these heads, public benefit must be proved and it is not enough that the settlor himself believes that the purpose is beneficial to the public: *Re Pinion* [1965] Ch 85, CA (where the testator tried to foist upon the public as a museum a 'mass of junk'). In a borderline case, as in *Re Pinion* or *Re Dupree's Deed Trusts* [1945] Ch 16 (chess tournaments for young males in Portsmouth up to the age of 21), the court may derive assistance from expert evidence. If necessary, the court will weigh the benefits of the proposed purpose against any detriments: *National Anti-Vivisection Society* v *IRC* [1948] AC 31, where a moral benefit was outweighed by a tangible detriment.

In the case of the relief of poverty, this aspect of the public benefit requirement is satisfied if the persons to be relieved are needy, which imports the notion of 'going short': *Re De Carteret* [1933] Ch 103. The third head of *Pemsel*, the advancement of religion, is in this respect, however, the most relaxed. The court assumes that the advancement of religion benefits the public and consequently the benefit does not have to be proven: *Re Watson* [1973] 1 WLR 1472, following *Thornton* v *Howe* (1862) 31 Beav 14. Evidence that the purpose is immoral or against religion will, however, deny charitable status. This has not been established in respect of the religious sect known as the Moonies, which remains a charity in English law. One reason advanced by the courts for not admitting charitable status to trusts for political purposes is that it has no means of judging whether a change in the law is for the public benefit: *National Anti-Vivisection Society* v *IRC* and *McGovern* v *A-G* [1982] Ch 321.

Secondly, public benefit can mean that the community, or the section of the community, to benefit must be sufficient. Essentially this is a matter of degree. In one case an appeal for the widows, orphans and dependants of six fishermen drowned at sea was held charitable: *Cross* v *Lloyd-Greame* (1909) 102 LT 163. In the context of the fourth head of charity in *Pemsel*, the requirement of public benefit in this sense is particularly stringent. Thus, if the description of persons to benefit comprises a class within a class, the trust cannot be charitable: see *IRC* v *Baddeley* [1955] AC 572, HL. The Recreational Charities Act 1958, s. 1, provides that nothing in that Act is to derogate from the principle that for a trust to be charitable it must be for the public benefit: and see *Guild* v *IRC* [1992] AC 310. On this basis it is arguable that the decision in *Baddeley* would still be the same today.

Furthermore, where the beneficiaries are defined by reference to a personal nexus, the trust cannot be charitable. This test was first established in the context of a blood relationship in *Re Compton* [1945] Ch 123, CA, and was applied by the House of Lords in *Oppenheim* v *Tobacco Securities Trust Co. Ltd* [1951] AC 297 to deny charitable status to a trust to educate the children of employees of a named company. Where however, the primary class to benefit does constitute a sufficient section of the community, a preference for a private class will not destroy the charitable nature of the trust, provided that the preference does not go to more than 75% of the trust income: *Re Koettgen's Will Trusts* [1954] Ch 252. This qualification does not, however, apply if the private class has a right in priority (*Caffoor* v *ITC* [1961] AC 584). Where no preference for a private class is specified in the trust, a de facto application by the trustees to a private class does not constitute an application for exclusively charitable purposes (*IRC* v *Educational Grants Association Ltd* [1967] Ch 993) and would appear to be a breach of trust.

There is one important exception to the personal nexus test, namely, it does not apply to trusts for the relief of poverty. Cases going back to the eighteenth century had held that a trust to relieve poor relations was charitable, and this principle had been extended for instance, in *Re Coulthurst* [1951] Ch 661, CA, to poor employees of a bank. In *Dingle* v *Turner* [1972] AC 601, the House of Lords affirmed that these earlier cases were not affected by the ruling in *Oppenheim*. In *Dingle* v *Turner*, Lord Cross opined that the *Oppenheim* test was established in order to prevent companies providing tax-free fringe benefits to their employees, and for this reason he thought that a trust to advance religion among the members of a company might be charitable, provided the benefits were purely spiritual. It should be noted, however, that the majority of their Lordships in that case expressly dissociated themselves from Lord Cross's view that, in determining charitable status, the courts ought to take tax benefits into account.

Even a trust for the relief of poverty cannot be charitable, however, if the persons to benefit, instead of being described merely by reference to a group (such as poor relations), are individually named: *Re Scarisbrick* [1944] Ch 229.

Although a trust for the advancement of religion is subject to the public benefit requirement in this second sense, such a requirement is generally applied less stringently. Thus, whereas in *Re Compton* (in the context of education) the court rejected the notion of indirect public benefit (viz, that the persons educated would mix with others in society), such a notion was admitted in the context of the advancement of religion in *Neville Estates Ltd* v *Madden* [1962] Ch 832. This was a trust to advance religion among members of the Catford Synagogue. Although this comprised only a small number of persons, the court held that the public benefit requirement was satisfied because such persons would mix with others in society and the benefit would thereby rub off. A similar approach is evident in *Re Hetherington, Gibbs* v *McDonnell* [1990] Ch 1, where a trust for the saying of masses for the soul of the testatrix was held charitable because the masses could be held in public.

There was no mixing with the public, however, in *Gilmour* v *Coates* [1949] AC 426, HL, where the purposes of a Carmelite convent were held not to be charitable. The nuns were a cloistered and purely contemplative order. Since they never mixed with society, the only public benefit could be that derived from spiritual edification or from intercessory prayer. The House of Lords held these benefits were not susceptible to judicial proof, and it was not sufficient that the Roman Catholic Church itself believed that these things benefited the public. *Gilmour* v *Coates* was distinguished from *Thornton* v *Howe* in *Re Watson* on the basis of the dissemination of the works in the earlier case. Nevertheless, the liberal approach adopted in recent cases involving the advancement of religion is not easy to reconcile with their Lordships' decision.

QUESTION 3

(a)   Consider the legal differences between a charitable trust and a private trust.

AND

(b)   By her will, Jemima (who died recently) left £100,000 'upon trust for charitable and deserving purposes'. Consider the validity of this disposition.

Commentary

Part (a) involves a broad range of knowledge. The skill here is not merely to show that you know what the differences are, but also to treat them in a balanced way. Given that this is only half of the question, you cannot be expected to go into great detail. The more fundamental differences are considered first, leaving the more technical ones (such as the numbers of trustees) until later. Taxation differences are also mentioned briefly at the end to indicate that the student is aware of them, but they are not elaborated upon since such differences do not relate to the substantive law of trusts. A possible variation of this question is to consider the advantages of charitable trusts over private trusts.

Part (b) illustrates the point that, where more than one construction can reasonably be placed upon a form of words, it is essential to consider all reasonable constructions.

Suggested Answer

(a) The primary legal difference is that a charitable trust aims to benefit society at large (or at least a sufficient section of it) whereas a private trust is designed to benefit specified persons or groups of persons, or (in a limited number of anomalous instances) for purposes which the law does not recognise as charitable. It is sometimes difficult to ascertain which has been created. This was illustrated by the uncertainty surrounding the legal status of the main fund raised following the Penlee Lifeboat Disaster. In the event, the Attorney-General decided not to contest that the fund had been raised for charitable purposes, and it was therefore treated as a private trust. Since then, many public disaster funds (such as the main appeal fund following the Bradford City Fire Disaster) have been specifically drafted as private discretionary trusts in order to give the trustees greater flexibility in the application of the fund.

Whereas private trusts are enforced by the beneficiaries (the beneficiary principle: *Morice* v *Bishop of Durham* (1804) 9 Ves 399), charitable trusts are enforced by the Attorney-General on behalf of the Crown. This itself leads to another difference between the two sorts of trusts. Thus, whereas certainty of objects is an essential requirement for a private trust (*Re Astor's Settlement Trusts* [1952] Ch 534), it is not necessary for a charitable trust. Provided the purposes of a trust are wholly and exclusively charitable and the public benefit element is satisfied, the trust will not fail merely because the purposes are vague. Thus a trust for 'charitable purposes' is a good charitable trust. Similarly, in *Re Smith* [1932] 1 Ch 153, a gift 'unto my country England' was held to be charitable. Where the purposes of a trust are wholly and exclusively charitable but vague, the court or the Charity Commissioners will settle a scheme applying the property to specific purposes. If, however, the expressed purposes are so vague that the property could, consistent with the terms of the trust, be applied to non-charitable purposes, the trust cannot be charitable. Thus a trust for 'the general welfare and benefit' of children in a children's home was held not charitable because it could be applied in the provision of television sets for juvenile delinquents. Such a purpose could not be considered to be within the spirit of the preamble to the Statute of Elizabeth 1601: *Re Cole* [1958] Ch 877.

If the objects of a private trust fail, the property (in the absence of any express provision) will usually go on a resulting trust for the settlor or the settlor's estate. By contrast, if the objects of a charitable trust fail, the property can sometimes be saved for charity by the application of a cy-près scheme; if the failure occurs before the property has vested in trust for the charity, a general charitable intention must be shown by the settlor: *Re Wilson* [1913] 1 Ch 314. Cy-près is also applicable to charitable trusts in the instances specified in the Charities Act 1993, s. 13; and there is provision for the alteration of the objects of small charities in s. 74. Funds raised for charitable purposes which fail may be applicable cy-près under the Charities Act 1993, s. 14.

Whereas private trusts are subject to both rules against perpetuities (the rule against remoteness of vesting and the rule against perpetual trusts), charitable trusts are subject only to the rule against remoteness of vesting. Even this is subject to the qualification that a gift over from one charity to another may validly occur outside the perpetuity period: *Christ's Hospital* v *Grainger* (1849) 1 Mac & G 460.

Further distinctions arise in regard to the trustees themselves. In the case of a private trust, subject to a contrary provision in the trust instrument, the decisions of the trustees must be unanimous: *Re Mayo* [1943] Ch 302. By contrast, in the case of a charitable trust, except where statute provides otherwise (e.g., in the Charities Act 1993, ss. 74, 75), decisions need only be by a simple majority: *Re Whiteley* [1910] 1 Ch 608. Again, whereas the maximum number of trustees of a private trust of land is four, there is no such limit if the trust is charitable: Trustee Act 1925, ss. 36(6), 34(3)(a).

It might also be mentioned briefly that charitable trusts enjoy certain important fiscal exemptions and reliefs as compared with private trusts: these include limited exemptions from income tax, capital gains tax and inheritance tax. They also enjoy relief from business rates.

(b) To be charitable a trust must be wholly and exclusively charitable. Although a trust for charitable purposes alone satisfies this requirement, a trust for charitable and deserving purposes may not do so. This is because 'deserving purposes' are not necessarily charitable. Whether the disposition in the problem is charitable depends, therefore, upon whether the word 'and' is construed conjunctively or disjunctively. The former construction means that every purpose to which the property can lawfully be applied must be both charitable and deserving; such a trust will therefore be charitable. The latter construction means that the property could be applied to purposes which are either charitable or deserving (but not necessarily both); such a trust is not wholly and exclusively charitable. In *Re Sutton* (1885) 28 ChD 464, a trust for 'charitable and deserving objects' was construed conjunctively and so held charitable. A similar construction was applied to the words 'charitable and benevolent' in *Re Best* [1904] 2 Ch 354. By contrast, 'charitable or public purposes' were construed disjunctively in *Blair* v *Duncan* [1902] AC 37, as were the words 'charitable or benevolent' in *Chichester Diocesan Fund* v *Simpson* [1944] AC 341.

These cases might suggest that 'and' tends to be construed conjunctively, whereas 'or' is usually construed disjunctively. Ultimately, however, it all turns on a construction of the particular gift in the context of the instrument as a whole. Thus in *A-G of the Bahamas* v *Royal Trust Co.* [1986] 1 WLR 1001, the Privy Council held that a gift for the 'education and welfare' of Bahamian children was to be construed disjunctively. The trust was therefore void because 'welfare' purposes were not wholly and exclusively charitable.

Thus, whilst Jemima's gift (because it uses the word 'and') appears to be prima facie charitable, whether this is so is essentially a matter of construction. If the gift is held not to be wholly and exclusively charitable, it will probably fail both for uncertainty of objects and for unenforceability: *Morice* v *Bishop of Durham* (1805) 10 Ves 522.

QUESTION 4

(a) Consider how the cy-près doctrine has been extended by statute.

AND

(b)   By his will made in 1975, Tommy gave his entire estate to his executors and trustees upon trust to use the same to build a hostel for the working people of Walkley. Tommy died last year. The value of his estate is insufficient to enable the hostel to be built. Tommy's next-of-kin are claiming his estate.

Discuss.

Commentary

Part (a) asks you to consider, not to describe. If you have the statutes in the examination room with you, there should be no problem with mere description, and clearly some description of the scope of the provisions is needed. The examiners, however, will be looking for more than a recitation of the statutory provisions. Simply copying out the statutory provisions will not achieve many marks: it is definitely not to be recommended!

Part (b) demands that you consider the charitable status of the gift before going on to consider a possible application cy-près.

Suggested Answer

(a)   Section 13 of the Charities Act 1993 re-enacts a provision in the Charities Act 1960 which extended the scope of the cy-près doctrine beyond cases of failure and surplus. The section specifies five circumstances in which the original purposes of a charitable gift can be altered. Paragraphs (a) and (b) apply where the purposes have been fulfilled, or cannot be carried out, or where they provide a use for part only of the gift. Paragraph (e)(i) and (ii) apply where the purposes have, since being laid down, been adequately provided for by other means, or have ceased to be charitable in law. This last provision might, for instance, be applicable if the courts were to hold the purposes of gun clubs (which can be charities under the principle in *Re Stephens* (1892) 8 TLR 792) no longer charitable. Essentially, however, these paragraphs merely put pre-existing cy-près circumstances onto a statutory basis.

Paragraph (c), however, was an important extension of the doctrine. It enables property to be applied cy-près where it, and other property applicable for similar purposes, can be more effectively used in conjunction and made applicable to common purposes. Before the Charities Act 1960, in the absence of failure or a surplus, neither the court nor the Charity Commissioners had power to alter the purposes of charities. Thus, whilst a scheme might facilitate the administration of several trusts for broadly similar charitable purposes, such scheme could not make any alteration to the specific purposes of each charitable trust: *Re Faraker* [1912] 2 Ch 488. This would now be possible.

Under paragraph (d), cy-près is permissible where the original purposes were laid down by reference to an area which has since ceased to be a unit for some other purposes, or by reference to a class of persons or to an area which has since ceased to be suitable or practical. Paragraph (e)(iii) applies where the original purposes have ceased 'in any other way' to provide a suitable and effective method of using the property.

All the paragraphs except (b) require reference to 'the spirit of the gift'. In *Re Lepton's Charity* [1972] Ch 276 it was stated that this means the basic intention underlying the gift. In that case the court used paragraphs (a)(ii) and (e)(iii) to authorise an increase, to allow for inflation, in the stipend payable to a minister out of the income of an eighteenth-century charitable trust. It should also be noted that s. 13(2) apparently preserves the need for a general charitable intention where that was required before the Act, i.e., in cases of initial failure only. A general charitable intention is not therefore needed in any other cy-près circumstances in s. 13.

The Charities Act 1985 (now repealed) gave small charities additional powers to modify their objects. This power was, however, rarely used — partly because of the complexity of the procedures. The power has been re-enacted (and procedurally simplified) in the Charities Act 1993, s. 74. The section applies only to a small charity, which means one with a gross annual income not exceeding £5,000, and it does not apply to a charity which holds land for its particular purposes. Under s. 74(2)(c) the charity trustees may resolve to modify the trusts of the charity by replacing its purposes with other charitable purposes. This power applies only if the charity trustees are satisfied that the existing purposes have ceased to be conducive to a suitable and effective application of the charity's resources, and that the specified purposes are as similar to those existing purposes as is practical in the circumstances: s. 74(5). No such scheme can take effect, however, without the Charity Commissioners' consent.

(b)   The specified purpose, a hostel for the working people, may be a charitable purpose. For a trust to be charitable its purpose must fall within the letter or the spirit of the preamble to the Statute of Elizabeth 1601. A simpler classification was the four-fold one of Lord Macnaghten in *Pemsel's Case* [1891] AC 531. The first head of charity listed by Lord Macnaghten was the relief of poverty. Poverty is not confined to destitution but includes simply going short. The trust may still be charitable for the relief of poverty if a poverty requirement can be inferred from the instrument — as occurred in *Re Cottam* [1955] 1 WLR 1299 — but not from extrinsic evidence alone: *Re Drummond* [1914] 2 Ch 90. In *Re Sanders' Will Trusts* [1954] Ch 265, a trust to provide dwellings for the working classes in Pembroke Dock was held not to be charitable: the judge did not consider the working classes were necessarily poor. By contrast, in *Re Niyazi's Will Trusts* [1978] 1 WLR 910, Megarry V-C held that a trust to build a working men's hostel in Cyprus was charitable: the case was near the borderline, but the two expressions together contained just enough indication that the purpose was to relieve poverty. On this basis, the present trust is likely to be held charitable.

If the trust is held to be charitable, the next issue is the insufficiency of the estate. This ranks as a failure of the purpose, which is a cy-près circumstance within the Charities Act 1993, s. 13. Since the trust fails *ab initio*, however, the court must be satisfied that the testator had a general charitable intention, i.e., an intention to benefit a wider purpose than that specified: *Biscoe* v *Jackson* (1887) 35 ChD 460. The issue is whether the testator intended the avowed purpose to be merely a means of effecting a wider purpose: see *Re Wilson* [1913] 1 Ch 314 and *Re Lysaght* [1966] 1 Ch 191. Whether a general charitable intention is present is ascertained by construing the words used in the context of the instrument as a whole and in the light of admissible extrinsic evidence: *Re Woodhams* [1981] 1 WLR 493. Generally, the more detailed the specified purpose, the more difficult it becomes to find the requisite intention: *Re Good's Will Trusts* [1950] 2 All ER 653. On the other hand, the fact that a gift is one of residue (or of the testator's entire estate) may indicate a general charitable intention, since no specified amount is provided: cf *Re Goldschmidt* [1957] 1 WLR 524.

If a general charitable intention is found, the property will be applied cy-près; if not, it will pass to Tommy's next-of-kin.

QUESTION 5

(a)   To what extent may charity trustees take ethical considerations into account when investing the charity's funds?

AND

(b)   Last year, the residents of the village of Eastwick decided to raise funds to build a cottage hospital. Money was raised for this purpose by means of street collections and the sale of raffle tickets. The appeal fund trustees also received a large number of cheques for various amounts. Unfortunately, the total sums raised proved insufficient to enable the hospital to be built.

Advise the trustees how they should deal with the funds raised.

Commentary

For essays on the statutory predecessor to the Charities Act 1993, s. 14, the student is referred to the valuable article by Wilson, [1983] Conv 40. There is also a general discussion of the impact of the original section in Luxton, *Charity Fund-raising and the Public Interest*, Avebury, 1990, pp. 136-149. Other sources of fund-raising which a question such as this might require you to deal with are membership subscriptions and deeds of covenant. The student should note carefully the amendments which were made when the original section was re-enacted in the Charities Act 1993.

Suggested Answer

(a)   It is a fundamental principle of trustee investment, established in the context of private trusts, that the trustees are under a duty to secure, so far as is consistent with commercial prudence, the best financial return for the trust regardless of ethical considerations. Thus in *Buttle* v *Saunders* [1950] 2 All ER 193, trustees of a private trust were held under a duty to gazump. More recently, in *Cowan* v *Scargill* [1985] Ch 270, miners' pension fund trustees were not permitted to pursue a policy (*inter alia*) of disinvestment in industries in competition with coal.

In the recent case of *Bishop of Oxford* v *Church Commissioners* [1992] 1 WLR 1241, Nicholls V-C affirmed the application of this fundamental principle to charitable trusts. He nevertheless indicated that, within prescribed limits, charity trustees may take ethical considerations into account.

First, charity trustees may (and, perhaps, must) have a policy of non-investment in companies whose objects conflict with the charity's purposes. Thus the trustees of a cancer charity might exclude shares in tobacco companies. Similarly, a temperance charity might exclude shares in brewery or distillery companies.

Secondly, trustees may take ethical considerations into account if this is provided for in the trust instrument.

Thirdly, there would be rare cases where trustees' holdings of particular investments might hamper a charity's work either by making potential recipients of aid unwilling to be helped because of the source of the charity's money, or by alienating some of those who support the charity financially. In these cases, the trustees will need to balance the difficulties they would encounter, or likely financial loss they would sustain, if they were to hold the investments against the risk of financial detriment if those investments were excluded from their portfolio.

Fourthly, some investments might be considered merely ethically unsuitable. The trustees must not use the property they hold to make moral statements at the charity's expense. But subject to that, and to there being no significant financial detriment, charity trustees may, in selecting investments, take ethical considerations into account. Nicholls V-C gave the example of a charitable trust where those who supported or benefited from a charity took widely differing views on a particular type of investment on moral grounds. In his view, so long as they were satisfied that the course would not involve a risk of significant financial detriment, trustees might accommodate such views.

In the *Bishop of Oxford* v *Church Commissioners* itself, declarations were sought that, in managing their assets, the Church Commissioners were obliged to have regard to the object of promoting the Christian faith through the established Church of England. Nicholls V-C refused the declarations (*inter alia*) because such a policy would exclude 37 per cent of UK listed companies (by value), including some of the largest, and could lead to significant financial detriment. The Church Commissioners' own policy, however, excluded investment only in companies whose main business was in armaments, gambling, alcohol or tobacco. Furthermore, this policy excluded merely 13 per cent of UK listed companies (by value). There was no risk of significant financial detriment because an adequate width of alternative investments remained open. There were also differing views in the church as to the morality of such investment. The Church Commissioners' ethical policy was therefore lawful.

(b)   The provision of a cottage hospital is clearly a charitable purpose: the relief of the 'impotent' is expressly mentioned in the Preamble to the Statute of Elizabeth 1601, and it falls within the fourth head of charity as classified by Lord Macnaghten in *Pemsel's Case* [1891] AC 531, namely, other purposes beneficial to the community (see *Re Resch* [1969] 1 AC 514).

The insufficiency of the funds raised means that the charitable purpose has failed *ab initio*. In such circumstances, equity itself does not permit an application cy-près unless the donors had a general charitable intention. Donors putting money in collecting boxes, however, might be presumed to be giving for a specific purpose and not with a general charitable intention. Thus, in *Re Gillingham Bus Disaster Fund* [1959] Ch 62, CA, anonymous contributions to a non-charitable fund were ordered to be held for such contributors on a resulting trust.

To avoid a similar outcome with failed charitable collections, the Charities Act 1993, s. 14 (which re-enacts with amendments provisions originally contained in the Charities Act 1960) provides that, in certain circumstances, funds given to charity are applicable cy-près, i.e., to other charitable purposes similar to those for which the funds were raised. Section 14(1) can apply only where (*inter alia*) the property belongs to donors who gave for specific charitable purposes which fail. It has been argued that the section has little impact on anonymous contributions, since these never belong to the donors: Wilson, [1983] Conv 40. First, anonymous contributions may be treated as abandoned and so pass as *bona vacantia* to the Crown, which results in an application cy-près: see dicta in *Re Ulverston* [1956] Ch 622). Secondly, they may be treated as having been given out and out: see dicta of Denning LJ in *Re Hillier* [1954] 1 WLR 700. Out and out gifts might be considered to be made with the widest possible general charitable intention: see Sheridan and Delaney, *The Cy-près Doctrine*, London: Sweet & Maxwell, 1959.

If, however, s. 14 applies, some donations made by cheque may be applicable cy-près under s. 14(1): first, where, after prescribed advertisements and inquiries, a donor cannot be identified or found; and, secondly, where a donor has executed a disclaimer in the prescribed form: s. 14(1). Some of remaining donors by cheque may have given such small amounts that it would be unreasonable to incur expense in returning their money. This is dealt with by s. 14(4), which enables the court to treat property as belonging to unidentifiable donors where it would be unreasonable either:

(i)   having regard to the amounts likely to be returned to the donors, to incur the expense of returning it; or

(ii)   having regard to the nature, circumstances and amount of the gifts, and the lapse of time since they were made, for the donors to expect them to be returned.

A donor who cannot be identified, but whose donation is applied cy-près other than by virtue of s. 14(3) or (4), must claim within six months of the making of the scheme. The charity trustees are permitted to deduct properly incurred expenses from any repayment: s. 14(5). This sub-section might deal, for instance, with a large donation made by a donor who cannot be identified or found.

The street collections and the money raised by raffles will be dealt with by s. 14(3). Thus the proceeds of cash collections made by means of collecting boxes and (*inter alia*) of any lottery (after allowing for prizes) are deemed (without advertisement or inquiry) to belong to unidentifiable donors. Such money will therefore be applicable cy-près.

7 Trusts of Imperfect Obligation

INTRODUCTION

This is a brief topic upon which it is possible to find discrete questions, but it may also be incorporated into questions on other topics such as certainties or charities. For an example of this, see Chapter 13, question 00. It is an important topic in that it deals with one of the fundamental principles of trusts. Comparatively recently, the courts have devised convenient interpretations of the rules to save dispositions which might otherwise fail as purpose trusts. These cases (referred to in the suggested answers) are important developments and a familiarity with them is essential to a study of this subject.

QUESTION 1

Daniel, who died recently, made the following dispositions in his will:

(a)   £5,000 to the Seaview District Council for the erection and maintenance of a statue on the promenade in memory of my late wife.

(b)   £5,000 for the care of my cat Tortoiseshell and any kittens she may have.

(c)   £20,000 for the fostering of cordial relations and understanding between countries.

(d)   The residue of my estate to the Cranford Cricket Club for the purpose of building a new pavilion and changing rooms.

The Cranford Cricket Club is a non-charitable unincorporated association.

Advise Daniel's executors as to the validity of these dispositions.

Commentary

This is a typical problem question on this area of the law, where the examiner chooses from the cases examples of trusts which may or may not fail for certainty of objects or perpetuity. Although it is a fairly compact area of law, you need to know the cases on it and the reasoning applied in them to answer the question well.

It is possible that such a question might also include a charitable disposition. For example, in part (a), if the disposition had been for the erection of a seat on the promenade, it might have been valid as a charitable disposition under the fourth head of charity (trusts for other purposes beneficial to the community).

To obtain good marks on such a question, you would probably have to demonstrate not merely a knowledge of any authorities which may be relevant to the precise terms of the gifts, but also a broader understanding of the underlying principles, for example, a knowledge of the cases on monuments in part (a) and of Cross J's analysis of gifts to unincorporated associations in part (d).

This area of the law being fairly self-contained should, however, be an area on which well-prepared students should be able to acquit themselves well.

Suggested Answer

(a)   To be valid, a trust must comply with the requirement for certainty of objects, that is, there must be ascertainable persons able to enforce the trust. In *Morice* v *Bishop of Durham* (1805) 10 Ves 522 a trust for 'such objects of benevolence and liberality as the Bishop of Durham in his own discretion shall most approve of' was held to be void. Grant MR said that such 'an uncontrollable power of disposition would be ownership and not trust'.

To be valid a trust must also comply with the rule against perpetuities, unless it is a charitable trust.

The gift in this clause is essentially a trust for a purpose and there are no particular objects that are able to enforce it. It cannot be brought within any of the four heads of charity in *Pemsel's Case* and is therefore a non-charitable purpose trust. It is not dissimilar to the disposition in *Re Endacott* [1960] Ch 232 where a testator left his residuary estate to the North Tawton parish council 'for the purpose of providing some useful memorial to myself'. The gift could not take effect as an outright gift to the parish council as the purpose attached to it created a trust. It was not charitable and was too wide and uncertain to fall within the anomalous cases 'when Homer has nodded' (per Harman J) namely, the maintenance of tombs.

The courts have made a concession for such trusts for the maintenance of tombs and monuments and of individual animals (such trusts having been described by Roxburgh J in *Re Astor's Settlement Trusts* [1952] Ch 534 at 547 as 'concessions to human weakness or sentiment'), but only as regards lack of objects and not perpetuity, so that a trust for the erection and maintenance of a monument limited to 21 years might be valid. The gift here is for the maintenance of the statue as well as its erection, and therefore will be void additionally as infringing the perpetuity rule.

If the statue could be regarded as a monument, then a donation for its erection, but not its maintenance, would be valid under this exception to the general rule.

(b)   Although a trust for the care of animals generally (*Re Wedgwood* [1915] 1 Ch 113) and the care of cats in particular (*Re Moss* [1949] 1 All ER 495) can be a charitable trust, a trust for the care of individual animals is not. Nevertheless, a trust for the care of individual animals can be valid as a private trust, this being another anomalous exception to the rule requiring certainty of objects. Again, however, any such trust must not infringe the rule against perpetuities.

Although there are cases such as *Re Haines, The Times*, 7 November 1952 and *Re Dean* (1889) 41 ChD 552 where the judges appear to have taken judicial notice of the fact that the particular animals concerned would be unlikely to live beyond the perpetuity period (a cat in *Re Haines* and horses and hounds in *Re Dean*), it would seem that such judicial indulgence is misguided. The rule against perpetual trusts, which was expressly preserved by the Perpetuities and Accumulations Act 1964, s. 15(4), must be applied at the time the trust is created and it must be possible to say at that time that the trust will not continue for longer than the perpetuity period, which in the present case is 21 years. Moreover, the rule against perpetuities has never recognised animal lives as lives in being for the purposes of calculating the perpetuity period (*Re Kelly* [1932] IR 255).

One must therefore conclude that the disposition to Tortoiseshell and her kittens is void, although had it been limited to 21 years or 'for so long as the law allows' then it could have been valid for 21 years. It could also have been limited to the life or lives in being of a person or persons living plus 21 years as in *Re Howard, The Times*, 30 October 1908, where the lifetime of a specified servant was used to measure the perpetuity period for the maintenance of a parrot.

(c)   This disposition would again be a purpose trust without objects able to enforce it and would therefore fail unless it could be brought under one of the heads of charitable trusts. However, a disposition with laudable objects is not necessarily charitable and it is unlikely that this one would be. Although similar objects were held to be charitable within the head of education in *Re Koeppler's WT* [1986] Ch 423, the disposition there was to 'Wilton Hall', a recognised series of lectures which the testator had organised during his lifetime. This is much more vague however in its application.

In *Re Astor's Settlement Trusts* a trust for (*inter alia*) the maintenance of good understanding between nations and the preservation of the independence and integrity of the newspapers was considered too vague and uncertain as to its application for the court to administer and was void.

(**d**)   A gift to a non-charitable unincorporated association may also fail for lack of certainty of objects and for perpetuity.

There have been cases where the courts have interpreted gifts to associations as being gifts to the current members beneficially as in *Re Clarke* (1901) 2 Ch 110, where a gift to the 'Corps. of Commissionaires' was held to be a valid gift to the members beneficially for the time being.

In *Re Lipinski's Will Trusts* [1976] Ch 235 however, Oliver J followed the principle of *Re Denley's Trust Deed* [1968] 1 Ch 373 by finding that although a trust for the erection of buildings for the Hull Judeans (Maccabi) Association was expressed as a purpose trust, it was in fact for the benefit of ascertainable individuals, namely, the members of the club, and he therefore held the trust to be valid. It was argued that because the testator had made the gift in memory of his late wife, this tended to a perpetuity and precluded the association members for the time being from enjoying the gift beneficially: this argument was rejected by Oliver J. Applying the principle of *Re Lipinski* to this disposition therefore, it might well not fail for certainty of objects.

The further requirement of compliance with the rule against perpetuities must also be satisfied as regards a disposition to an unincorporated association. Gifts to members of an unincorporated association were considered in detail by Cross J in *Neville Estates Ltd* v *Madden* [1962] Ch 832. He identified two categories of unincorporated associations where any gift would not infringe the perpetuity rule, namely, where the gift is to the members themselves as joint tenants beneficially, or to the members as members of the association, but there is nothing in the rules of the association to preclude the members from deciding, if they so choose, to divide the gift up between them. In both these cases the possibility of immediate division of the gift makes it inoffensive to the rule against perpetuities. Cross J's third category however is where there is some factor, such as the rules of the association (see *Re Grant's Will Trusts* [1980] 1 WLR 360), or the nature of the gift (see *Leahy* v *A-G* (NSW) [1959] AC 457), which precludes any immediate division of it between the members of the association for the time being. Such gifts will be void. This analysis by Cross J was adopted by Brightman J in *Re Recher* [1972] 1 Ch 526 where he was prepared to accept as valid a gift to the members of an association on a contractual basis according to the terms of the association's rules, which did not preclude the members from dividing up the gift between themselves if they so decided.

Assuming that there is nothing in the rules of the Cranford Cricket Club which would preclude the members for the time being from dividing the gift between themselves if they decided to do so, the gift would not fail for perpetuity and could therefore be a valid trust.

QUESTION 2

There can be no trust over the exercise of which this court will not assume control . . . (Grant MR in *Morice* v *Bishop of Durham* (1804) 9 Ves 399).

Keeton and Sheridan, *The Law of Trusts*, 10th edn, London: Professional Books Ltd, 1974, wrote:

Modern cases regard (Grant MR) as saying that a trust must have definite human or corporate objects or be charitable. Construing his judgment in this sense has impeded the development of purpose trusts.

Explain the rationale for Grant MR's dictum and discuss the solutions which the courts have found to some of the problems raised by the rule.

Commentary

This is a fairly typical essay question on trusts of imperfect obligation which requires you to demonstrate an understanding of the rationale for such a rule. You should also be aware of the criticisms of the rule and the ways in which the courts have mitigated the harshness of it in some of the more recent cases.

Suggested Answer

One of the three requirements for certainty for a trust is certainty of objects. The reason expressed for this by Grant MR was that there must be a person or persons able to enforce the obligations of the trust against the trustees, as otherwise property would be left in their hands entirely without obligation attaching to it. This would abnegate the essential nature of a trust of division of legal and equitable ownership and would be equivalent to unfettered ownership.

Trust for charitable purposes are enforced by the Attorney-General so that this problem does not arise. However, trusts for non-charitable purposes clearly do present a problem in this respect.

A further objection to enforcing a non-charitable purpose trust is the difficulty of interpreting and applying the purpose. This was illustrated in *Re Astor's Settlement Trust* [1952] Ch 534. The court must be able to control and administer a trust itself if necessary. Any uncertainty or ambiguity as to the purpose to be carried out will make this impossible and is a further reason for the invalidity of such trusts.

A further problem with non-charitable purpose trusts is the unlimited scope of purpose which the courts might be called upon to recognise as valid. Although many non-charitable purpose trusts might be useful and beneficial to some persons, other such purported trusts may benefit nobody. The case of *Brown v Burdett* (1882) 21 ChD 667, where a house was left in trust to be shut up for 20 years, illustrates the undesirable purposes for which eccentric testators might create trusts. Such capricious trusts will not be recognised. However, any decision on the desirability or otherwise of any particular purpose necessarily involves a difficult value judgment. From a practical point of view, Roxburgh J said in *Re Astor's Settlement Trusts*:

> it is not possible to contemplate with equanimity the creation of large funds devoted to non-charitable purposes which no court and no department of State can control, or in the case of maladministration, reform.

Non-charitable purpose trusts must also comply with the perpetuity rule. An application of this rule invalidates any non-charitable purpose trust which might subsist for more than 21 years. Purpose trusts infringe this rule if they provide for the tying up of capital for more than the permitted period. If all the capital can be spent at once, this problem does not arise: *Re Lipinski's Will Trusts* [1976] Ch 235.

Nevertheless, it must be conceded that many purpose trusts may be valuable and for the law automatically to deny validity to them is harsh.

There are certain exceptions to the rule therefore which have always been recognised, and more recently the courts have been prepared to interpret purpose trusts more generously where possible to recognise 'indirect' objects and so validate them.

The clearly recognised anomalous exceptions are trusts for the maintenance of tombs and monuments and of individual animals. All such trusts must however comply with the perpetuity rule.

A gift to an unincorporated association may necessarily involve problems as to both certainty of objects and perpetuity, as the association is a fluctuating body of people which may include future members, and may have purposes which are perpetual. This problem was addressed by Cross J in *Neville Estates Ltd* v *Madden* [1962] Ch 832 who was able to find that a disposition to the members for the time being beneficially (either as joint tenants or tenants in common) is unobjectionable. They themselves are the object of the gift and so they may, if they wish, divide the gift between themselves at any time. Such a disposition is also unobjectionable on the point of perpetuity.

A second possibility is that the gift is one to the members as members of the association, in which case they take beneficially, but subject to the contractual rules of the association. Provided that there is nothing in the rules to prevent the members from agreeing to change them if necessary in order to take the gift beneficially, then the gift will again be unobjectionable on grounds of certainty of objects or perpetuity. If however, there is something in the nature or terms of the gift, or the rules of the association, which precludes the members from taking beneficially, then the gift will be for the purposes of the association and will offend the certainty of objects rule and possibly also the perpetuity rule. In *Re Grant's Will Trusts* [1980] 1 WLR 260 the rules of the local Chertsey and Walton Constituency Labour Party were subject to the rules of the National Labour Party and could not be altered by the local party. The members could not alter the rules to make the gift one which they had control over and it therefore failed.

In *Re Recher's Will Trusts* [1972] 1 Ch 526 Brightman J found that a gift to an anti-vivisection society would have been valid as within Cross J's second category, although it might have surprised the testatrix to know that this was the legal position! (In this case, a gift to an amalgamated association which was incorporated after the testatrix's death was void, as it contemplated a different contractual situation from that subsisting at death.)

In *Re Denley's Trust Deed* [1968] 1 Ch 373 land was left on trust for use as a recreation ground for the employees of a company. Goff J upheld the trust as he was able to find that the employees were the *de facto* beneficiaries, even though the trust was expressed as a purpose trust. This was followed in *Re Lipinski's Will Trusts* where a trust 'solely' for the erection and improvement of new buildings for the Hull Judeans (Maccabi) Association was held to be valid on two separate grounds, one of them being that the members of the association could be treated as the *de facto* objects of the trust. The other ground was on the contract-holding construction described in *Re Recher's Will Trusts*. Oliver J held in that case that the expressed purpose of the gift being 'in memory of my late wife' did not imply an intention to create a permanent endowment but was merely a tribute to the testator's wife and therefore did not necessarily tend to a perpetuity.

Clearly legal recognition afforded only to trusts with objects able to enforce them is open to criticism on the grounds of harshness and inflexibility and creates difficulties with endowments for unincorporated associations. Whilst any general abrogation of the rule would be undesirable, the modifications made by the courts where there are discernible 'indirect' objects are to be welcomed.

8 Implied and Resulting Trusts

INTRODUCTION

Apart from difficulties of classification, this topic should not cause great intellectual difficulties. This area, which takes well to problem questions, may well be mixed with another — there is often a combination with constructive trusts.

QUESTION 1

Distinguish a resulting trust from an implied trust and a constructive trust.

Commentary

This question raises difficult, but absorbing, issues. Students deeply interested should read Birks, P., *An Introduction to the Law of Restitution*, Oxford University Press, 1985, which places many different areas of law, including the law of trusts and the rules relating to tracing, in a restitutionary framework.

Suggested Answer

The Law of Property Act 1925, s. 53(2) excludes from the scope of s. 53(1) the creation or operation of 'resulting, implied or constructive trusts'. This might suggest that these are different examples within a single classification; but this is not so. These are, in fact, examples drawn from different methods of classification, and the terms are not therefore necessarily mutually exclusive.

The term 'resulting trust', is ambiguous. As Professor Birks has indicated, it appears to be used in two distinct senses: Birks, *An Introduction to the Law of Restitution*, pp. 57-64. First, it is used merely descriptively, i.e., to denote a trust under which a transferor or settlor retains a beneficial interest. Birks calls such a trust 'resulting in pattern'. In this sense, a beneficial interest, retained by a settlor under even an express trust, can be described as resulting: e.g., where S transfers property to T in trust for B for life, remainder for S himself. Secondly, the term is used to denote, additionally, that the settlor's interest under such a trust arises only by implication — which therefore makes it a particular species of implied (or presumed) trust. Birks calls such a trust 'resulting in origin'.

An implied trust is a trust which arises from the presumed intention of the transferor. Thus if A transfers property into the name of B, who is in law a stranger, there is an equitable presumption (except, perhaps, in the case of land) that B holds the legal title in trust for A: *Re Vinogradoff* [1935] WN 68. The presumption (which can easily be rebutted by evidence of a contrary intention) is therefore one of resulting trust. Where an implied trust leaves the beneficial interest with the settlor, it is also (in both senses) a resulting trust.

Because of this closeness of identity, resulting trusts have sometimes been
treated as synonymous with implied trusts. This, however, disregards the
fact that some trusts classifiable as implied (e.g., those arising under
mutual wills) are not resulting. It is equally wrong to treat resulting trusts
solely as a sub-species of implied trust because, as Megarry J lucidly
explained at first instance in *Re Vandervell's Trusts (No. 2)* [1974] Ch 269,
not all resulting trusts are implied. Megarry J there distinguished between
'presumed resulting trusts', which arise from the implied intention of the
transferor, and 'automatic resulting trusts', which do not depend upon
intentions or presumptions, but are an automatic consequence of the
transferor's failure to dispose of what is vested in him. An automatic
resulting trust therefore arises where, for instance, S transfers property to
T upon trust for B for life, but does not state what is to happen to the
property on B's death. In this instance, the resulting trust arises, not from
S's implied intention, but merely from S's failure to dispose of the entire
beneficial interest in the property transferred to T.

The distinction between the two types of resulting trust emerged in the
litigation involving the Vandervell family. In *Vandervell v IRC* [1967] 2
AC 291, the House of Lords held that Mr Vandervell was liable to pay tax
on dividends declared paid on shares which he had transferred to a
charity. One reason was that he had failed to dispose of his interest in a
resulting trust of an option to repurchase the shares. The retention of an
interest under a resulting trust was probably the last thing Mr Vandervell
intended, since it deprived the scheme of the very tax advantages which it
was designed to secure. As Megarry J pointed out in *Re Vandervell's
Trusts (No. 2)*, however, Mr Vandervell's interest under a resulting trust
was automatic, and not based upon his presumed intention.

Its arising independently of any intention on the part of the settlor is a
characteristic which an automatic resulting trust shares with a
constructive trust. A constructive trust, however, is not automatic: it is
imposed by equity in specific circumstances in order (broadly speaking)
to promote justice and good conscience.

There is a further important difference between resulting trusts (whether
presumed or automatic) and constructive trusts. Resulting trusts are
always substantive trusts: they can arise only where the property subject
to the trust is vested in the trustee. This is not always true of a constructive
trust. Thus, although in English law the constructive trust is considered to
be a real trust, in certain instances it seems to have a remedial function.

The trust which arises under mutual wills is often treated as constructive; yet, considered as a substantive trust, it can give rise to problems (never satisfactorily addressed in the cases) of certainty of subject-matter.

Furthermore, it appears that the courts sometimes use the language of a constructive trust as a means of imposing merely a personal liability to account: as, for instance, in *Boardman* v *Phipps* [1967] 2 AC 46, HL. It is not clear whether the beneficiaries of the Phipps Trust had a proprietary interest in the shares which Boardman had purchased.

A resulting trust can arise only in respect of property which the beneficiary under the resulting trust himself transferred, or through the purchase of property to which the beneficiary has made a direct contribution in money or money's worth. Thus where land conveyed into the name of A alone is purchased with a direct monetary contribution from B, B acquires an interest under a presumed resulting trust.

In other common situations, however, the distinction between a resulting and a constructive trust is less clear. This springs partly from dicta of Lord Diplock in *Gissing* v *Gissing* [1971] AC 886, HL, which Lord Denning MR seized upon in order to develop, in a number of judgments, such as *Eves* v *Eves* [1975] 1 WLR 1338, CA, the concept of a new model constructive trust of a remedial nature. In *Hussey* v *Palmer* [1972] 1 WLR 1286, CA, Lord Denning MR for instance, did not think it mattered whether the trust was considered to be resulting or constructive. Since *Burns* v *Burns* [1984] Ch 317, however, there has been a return to more traditional principles.

A mere agreement between the parties that B is to have an equal share in land conveyed into A's sole name, unless evidenced in writing, infringes the Law of Property Act 1925, s. 53(1)(b). If, however, B performs her part of an agreement which means using her own earnings to pay the household expenses, thus freeing A's salary for the payment of the mortgage contributions, B will acquire a beneficial interest. This cannot be an interest under a resulting trust, since her contribution is not a direct one. Her interest might be treated as an interest under a constructive trust on the basis that, by making the payments in pursuance of the agreement, B is acting to her detriment, and it would therefore be a fraud on A's part to seek to escape from the agreement by relying on s. 53(1)(b). Such reference to the agreement indicates, however, that the trust which arises, even if it is termed constructive, does take cognisance of the parties' common intention. In *Grant* v *Edwards* [1986] Ch 638, the court, on similar facts, treated this as a constructive trust. It might appositely be termed a common intention constructive trust: Hayton and Marshall, *Cases and Commentary on the Law of Trusts*, 9th edn, London: Sweet & Maxwell, 1991, p. 498.

QUESTION 2

In 1987, Rook bought shares which he transferred into the name of his nephew, Pawn, then aged 17. Pawn, however, delivered the share certificate to Rook, and always paid the dividends he received in respect of the shares into Rook's own bank account.

In 1989 Rook voluntarily, and without any expression of intention, conveyed his freehold land known as 'Castle' into Pawn's name.

Last year Rook handed Pawn a cheque in the sum of £5,000 which he had made out in Pawn's favour. At the same time Rook declared: 'This is to enable you to pay your creditors.' In fact Pawn's debts at the time amounted only to £3,000. Having paid off his creditors, Pawn gave the balance of £2,000 to his girlfriend, Queenie.

Rook died recently. In his will he gave all his property to Knight.

Advise Knight whether he has any claim to the shares, to 'Castle', or to the money received by Queenie.

Commentary

Only candidates who think that the expression '*in loco parentis*' means that you father is a train driver should experience difficulty with this question. Note that, as all the issues depend upon matters of construction and evidence, no definite conclusions are reached upon the facts.

Suggested Answer

As the sole beneficiary under Rook's will, Knight will have a claim to these items of property if he can establish that Rook retained a beneficial interest in them by way of a resulting trust. Let us deal with each item in turn.

The Shares

In certain cases, where a person puts his property into the name of another, it is presumed (in the absence of evidence to the contrary) that he intended the legal title to carry with it the beneficial interest. This is known as the presumption of advancement. It arises in three instances: transfers from husband to wife; transfers from a father to his legitimate child; and transfers from a person *in loco parentis* to his quasi-child. Transfers which do not fall within these three categories are known as transfers to strangers. Here the presumption is reversed, i.e., there is a presumption of resulting trust. It is presumed that the transferor did not intend the legal title to carry with it the beneficial interest. These presumptions are weak and are easily rebutted by evidence of the transferor's intention. Even evidence of a close relationship between the parties may be sufficient: *Fowkes* v *Pascoe* (1875) 10 Ch App 343; contrast *Re Vinogradoff* [1935] WN 68.

There is nothing in the question to indicate that, at the time he transferred the shares into the name of his nephew, Pawn, Rook stood *in loco parentis* to Pawn. In the absence of contrary evidence, therefore, the presumption is that Pawn holds the shares on a resulting trust for Rook. It is necessary to consider the impact upon this presumption of Pawn's acts subsequent to the transfer. The payment of the dividends to Rook is somewhat equivocal: it could indicate that Pawn considers himself merely a trustee for Rook, who (under a resulting trust) would have the entire equitable interest under the trust and thus (*inter alia*) a right to the dividends received. On the other hand, the payment to Rook of the dividends could be characterised as merely a series of independent gifts to Rook, of property which is now Pawn's both at law and in equity: see the judgment of Lord Denning MR in *Re Vandervell's Trusts (No. 2)* [1974] Ch 269, CA.

Pawn's delivery of the share certificate to Rook per se is evidence of a resulting trust, since it effectively puts it out of Pawn's power to deal with the shares. Unless this can be explained on some other basis — that the certificate was returned, for instance, to Rook for safe-keeping — it points away from Pawn having the beneficial interest in the shares. However, were Rook found to be *in loco parentis* to Pawn in 1987, the mere delivery to Rook of the share certificate might not be sufficient to rebut the presumption of advancement: see *Scawin* v *Scawin* (1841) 1 Y & CCC 65. Some additional evidence may be needed: in *Warren* v *Gurney*

[1944] 2 All ER 472, CA, this was supplied by a contemporaneous declaration by the father that no gift was intended. In the present case, the additional factor may be the gift of the dividends. Such evidence is not as cogent, however, as that in *Re Gooch* (1890) 62 LT 384. There, a father bought shares in a company in the name of his son, but the latter always paid the dividends to his father and even handed him the share certificate. Additionally, however, it was shown that the shares were transferred to the son in order that he could qualify as a director of the company. The presumption of advancement was rebutted.

'Castle'

Although the normal presumption upon a transfer to a stranger is one of resulting trust, this presumption may not apply in the case of a transfer of land. This is because the Law of Property Act 1925, s. 60(3), states: 'In a voluntary conveyance a resulting trust for the grantor shall not be implied merely by reason that the property is not expressed to be conveyed for the use of benefit of the grantee.' Section 60(3) could be interpreted to mean that in a voluntary conveyance of land there is always a presumption that the equitable interest passes to the grantee even if the conveyance does not state that it is for his use or benefit. Another interpretation, however, is that s. 60(3) is merely intended to ensure that, with the repeal of the Statute of Uses 1540, a beneficial interest can pass post-1925 if intended to pass even where the words 'use or benefit' are not contained in the conveyance. In *Hodgson* v *Marks* [1971] Ch 892, the court found evidence of the transferor's intention and therefore found it unnecessary to consider the effect of s. 60(3), which Russell LJ considered to be debatable.

In the absence of evidence of Rook's intention, Knight's claim depends upon the court's preferring the former interpretation.

The Money Received by Queenie

In order to determine whether Knight has a claim to the surplus, it is necessary to construe Rook's intention when he handed Pawn the cheque.

First, if certainty of intention can be found, his words might be interpreted as creating a trust in favour of Pawn's creditors. If this is so, the normal principle is that once the trust has been performed, the surplus is held on a resulting trust for the settlor — in this case, Rook. Other outcomes are, however, possible, depending upon a construction of Rook's intention. Thus, it might be found that he intended that, once the trust had been performed, any surplus should belong to the trustee (Pawn) beneficially: *Re Foord* [1922] 2 Ch 519. This might be presumed if Rook stands *in loco parentis* to Rook. Yet again, it might be found, as in *Smith* v *Cooke* [1891] AC 297, that Rook intended that the beneficiaries (in this case the creditors) should take any surplus.

Secondly, Rook's words could be held to indicate a gift of the money subject to an equitable charge in favour of the creditors. Upon this construction, it is presumed that the recipient of the fund (in this case Pawn) takes the beneficial interest in it subject only to the payment of the creditors.

Thirdly, the matter could be construed as a contract, whereby Rook pays Pawn £5,000 in consideration for Pawn's paying off his own creditors. On this basis, Pawn has performed his part of the agreement. Strictly, there is no surplus because no debts are charged upon the £5,000, but, in effect, the remaining £2,000 is Pawn's own.

Fourthly, it might be possible to treat Rook as making Pawn a conditional gift of £5,000, i.e., a gift subject to a condition that Pawn pays his own creditors.

In each of these last three constructions, neither Rook nor Knight, as the beneficiary under Rook's will, has any claim to the money paid to Queenie. Knight will therefore have a claim to trace the money into the hands of Queenie only if the first construction is adopted with a resulting trust of the surplus.

QUESTION 3

Three years ago, a bowling club was set up in Plymouth as an unincorporated non-charitable association. Under the rules of the club, members were required to pay an annual subscription of £20, which entitled them to play bowls at the club throughout the year, to use its tea-room and other facilities, and to be considered for inclusion in the team for matches with other clubs. Non-members could also play bowls at the club, subject to the payment of £2 per game. Additional funds to support the club were raised through street collections in Plymouth.

The opening of a massive new sports complex in Plymouth has caused interest in the bowling club to decline, and the club's committee has now decided to disband the club. At present, some £20,000 remains in the club's 'Common Fund', into which all payments and donations had been placed.

Advise the club's committee how they should deal with this fund.

Commentary

This is the sort of question frequently found in examinations. Sometimes it will involve a members' club, sometimes more outward-looking types of association. Make sure you deal with the allocation of each part of the fund. Note that the question-setters have been kind, and have expressly told you that the club is a non-charitable unincorporated association. Do not look this gift horse in the mouth. For additional discussion in essays, the student will find valuable analyses by Rickett, (1980) 39 CLJ 88, and by Green, (1980) 43 MLR 626.

Suggested Answer

A number of different legal approaches has been applied to resolve the issue of entitlement to the surplus funds of an unincorporated association upon its dissolution.

One approach is to treat the contributors to the fund as entitled to the surplus by way of a resulting trust. Such a trust arises because the court will presume, in the absence of an expression of intention on the part of the contributors, that they did not intend to part with their contributions out and out. This principle was applied in *Re Hobourn Air Raid Distress Fund* [1946] Ch 194, where factory employees raised a fund to provide for those amongst them who suffered in air raids. The Court of Appeal held that the surplus was held on a resulting trust for the contributors in proportion to the amount each had paid in.

This approach can cause administrative problems, however, where there are many contributors and where the fund has existed for a long time. In such circumstances, two alternative outcomes are possible without abandoning the concept of the resulting trust.

First, it might be presumed that each contributor initially retained an interest in his contribution under a resulting trust until his contribution is spent. On this basis, withdrawals from the fund could be treated as being made according to the rule in *Clayton's Case* (1816) 1 Mer 572, i.e., first in, first out. This would clearly favour later contributors over earlier ones. No reported decision, however, has applied *Clayton's Case* in this context.

Secondly, in *Re Printers* [1899] 2 Ch 184, upon dissolution of a trade union, the surplus of the funds (which had been raised by weekly contributions from members) was held by way of resulting trusts for existing members only, rateably according to their contributions. As was pointed out in *Re St Andrews Allotment Association* [1969] 1 WLR 229, however, it is difficult to see how the existing members could take by way of resulting trust a surplus partly derived from the contributions of past members.

An alternative approach is to treat the matter, not as one of trust, but as one of contract. Thus in *Cunnack* v *Edwards* [1896] 2 Ch 679, a surplus remained in a friendly society's funds after the death of the last widow annuitant. The Court of Appeal held that the members had contributed on the basis of contract, i.e., each payment was made in consideration for the payment of an annuity to the subscriber's widow. Each member had therefore enjoyed their full contractual entitlement from the fund. Thus the surplus went *bona vacantia* to the Crown. This contractual approach was also used in *Re West Sussex Constabulary's Widows, Children and Benevolent (1930) Fund Trusts* [1971] Ch 1, to deal with parts of the surplus remaining on the dissolution of a police benevolent fund. Goff J held that members' contributions, together with funds raised by way of entertainments and raffles, had all been given on a contractual basis, and should therefore go *bona vacantia* to the Crown. There, in contrast to *Re Gillingham Bus Disaster Fund* [1958] Ch 300, the judge said that anonymous contributors must be taken to have given out and out, so that this part of the surplus also went to the Crown. That part which represented the contributions of identifiable donors, however, was held for such donors on a resulting trust.

A different line of reasoning, however, emerges from a more recent line of authorities. Thus in *Re Recher's Will Trusts* [1972] Ch 526, Brightman J considered that the property of an unincorporated association was held for the members beneficially for the time being subject to the contract which exists between them, i.e., the association's rules. On this basis, unless the rules provide otherwise, the assets are held for the members at the date of dissolution equally, not on any principle of resulting trust, but simply because it is their property.

Problems with the contract holding approach remain to be addressed: how, for instance, interests can be acquired and lost by new and old members respectively without written assignments complying with the Law of Property Act 1925, s. 53(1)(c). Nevertheless, for the time being at least, this approach has found favour with the courts, e.g., in *Re Sick and Funeral Society of St. John's Sunday School, Golcar* [1973] Ch 51, *Re GKN Bolts & Nuts Ltd (Automotive Division) Birmingham Works Sports and Social Club* [1982] 1 WLR 774, and it could also explain *Re St Andrews Allotment Association* [1969] 1 WLR 229. The contract-holding approach was applied to a friendly society in *Re Bucks Constabulary Friendly Society (No. 2)* [1979] 1 WLR 936. Walton J considered that the judge in *Re West Sussex* was wrong to rely on *Cunnack* v *Edwards*. In Walton J's view, *Cunnack* v *Edwards* turned on the friendly society statutes then in force which forbade distribution of surplus to the members.

In the context of outward-looking associations and those which benefit members' widows and orphans, the authorities are therefore in some disarray. Furthermore, pension funds may be a special case, where contractual principles are not necessarily incompatible with a resulting trust: *Davis* v *Richards & Wallington Ltd* [1990] 1 WLR 1511. In the context of members' clubs, however, such as the bowling club in the problem, where the benefits are confined to the members alone, there is now a fair body of opinion favouring the contract-holding approach of *Re Recher*. Thus, subject to a contrary indication in the bowling club's rules, that part of the surplus representing members' subscriptions belongs to the members at the date of dissolution.

The members' club cases, however, have not substantially had to deal with outside contributions. Assuming the criticisms of *Re West Sussex* made in *Re Bucks* are sound, the receipts from non-members for use of the green are paid under a contract and therefore form part of the general assets of the club. The contributions from street collections will probably be treated as absolute gifts, whether or not for the reasons stated in *Re West Sussex*. Greater difficulties might arise in the case of donations from identifiable donors. Dicta in *Re Bucks* suggest that even these would belong to the present members.

In conclusion then, in the absence of anything to the contrary in the club's rules, it is probable that the whole 'Common Fund' belongs equally to those who were members at the date of dissolution.

9 Constructive Trusts

INTRODUCTION

This subject lends itself to both problem and essay questions. The knowledge gained from studying the topic may also make a useful contribution to general questions on equity such as 'Is equity as long as the Chancellor's foot?' or 'Is equity past the age of child-bearing?'

Whilst some of the concepts, such as unconscionable behaviour, unjust enrichment and fiduciary duties, are straightforward, others such as mutual wills and a stranger's liability for breach of trust, are complex and involve difficult cases. This is particularly true of the applications of an agent's liability to complicated fraud cases. The plots (and the length) of some of these would compare favourably with many novels!

Constructive trusts cover some of the 'high growth' areas of equity. For example, the 'new model constructive trust' of property owned by cohabitees has been developed by the courts over the last 23 years or so. There has, more recently, been a number of cases dealing with the liability of agents and receivers who deal with 'trust' property. The principles relating to cohabitees now appear to be fairly well settled, but those relating to agents and receivers are in some turmoil. This is an area where you should be on the look-out for new cases which further refine the principles for the application of a constructive trust.

Because it is a developing area, articles are frequently published on it in journals such as the Law Quarterly Review or the Conveyancer, and for any assessed essay you would need to refer to these. Reference has been made to some articles in the answers. The articles may be helpful too in shedding light on particularly difficult subjects, or in discussion of recent cases. Oakley's book *Constructive Trusts*, 2nd edn, London: Sweet & Maxwell, 1987, is small and readable, and although sadly not recent, would give you a sound understanding of the basic concepts.

Equity and Trusts courses vary as to the emphasis they give to constructive trusts, although all courses will include it in the syllabus to some extent. You must therefore be guided by your lecturer as to the emphasis which you should give the subject in preparing for your examination. There is of course no point in reading in depth a topic which your lecturer has barely mentioned — it will almost certainly not be examined in depth.

The general advice for all examinations holds good for this subject. Think hard about the question before you start to write. And if you have a two-part question, allocate your time roughly equally between the two parts, unless the examination paper indicates that one part is worth more marks than the other.

QUESTION 1

'English law provides no clear and all-embracing definition of a constructive trust. Its boundaries have been left perhaps deliberately vague . . .' (Edmund Davies LJ in *Carl Zeiss Stiftung* v *Herbert Smith & Co. (No. 2)* [1969] 2 Ch 276.

Discuss with reference to decided cases.

Commentary

This is a very general essay question on the nature of constructive trusts — the sort of question for which you might achieve a pass if you had not actually revised constructive trusts too specifically but had a general overall knowledge of the subject. However, to do well on it, you would need to have a good knowledge of the cases and the recent developments.

The material in this essay answer might well be adapted to similar essays on constructive trusts, such as a discussion of Lord Denning's statement in *Hussey* v *Palmer* [1972] 1 WLR 1286, CA, that 'a constructive trust is one imposed by equity whenever justice and good conscience require it'. However, do always remember that no matter how similar two essay questions may be, you should always slant your answer to the particular question asked.

Suggested Answer

A constructive trust is one imposed by the court on a person in whom the legal title to property is vested. It has the effect of divesting such persons of the whole, or part, of the equitable beneficial interest which they then hold as trustee for someone else.

The underlying rationale for the imposition of most constructive trusts is the unjust enrichment of the legal owner, which would result if they were allowed to retain the whole of the beneficial interest, and a constructive trust usually involves some fraudulent or unconscionable behaviour on the part of the legal owner. This is the application of a very general equitable principle and it is hardly surprising that the circumstances in which the courts have been prepared to impose a constructive trust are wide and varied. Moreover, it is an ever evolving area of equity where the courts are constantly defining and reviewing the principles on which a constructive trust will be imposed in new cases.

Oakley in his book *Constructive Trusts* 2nd edn 1987, identifies three well established categories of constructive trusts. These are where someone obtains an advantage from fraudulent or unconscionable behaviour, where a fiduciary derives a profit from the fiduciary relationship and where there is a disposition of property in breach of trust. Other less certain classifications he suggests are secret trusts and mutual wills (sometimes regarded as express or implied trusts), and trusts arising on the incomplete transfer of a legal title and on a specifically enforceable contract for sale.

The application of such a wide equitable jurisdiction as the constructive trust has inevitably led to different approaches by the judges. Lord Denning was always a judge with a strongly developed sense of justice and he said in *Hussey* v *Palmer* [1972] 1 WLR 1286, CA, that a constructive trust 'is a trust imposed by law whenever justice and good conscience require it. It is a liberal process, founded on large principles of equity, to be applied in cases where the defendant cannot conscientiously keep the property for himself alone, but ought to allow another to have the property or a share of it'. This suggests very much that a constructive trust is really another equitable remedy, as it is in American law, but A J Oakley argues that it should not be so regarded as it imposes heavy duties of accountability on the trustee and affects property rights. The contrary view, that the constructive trust should be constrained in its application, is put by Bagnall J in *Cowcher* v *Cowcher* [1972] 1 WLR 425, where he says that it should only be imposed on 'sure and settled principles' as otherwise 'no lawyer could safely advise on the client's title and every quarrel would lead to a law suit'. The reality is probably somewhere between the two views in that the courts do apply settled principles, but the principles themselves are frequently reviewed and modified or extended.

A good illustration of the development of constructive trusts in the context of a desire to effect justice on the one hand and a desire to keep within well defined boundaries on the other hand are the cases involving co-ownership of property where the legal title is vested in one co-owner only. In *Gissing* v *Gissing* [1971] AC 886, the House of Lords laid down the requirements for a party whose name was not on the legal title to property to acquire a beneficial interest. These were that there should be an agreement between the two co-owners, or an intention, that the co-owner whose name is not on the title should have a beneficial share and that that co-owner should act upon this to his detriment with regard to the property. However, some subsequent cases such as *Cooke* v *Head* [1972]

1 WLR 518, CA and Lord Denning MR in *Eves* v *Eves* [1975] 1 WLR
1338, CA, adopt a more liberal view in order to achieve justice in the
instant case. This approach was however, disapproved of by the Court of
Appeal in *Burns* v *Burns* [1984] Ch 317, which returned to the principles
laid down by the House of Lords in *Gissing* v *Gissing*. The principles have
received fairly recent confirmation and some refinement by Lord Bridge
in *Lloyds Bank Ltd* v *Rosset* [1991] AC 107.

Constructive trusts have been used in widely differing situations to give
effect to the maxim of equity, applied in *Rochefoucauld* v *Bousted* [1897]
1 Ch 196, that 'Equity will not allow a Statute to be used as an instrument
of fraud'. Evidence of secret trusts is admissible in contravention of the
Wills Act 1837, as to refuse to admit evidence of the trust could result in
the perpetration of a fraud on the intended beneficiary or the testator. In
Bannister v *Bannister* [1948] 2 All ER 133, CA, evidence was accepted of
an oral agreement between the plaintiff and the defendant that the
defendant should be allowed to occupy the cottage which she had sold to
the plaintiff at below the market price. This did not comply with the Law
of Property Act 1925, s. 40 as the plaintiff would otherwise have obtained
an unfair advantage by fraud. More recently, in *Lyus* v *Prowsa
Developments Ltd* [1982] 1 WLR 1044, the court accepted that a
purchaser who took property expressly subject to the right of another was
bound by that right even if it was not registered under the Land
Registration Act 1925, as it could have been.

The courts have shown themselves ready to apply a constructive trust to
the profits derived by a fiduciary from his fiduciary relationship in a
number of differing circumstances, and in *Boardman* v *Phipps* [1967] 2
AC 46 the House of Lords decided (Lord Upjohn dissenting) that a profit
made as a result of information acquired from the fiduciary relationship
was within the principle. In *Reading* v *A-G* [1951] AC 507, HL, the
concept of fiduciary relationship was extended to that of an army officer
and the Crown. The principle means that a trustee may not profit from his
position and the courts have applied this to widely differing
circumstances. For example, in *Keech* v *Sandford* (1726) Sel Cas Ch 61, a
trustee in whose name a lease was renewed was held to be a constructive
trustee of it for the trust, and in *Re Macadam* [1946] Ch 73, a trustee who
was able to use his position as trustee to appoint himself as director of a
company was held to be a constructive trustee for the trust of his director's
fees.

One of the constructive trusts which has seen the most development in recent years however, is the trust imposed where a person knowingly receives or deals with trust property in breach of trust. This type of constructive trust was recognised by Lord Selborne in *Barnes* v *Addy* (1874) 9 Ch App 244, but the definition of its requirements has been judicially considered in a number of recent cases, often involving fraud. An attempt was made by Gibson J in *Baden, Delvaux and Lecuit* v *Societé General* [1983] BCLC 325 to define the types of knowledge which would make an agent accountable as a constructive trustee, but the law in this area is by no means settled. Thus, whilst some decisions have regarded constructive notice as sufficient (*Selangor United Rubber Estate Ltd* v *Cradock (Bankrupt) (No. 3)* [1968] 1 WLR 1555), others have not, and have required evidence of 'a want of probity' in failing to enquire further (*Cowan de Groot Properties Ltd* v *Eagle Trust plc* [1992] 4 All ER 700). This latter approach would seem to be more in line with the general principles of constructive trusts that the defendant's conscience must be affected. It is arguable too that the constructive trust imposed upon an agent is not a true constructive trust in the sense that such an agent is not holding the property itself on trust. It may be that the court simply declares the agent a constructive trustee in order to impose a more personal liability to account.

It is clear from the widely differing situations in which constructive trusts have been applied that it is a versatile and flexible weapon of equity, capable of apparently unlimited adaptability to changing social and commercial circumstances. It justifies the statement by Lord Denning MR in *Eves* v *Eves* that 'Equity is not past the age of childbearing'. However, its adaptability necessarily requires that its boundaries should not be too rigidly defined.

QUESTION 2

Angela was the Council tenant of a house when Bertram, a married man, went to live with her there 10 years ago. A year later, the Council offered to sell the house to Angela at a discounted price, being 40 per cent less than the market price, and Angela discussed this with Bertram. They agreed that the house should be conveyed into Angela's name alone as she was the tenant with the right to buy and Bertram was involved in divorce proceedings and property claims from his wife. Of the £30,000 discounted price, £5,000 was contributed by Bertram and the remaining £25,000 was raised by a mortgage in Angela's name which was guaranteed by Bertram.

Angela and Bertram contributed equally to the mortgage repayments until Angela had a baby about a year later, after which Bertram paid them. Angela and Bertram decided to modernise the kitchen and the bathroom, and Bertram, being a qualified carpenter, made all the fitments and did most of the work. Three years ago, they decided to build an extension and Angela took a further mortgage with the Quicklend Bank plc for £30,000 to pay for this. Repayments on this mortgage were also made by Bertram.

Six months ago Bertram left Angela and is now claiming a share of the house. Angela has defaulted on the mortgage instalments to the Quicklend Bank plc who are claiming possession.

Advise Bertram and the Quicklend Bank plc.

Commentary

This is the type of question which could arise in land law, family law or trusts, although each might have a particular slant. There has been much litigation surrounding the area of constructive trusts, but the principles are now fairly well settled.

It is also an area which has developed since its early recognition in *Gissing* v *Gissing* [1971] AC 886 where Lord Diplock said at 905, 'A resulting, implied or constructive trust — and it is unnecessary for present purposes to distinguish between these three classes of trust . . .'. D J Hayton (in his article referred to below) puts forward some sound reasons for distinguishing a resulting from a constructive trust. In any answer to this type of question on a trusts paper, you should do the same.

It may be possible to calculate a party's interest under a resulting trust when the property is first bought, but examiners are not likely to want you to attempt complicated calculations to ascertain an exact share. All that you can be expected to do is to know factors which have been taken into account in the cases as increasing a party's share.

The parties in this question are not married, but you should of course remember that in the case of married couples there is legislation governing the distribution of matrimonial property on divorce, notably the Matrimonial Proceedings and Property Act 1970, s. 37 and the Matrimonial Causes Act 1973, but you would not be expected to deal with these in any depth in a trusts examination. Lord Denning MR has said that s. 37 is merely declaratory of the existing law as to constructive trusts, but there could be a different result in that the section applies 'subject to any agreement to the contrary'.

Suggested Answer

If the original purchase price of £30,000 represented a discount of 40 per cent, then the market price was £50,000 and £20,000 was allowed to Angela as a Council tenant exercising her right to buy. Of the original purchase price therefore £20,000 is to be regarded as having been contributed by Angela, £5,000 by Bertram and £25,000 by a mortgage to which they originally contributed equally but latterly Bertram has paid. In *Springette* v *Defoe* (1992) 24 HLR 552, CA, the discount on the market price on a sale to a council tenant from the market price was credited to the tenant who was entitled to it under the legislation.

Where a person contributes to the purchase price of property and there is no evidence of an intention of gift and no circumstances from which a presumption of advancement arises, there will be a resulting trust for that person of a proportionate part of the equitable interest according to their contribution. There would therefore be a resulting trust for Bertram of one tenth of the equitable interest and some part of the one half for which they both contributed to the mortgage.

A person whose name is not on the title deeds may also acquire an equitable interest in property under a constructive trust if they comply with the requirements laid down in *Gissing* v *Gissing* [1971] AC 886, HL. There must be evidence of an agreement (express or inferred) or a common intention that that person is to have a beneficial interest in the property at the time of its acquisition, and he or she must have acted on this understanding to their detriment. In *Lloyds Bank Ltd* v *Rosset* [1991] AC 107, HL, Lord Bridge expressed the view that the detriment could be some material alteration in a party's position in the case of an express agreement, but that in the case of an inferred agreement some direct contributions to the purchase price of the property, either initially or by way of contribution to the mortgage instalments, would be necessary.

It is possible to infer such a common intention from what was said when the property was purchased and a party who has impliedly agreed to this may be estopped from denying it later. In *Eves* v *Eves* [1975] 1 WLR 1338,

CA, the man said that the woman's name could not be included on the legal title because she was under age, and in *Grant* v *Edwards* [1986] Ch 638 it could not be included because it would prejudice any settlement in the woman's divorce proceedings. In both cases, the reasons given for omitting the woman's name implied that her name would otherwise have been included on the legal title, and it was possible to draw an inference from this that she was intended to have a share of the beneficial interest in the property.

The parties' agreement in this case as to why Bertram's name should be left off the legal title might similarly lead to the inference of a common intention that he should have a share of the beneficial interest. His initial contribution of £5,000 and his guarantee of the mortgage (as in *Falconer* v *Falconer* [1970] 1 WLR 1333, CA) would also assist in reaching this conclusion.

Assuming this to be so, Bertram would then have to show that he subsequently acted to his detriment in reliance upon this. He has contributed substantially to the mortgage repayments and carried out improvements to the property, and these might both be regarded as sufficient conduct to his detriment to enable him to acquire an interest under a constructive trust, thereby increasing his original equitable interest.

The extension appears to have been a joint venture in that the mortgage to finance it was in Angela's name but Bertram has made the repayments. In *Hussey* v *Palmer* [1972] 1 WLR 1286, CA, a mother-in-law's payment for an extension to her son-in-law's house was held to give rise to a constructive trust in her favour. Similarly here Bertram could again have an increased share of the equitable interest in the increased value of the property under a constructive trust.

The Quicklend Bank plc have made a further loan to Angela and it is necessary to consider whether they are bound by any equitable interest in the property which Bertram has. In his article 'Equitable rights of cohabitees' (1990) Conv 370, D J Hayton suggests that, as regards third parties, an interest acquired under a resulting trust is more likely to be binding than one acquired under a constructive trust. An interest under a resulting trust is acquired for money or money's worth at the time when the property is purchased, whereas an interest under a constructive trust may have an element of voluntary settlement, and in any event will not be acquired until the party has acted to his detriment, which will necessarily be subsequent to the purchase. In *Re Densham* [1975] 1 WLR 1519, the original contribution of half the deposit on a house which the wife made towards the purchase price was held to give her a one ninth share in the equitable interest under a resulting trust which was good subsequently against the husband's trustee in bankruptcy, but any increased share which she might have acquired under a constructive trust was void under bankruptcy law as there was an element of voluntary settlement in it.

On this basis, it would appear that the Quicklend Bank plc might take subject to Bertram's initial interest under the resulting trust, but free from at least some part of his subsequently acquired interest under a constructive trust.

QUESTION 3

Five years ago Olga, a spinster, married Clive, a widower with three children. They agreed to make wills in identical terms leaving their property to each other and then to Clive's two daughters, Amy and Bea. Wills in accordance with this agreement were executed by both of them shortly after they married. Clive had quarrelled with his son Nigel and did not want him to benefit from his estate.

About three years ago Clive became seriously and terminally ill. Amy was a nurse and Clive told her that if she would take unpaid leave to go and live with him to look after him, as Olga was not strong enough, he and Olga would ensure that his house 'Greensleeves' would be left to her. Amy took unpaid leave and nursed her father for nine months before he died. While living at the house, she paid for the modernisation of the kitchen and bathroom.

Some three months before he died Clive and Olga executed identical codicils to their wills, both signed on the same day, varying the ultimate disposition of 'Greensleeves' so that Amy should receive it from the survivor of them and the remainder of their property should ultimately be divided between Amy and Bea.

After Clive died, Olga gave away considerable property which had belonged to Clive to charity. She also won £500,000 on the football pools. Nigel, who lived near to Olga, visited her regularly and did small jobs for her. Olga died recently and a will was found among her papers, dated a few days before she died, revoking all previous wills and testamentary dispositions and leaving all her property 'to my wonderful stepson Nigel'.

Advise Amy and Bea.

Commentary

This question raises some of the unresolved difficulties relating to mutual wills. You should be aware of these problems and also of the necessary requirements to establish mutual wills. Apart from this, however, the question is fairly straightforward.

The facts of the question disclose two possible causes of action available to one of the parties (Amy) whom you are asked to advise. If you come to the conclusion that Amy is likely to succeed on one ground, you should of course nevertheless go on to consider the other ground also. REAL cases are often pleaded in the alternative!

Although the times referred to in this question are sufficiently vague to admit of a consideration of the equitable doctrine of part performance, this will presumably become rarer in its applications as time passes. It is probably safe to assume that many courses will not now include this, so if it is not something to which your lecturer has referred, you can probably ignore it.

Suggested Answer

The enforceability of mutual wills depends upon an agreement between the parties making them. The agreement is that they will both make wills in substantially the same form, leaving property in accordance with the agreement, and they agree not to revoke the wills. It will be an unenforceable agreement until such time as the first of the parties dies, as it will not be supported by consideration until then. However, when the first party dies, the consideration is the benefit which the survivor receives under their will, and the agreement then becomes binding on the conscience of the survivor, who has received a benefit.

It is often difficult to find sufficient evidence of the agreement to establish that the parties did intend to make mutual wills. The fact that the wills are identical is some evidence but is not in itself sufficient (*Re Oldham* [1925] Ch 75) as there should also be an agreement not to revoke the wills.

However, in *Re Cleaver* [1981] 1 WLR 939, where two sets of wills were made by a husband and wife in identical form and a further will by the surviving wife consistent with her second identical will, this was held to be sufficient evidence of an agreement. The identical wills made here, together with identical codicils giving effect to identical changes, would probably be sufficient to establish the necessary agreement as in *Re Cleaver*.

It is probable therefore that Amy and Bea will be able to challenge Olga's will leaving all her property to Nigel, and require her estate to be administered according to the terms of her will and codicil made shortly before Clive died.

There are a number of vexed questions with regard to the property which is subject to any trust created by mutual wills and there do not seem to be any very satisfactory answers.

Does any trust arising attach only to the property which the survivor receives from the other party to the agreement, or does it attach to all the survivor's property on death? If the latter, then the £500,000 which Olga won on the football pools would also be subject to any trust arising. As the survivor entered into an agreement to leave all their own property to the same third party too, this would seem to be a tenable argument. In *Re Estate of Monica Dale (deceased), The Times*, 16 February 1993, it was held that the trust attached to all the property held by the survivor at the date of the survivor's death. In *Re Hagger* [1930] 2 Ch 190, also a first instance decision, it was considered that the trust should at least attach to all the property held by the survivor at the date of the first death.

Does the trust arising prevent the survivor from disposing of any property they receive under the will of the first to die? If so, it would effectively be only a life interest in that property which the survivor has. In the Australian case of *Birmingham* v *Renfrew* (1937) 57 CLR 666, Dixon J said that the survivor could enjoy the property as if an absolute owner, subject to restrictions on his rights of alienability, but that on his death there was a 'floating obligation' which crystallised and attached to the property. If this is correct, presumably an action could have been brought during Olga's lifetime to prevent her from disposing of any very large sums of money. This point was not considered in *Re Estate of Monica Dale (deceased)*.

Additionally, Amy may have a ground to claim the house 'Greensleeves' under either the equitable doctrine of part performance or proprietary estoppel.

If Amy went to nurse Clive, and the statement with regard to the house 'Greensleeves' was made before 27 September 1989 (when the Law of Property (Miscellaneous Provisions) Act 1989 became operative as regards contracts for the disposition of land), Amy might be able to enforce the agreement to give her the house under the doctrine of part performance. A similar claim was successful in *Wakeham* v *Mackenzie* [1968] 1 WLR 1175 where a housekeeper was able to enforce an oral contract to give her the house in return for work which she had carried out.

However, the 1989 Act repealed the Law of Property Act 1925 s. 40, and provided that contracts for the sale or disposition of land have to be in writing and signed by both parties. So if the agreement as regards the house and Amy's actions were on or after 27 September 1989, she would (probably) not be able to plead part performance. She might well have a claim under the equitable doctrine of proprietary estoppel however. This operates where a party makes a promise to someone and the promisee acts to their detriment on that promise. The promisor is then estopped from going back on their promise and an equity attaches to the property to which it relates, not only in the hands of the promisor himself but also in the hands of a volunteer acquiring the property from him. Thus in *Inwards* v *Baker* [1965] 2 QB 29, CA, a son who was persuaded by his father to build a bungalow on a plot of land belonging to the father was able to remain there after the father died and the land passed to his mistress. In *Pascoe* v *Turner* [1979] 1 WLR 431 a man who told a cohabitee with whom he lived that his house and contents all belonged to her, and was aware that she was spending her frugal savings on repairing and redecorating the house after he had left, was estopped from denying this and was obliged to convey the fee simple in the property to her.

Although at one time proprietary estoppel could only be used to defend an action and not to found one, it has developed so that it may now also found an action. The acquiescence relied upon to found an action of proprietary estoppel should relate to the property, Amy has acted to her detriment in modernising the property, and if this was in reliance upon her father's promise, this may well be sufficient. Both Olga and Nigel are volunteers, so that Amy's claim to the house, which is necessarily equitable and not registrable under the Land Charges Act 1972 (per Denning LJ in *Ives (ER) Investment Ltd* v *High* [1967] 2 QB 379) might succeed on this ground also.

QUESTION 4

By his will Peter bequeathed 50 casks of brandy to Smee absolutely. Shortly after the will was made, Peter handed Smee a sealed envelope marked 'Not to be opened until after my death'. He asked Smee to hold the brandy on the terms contained therein, and Smee agreed. The sealed instructions state that Smee can drink as much of the brandy as he likes during his life, but that he must, by his will, bequeath whatever is left to Peter's mistress Tinkerbell.

Peter and Tinkerbell were in a flying accident last month. Tinkerbell was killed instantly and Peter died the next day. Tinkerbell had witnessed Peter's will. Smee says he intends to sell the brandy and spend the proceeds on a world cruise. Advise Tinkerbell's executors.

Commentary

This is a particularly difficult problem question which you might want to avoid even if you have revised secret trusts and mutual wills very well! If you fail to appreciate all its different aspects however, you should nevertheless be able to pick up some marks fairly easily for knowing some of the points involved, such as what happens if the secret beneficiary witnesses the will or predeceases the testator.

Definitely a question to think hard about, however, before you set pen to paper!

Suggested Answer

As the brandy is bequeathed to Smee absolutely with no indication on the face of the will that it is to be held by him on trust, this purports to create a fully secret trust.

For a fully secret trust to be valid, it must be accepted by the trustee at any time before the death of the testator. Provided that the trust itself has been accepted, it is probably sufficient if the exact terms are contained in a sealed envelope which is not to be opened until after the testator's death

(Lord Wright MR obiter in *Re Keen* [1937] Ch 236, CA). Although *Re Keen* was concerned with a half secret trust, there would seem to be no reason why the principle should not be applicable also to a fully secret trust. It is possible that in the case of a half secret trust, communication has to be by handing over the sealed envelope before the execution of the will (*Re Bateman's Will Trusts* [1970] 1 WLR 1463), but in the case of a fully secret trust, it could be handed over at any time before death.

Assuming that these circumstances create a valid secret trust for Tinkerbell, it will not matter that Tinkerbell, who was a beneficiary under the trust, witnessed Peter's will: *Re Young* [1951] Ch 344, where it was held that a beneficiary under a half secret trust who had witnessed the will was nevertheless able to take under it. The reason is that the beneficiary took under the secret trust and not under the will. There would seem to be no reason why this principle should not apply also to a fully secret trust.

It is more questionable however, whether Tinkerbell's predeceasing Peter will render the trust void. In *Re Gardner (No. 2)* [1923] 2 Ch 230, where the secret beneficiary predeceased the testatrix, Romer J held that there was a valid trust for her estate, but this decision has been criticised. Normally a gift to a beneficiary who predeceases the testator will lapse. Even if the doctrine of lapse is avoided by construing the secret trust as one which arises at the moment it is accepted by the secret trustee during the lifetime of the testator, it cannot be fully constituted until his death, and it must be fully constituted to be valid. Nevertheless, if the decision in *Re Gardner (No. 2)* is applied, then Tinkerbell's estate would be able to benefit.

A more serious problem in construing Peter's arrangement as a secret trust is that of certainty of subject matter. In *Sprange* v *Barnard* (1789) 2 Bro CC 585, where a testatrix left property to her husband for his sole use and at his death 'the remaining part of what is left' was to be divided between a brother and sister, the trust failed for certainty of subject matter. So a secret trust of whatever brandy Smee does not drink may well similarly fail for certainty of subject matter.

However, it might be possible to argue that the arrangement resembles the type of agreement necessary for mutual wills. Smee agrees to hold the brandy on the terms contained in the envelope and he is thereby (although he does not realise it) agreeing to dispose of it in a certain way by his will. In *Ottaway* v *Norman* [1972] Ch 698, a similar sort of arrangement was successfully enforced by the secret beneficiary, but the case was pleaded as a secret trust and not as mutual wills, and as such was only valid as regards that property which was certain, namely a bungalow. However, mutual wills may be valid even if they involve just the type of uncertainty of subject matter as here (see Dixon J in an Australian case *Birmingham* v *Renfrew* (1937) 57 CLR 666, as to the nature of enjoyment and obligation under such an arrangement, namely, rights of virtually full ownership during the survivor's lifetime and an obligation as regards the property which crystallises on his death).

The usual type of agreement for mutual wills is that the parties to it agree to benefit each other and then an agreed third party, but there would seem to be no reason why one party who accepts a benefit should not do so on terms which require him to confer a benefit on a third party, as indeed was the case in *Ottaway* v *Norman*. In *Re Estate of Monica Dale (deceased), The Times*, 16 February 1993, it was not even considered necessary for the survivor to receive a personal benefit. It would be necessary however to establish a clear agreement, and it would be arguable that it could not be a binding agreement if Smee did not know the full terms of what he was agreeing to.

Therefore it is just possible, although unlikely, that an action by Tinkerbell's executors might succeed if pleaded as a mutual will.

QUESTION 5

(a) '. . . the whole basis of secret trusts . . . is that they operate outside the will' (Megarry V-C in *Re Snowden (deceased)* [1979] Ch 528).

Discuss.

(b) Meg, a wealthy but eccentric elderly spinster, decided to leave a large legacy to the Battersea Dogs' Home but did not want her family to know. She therefore asked her old friend James if he and his son Sam would hold any property she left to them in her will in trust for the Home. James agreed. Meg made a will the following week leaving £50,000 to James and Sam. James did not tell Sam of Meg's wishes and Meg also forgot to mention anything about it to Sam. Subsequently, Meg decided to increase the legacy to £100,000 and executed a codicil to this effect. She told neither James nor Sam about the codicil however.

Advise Meg's executors as to what extent the secret trust is effective. Would your answer differ if the legacy had been left to James and Sam as tenants in common?

Commentary

The two parts of this question make it a fairly lengthy one. You should not be deterred by this as it means that there are a lot of points for you to pick up. However, it does mean that your answer to the essay part must be fairly concise and you must avoid going into too much detail on it at the expense of the time required to answer the problem part.

Suggested Answer

(a)   Equity's enforcement of secret trusts necessarily involves accepting evidence of a testator's intentions which were not embodied in his will and which do not therefore comply with the Wills Act 1837, s. 9.

To be valid, a secret trust must be accepted by the secret trustee although the time of acceptance varies according to whether the trust is a fully secret trust or a half-secret trust. To allow the secret trustee to renege on this agreement would amount to a fraud on the beneficiaries of the trust and on the testator, in that he would not have left property to the secret trustee if he had not agreed to the trust. Such rationale may also explain equity's intervention in half-secret trusts, under which the trustee himself cannot derive any benefit as legatee or devisee. Fraud on the beneficiary was the rationale accepted for secret trusts in *McCormick* v *Grogan* (1869) LR 4 HL 82 but this applied only to fully secret trusts. In *Blackwell* v *Blackwell* [1929] AC 318, however, Viscount Sumner took the view that a secret trust is created and becomes binding as a result of the communication of it by the testator to the secret trustee and his acceptance of it during the testator's lifetime, and that the trust which consequently arises is therefore governed by the law relating to trusts and is outside the scope of the Wills Act 1837.

Although this is a better explanation for the operation of secret trusts, it is not entirely satisfactory because the secret trust depends upon the proving of the will for its constitution. This dependence has thrown up some unhappy conflicts in cases where strict adherence to the Wills Act 1837 would have invalidated a secret trust, but the courts have nevertheless been prepared to recognise its existence.

Constructive Trusts

It is debatable, for example, to what extent a secret trust will be enforceable if the secret trustee predeceases the testator or disclaims the gift under the will, and this may vary according to whether the secret trust is fully secret or half-secret. In the case of a half-secret trust the principle that equity will not allow a trust to fail for want of a trustee would probably apply to save the trust. However, Cozens-Hardy LJ in *Re Maddock* [1902] 2 Ch 220, CA, expressed the opinion that a fully secret trust would fail if the secret trustee renounced or disclaimed the gift or died in the lifetime of the testator.

In *Re Gardner (No. 2)* [1923] 2 Ch 230 the beneficiary under a half-secret trust had predeceased the testatrix. This should have resulted in the gift to her lapsing, but Romer LJ held that it went to her personal representatives. Note, however, that this decision has been criticised.

In *Re Young* [1951] Ch 344 one of the beneficiaries of a half-secret trust witnessed the testator's will which would have invalidated any gift to him in the will itself. The court held that the legacy was nevertheless valid because the beneficiary took under the trust and not under the will.

Many of the decisions therefore illustrate the courts' willingness to modify the strict requirements of the Wills Act 1837 where necessary to give effect to a secret trust. This suggests that the tendency is indeed to regard secret trusts as being governed by the law relating to trusts, deriving from the agreement between the testator and the trustee.

(b)   In *Re Stead* [1900] 1 Ch 237, Farwell J had to consider the situation where a fully secret trust was communicated to one joint tenant trustee but not the other. He stated the rules applicable in a technical way, distinguishing between secret trustees who were joint tenants and secret trustees who were tenants in common. In the case of tenants in common, an acceptance of the secret trust by one only will never bind his co-trustee, as tenants in common take a distinct and separate share in property left to them. In the case of joint tenants, however, communication to one of them before the will is made binds all of them, but communication after the will binds only those to whom communication is made.

In his article 'Can you keep half a secret?' (1972) 88 LQR 225, Bryn Perrins suggests that the distinction between joint tenants and tenants in common arises from a misinterpretation of early cases, notably *Huguenin* v *Baseley* (1807) 14 Ves 273, in which the rationale for deciding whether a co-trustee, with whom there was no communication, was bound or not, was whether the testator was induced by the promise of the secret trustee to make (or to leave unrevoked) the gift to him in the will. As the relationship between joint tenants is closer than that between tenants in common, a testator is more likely to assume that a joint tenant will readily accept an obligation imposed on a fellow joint tenant and this could therefore induce the gift to them jointly in the will. Thus communication to one of them before the will is made should bind both of them. It is probably more difficult, however, to prove that a gift previously made was left unrevoked by a subsequent promise, so that even a joint tenant trustee where communication is after the will would not generally be bound. A gift to tenants in common gives each of them a distinct and separate share and it is clearly inappropriate to expect that communication to one of them should bind the others whether before or after the execution of the will.

Applying these rules to the question, the secret trustees are joint tenants as there are no words of severance used in the gift. Communication was made to one of them before the will was made, and following the 'inducement' rationale behind the technical statement of the rules in *Re Stead*, the communication will bind both of them. Both James and Sam are bound by the secret trust for £50,000.

However, the subsequent codicil has to be communicated to the secret trustee and accepted in the same way or it will not bind the trustees: *Re Colin Cooper* [1939] Ch 811. Meg's failure to inform either James or Sam will mean that neither of them are bound by the trust as regards the increased legacy and the trust will not affect the further £50,000. If the legacy had been left to James and Sam as tenants in common, then only James would have been bound by the secret trust of the first gift of £50,000 in Meg's will, as tenants in common are presumed to take distinct and separate shares and a communication to one will never bind another. As far as the codicil is concerned, neither of them is bound.

QUESTION 6

Alf is a trustee of the Beta Trust which has a 30 per cent shareholding in Gamma Ltd, a pharmaceutical company developing a new drug to stimulate memory, primarily for students taking examinations. In his position as trustee, Alf learned that tests on the drug were indicative of a successful outcome, and he therefore purchased a 25 per cent shareholding in the company himself. He was subsequently elected as a director of the company and has received considerable sums in director's fees.

Shortly after Alf became a director, the company's lease on its factory premises expired and its landlord wanted to sell the reversion for £100,000. The company could not afford this, so Alf and the company's solicitor, Delta, purchased the reversion themselves jointly. They then granted a new lease to the company at a lower rent than under the previous lease.

The company were also interested in a new drug for improving concentration which had been patented. It was agreed between Alf and Delta that Alf would negotiate to buy the patent and, if successful, would receive for his efforts one per cent of the purchase price. He negotiated a purchase for £20,000.

Alf began to have doubts about the company's future and decided to sell his shareholding and retire from the directorship. Having retired as a trustee from the Beta Trust six months previously, he sold his shares in Gamma Ltd to the trust for £5,000 above the market value.

The new drugs which the company were developing have recently failed pharmaceutical tests and the company's shares are now almost worthless.

Alf and Delta have received an offer of £150,000 for the freehold of the factory premises and would like to sell it.

Discuss Alf's liability as a fiduciary in the various circumstances.

Commentary

This is a fairly lengthy question involving different fiduciary relationships and different breaches of fiduciary duties. It is the type of question which you should therefore spend some time thinking through, jotting down different points and any relevant cases before embarking on the answer. The risk is, if you do not do this, that you will get to the end and find that there are some points or cases which you have omitted. The question is wide in its scope and requires a fair knowledge of the subject to produce a reasonable answer.

Suggested Answer

Equity has consistently demonstrated a harsh attitude to the rule that a fiduciary may not benefit from his position. The rule has been applied even where there is no conflict of interest between the fiduciary and the principal and no evidence of an actual consequent injury to the principal. Even in these circumstances, a fiduciary will still be accountable for a profit derived from his fiduciary relationship.

Moreover, a fiduciary relationship has been very broadly defined and is not restricted to the narrow relationship between a trustee and beneficiary. A director is in a fiduciary position to his company, an agent to his principal, and an employee may also be in a fiduciary relationship to his employer: *Agip (Africa) Ltd* v *Jackson* [1991] Ch 547, CA. In *Reading* v *A-G* [1951] AC 507 it was held that an army officer was in a fiduciary position to the Crown.

A trustee who uses his position to appoint himself as a director of a company is prima facie accountable to the trust for any remuneration he receives as a director: *Re Macadam* [1946] Ch 73. In order to be able to keep his director's fees, Alf would have to show that his appointment as a director would have been made even if the votes attaching to the trust's shares had been used against him (per Harman J in *Re Gee* [1948] Ch 284). So if Alf can show that he would still have been elected as a director, notwithstanding that the voting rights of the Beta Trust's shares had been used to vote against him, then he will be able to keep his director's fees. Otherwise, he will be prima facie accountable to the Trust for them. He would also be able to retain his director's fees if authorised in the trust instrument: *Re Llewellin* [1949] Ch 225.

If the trust property includes a lease, a trustee to whom the lease is renewed (*Keech* v *Sandford* (1726) Sel Cas Ch 61), or who purchases a reversion on the lease (*Protheroe* v *Protheroe* [1968] 1 WLR 519, CA), will become a constructive trustee of the lease or reversion for the beneficiaries. In *Protheroe* a husband and wife were co-owners of a leasehold interest in their matrimonial home. They separated and the husband subsequently purchased the reversion on the lease. It was held that this became trust property in which his wife also had an interest. As a director of Gamma Ltd, Alf is in a fiduciary position to the company and would therefore hold one-half of the reversion on the lease as a constructive trustee for the company. He would similarly be accountable for one-half of any profit made on its sale. It is irrelevant that the company itself could not have purchased the reversion, or that the company itself benefited from the transaction. In *Regal (Hastings) Ltd* v *Gulliver* [1942] 1 All ER 378, HL, directors purchased shares, which the company could not afford to purchase, in order to enable the company to take a lease of a cinema, and subsequently to sell it with other property owned by the company at a profit. They were nevertheless held accountable for their profits as they had acquired their shares through their fiduciary position.

In *Guinness plc* v *Saunders* [1990] 2 AC 663 a director who received an unauthorised fee of 0.2 per cent of the value of a takeover bid was held by the House of Lords to be a constructive trustee of this for the company. Nor was he able to claim payment for his services on a *quantum meruit* as he had created a conflict of interest between himself (in whose interest it was to pay a high price) and the company. Assuming that Delta was not authorised to award director's remuneration, the agreement between Delta and Alf would not be binding on the company, and any commission would be a profit derived from Alf's fiduciary position as a director. He would therefore not be able to claim any such commission. As in *Guinness* v *Saunders*, any such agreement would also create a conflict of interest between Alf and the company in that Alf has an interest in purchasing for a high price and the company in purchasing for a low price. He would similarly not have any claim for work undertaken in this connection on a *quantum meruit*.

The case of *Boardman* v *Phipps* [1967] 2 AC 46, HL, indicates that a trustee who uses information obtained as a result of his fiduciary position to make a profit will be a constructive trustee of that profit for the trust. If it could be shown, therefore, that Alf had serious doubts about the company's future when he sold the shares to the Trust, this would amount to a breach of his fiduciary duty and he might be made liable for the subsequent loss to the Trust.

The rule in *ex parte Lacey* (1802) 6 Ves 625, which is strictly applied, precludes a trustee from purchasing trust property, and this applies even after a trustee has retired: *Wright* v *Morgan* [1926] AC 788. A trustee's liability does not necessarily cease on his retirement: he or his estate will remain liable for breaches of trust committed during his trusteeship. The rule in *ex parte Lacey* applies to any dealing between the trustee in his personal capacity and in his capacity as trustee. In *Bentley* v *Craven*

(1853) 18 Beav 75, it was held that an agent employed to purchase sugar for a company could not sell to the company sugar he had purchased himself, even at the market price, unless his interest was declared and accepted by the company. In that case, Romilly MR said (obiter) that the same principle would apply to other fiduciary relationships, including a dealing by a trustee with a trust. The transaction necessarily puts the agent in a position of conflict with his principal as to price. Unless there is a full disclosure as to the agent's interest, which is accepted by the principal, the principal may either repudiate the transaction or claim any profit which the agent makes on it. It is quite possible here therefore that the Trust could repudiate the sale to them and claim back the purchase price. It is irrelevant that it was an advantageous sale to the Trust at the time when it was made.

QUESTION 7

> . . . strangers are not to be made constructive trustees merely because they act as the agents of trustees in transactions within their legal powers . . . unless those agents receive and become chargeable with some part of the trust property or unless they assist with knowledge in a dishonest and fraudulent design on the part of the trustees. (Lord Selborne LC in *Barnes* v *Addy* (1874) 9 Ch App 244.)

Discuss.

Commentary

This is a very difficult area of law with many quite recent decisions, often involving complicated fraud cases. The authorities are in some disarray and you should be aware of any further cases in the area that may have been decided since this book was written! It seems to be a developing area of trusts law.

It would probably be fair to say that the law here represents a challenge to those who want to get their teeth into something! If, however, you are seeking an easy life, and an uncomplicated passage, then this subject may not be for you. However, assuming that many students may want just this and will not venture too far into the subject, it could present a good student who has time to tussle with it, with an opportunity to demonstrate their ability in analysing legal decisions. Such a student should be able to produce an answer that would score well in an examination.

Suggested Answer

Lord Selborne's dictum is the classic statement of the scope of an agent's liability for involvement in a breach of trust. It recognises the necessity of instructing agents in the ordinary course of business, and that commercial expediency precludes an agent from making exhaustive enquiries before acting as to the honesty of every transaction in which he is instructed. There is a pragmatic commercial rationale for the protection afforded to agents.

The earlier cases adhered strictly to this protection, and even negligence would not make an agent liable (*Williams-Ashman* v *Price and Williams* [1942]1 Ch 219) although nowadays it would of course raise the possibility of an action in tort. However, some more recent decisions (*Selangor United Rubber Estates* v *Cradock (No. 3)* [1968] 1 WLR 1555 and *Karak Rubber Co. Ltd* v *Burden (No. 2)* [1972] 1 WLR 602 (as to which see below)), have taken a more stringent view of the degree of knowledge that an agent can be expected to have of a transaction and have found liability on constructive knowledge.

Peter Gibson J in *Baden Delvaux and Lecuit* v *Societé Generale* [1983] BCLC 325 defined five kinds of knowledge, the last four of which would all fall within the concept of constructive notice in property transactions (per Megarry V-C in *Re Montagu's Settlement Trusts* [1987] 1 Ch 264). These are:

(a) actual knowledge;

(b) wilfully shutting one's eyes to the obvious ('Nelsonian knowledge');

(c) wilfully and recklessly failing to make the enquiries which a reasonable and honest man would make (called by David Hayton 'naughty knowledge');

(d) knowledge of circumstances which would indicate the facts to an honest and reasonable man; and

(e) knowledge of circumstances which would put an honest and reasonable man on enquiry.

Although Peter Gibson J in *Baden Delvaux* accepted (without argument) counsel's concessions that all five types of knowledge would suffice to impose a constructive trust on an agent (which was in line with the decisions at first instance in *Selangor* and *Karak*), the Court of Appeal in *Belmont Finance Corporation Ltd* v *Williams Furniture Ltd* [1979] Ch 250 had expressed the opinion (obiter) that only the first three types of knowledge of fraud would suffice. In both *Selangor* and *Karak* the agents were banks who had enabled the execution of a fraudulent scheme whereby companies' monies were used to purchase their own shares contrary to the Companies Act 1948 (now the Companies Act 1985). In both cases it was said that the banks ought to have realised that they were assisting in a fraudulent scheme. *Belmont* involved a similar breach of fiduciary duty, but the Court of Appeal found as a fact that the director of a company which purchased another company at a vast over-value, genuinely failed to appreciate this and there was therefore no liability. In *Baden Delvaux* it was decided that a bank which transferred large sums of money to Panama did not have notice of a fraudulent design as their suspicions were allayed by an erroneous court order, reassurances given to them and the plaintiff's inaction.

The whole issue has become further confused by the courts having applied the same tests of sufficient knowledge to impose a constructive trust on persons who receive trust property (either for their own benefit, or with which they subsequently deal with notice of a breach of trust) and agents who knowingly assist in a breach of trust. It is not even always clear whether a person is to be regarded as an agent or a receiver, and as Harpum has pointed out, although a bank handling a transaction for a client will usually be an agent, if the client has an overdraft, they may become a receiver (Harpum (1986) 102 LQR 114). A J Oakley in *Constructive Trusts* has doubted whether an agent's assisting in a breach of trust can be a true constructive trust at all as he no longer holds the property, and suggests that this type of case is perhaps better regarded as an action to account.

As regards knowing receipt of trust property, Megarry V-C in *Re Montagu's Settlement Trusts* thought the first three categories of knowledge were required to make a person liable as a constructive trustee, and this was applied by Alliott J at first instance in *Lipkin Gorman* v *Karpnale* (1986) NLJ 659. Megarry V-C criticised the importation of the doctrine of constructive notice, applicable in property law to determine whether a purchaser is bound by third-party interests in land, into commercial transactions, where commercial expediency is a relevant factor. This criticism found favour with Vinelott J in *Eagle Trust plc* v *SBC Securities Ltd* [1992] 4 All ER 488 where he again found that the constructive knowledge of categories (four) and (five) of *Baden Delvaux* were inappropriate to commercial transactions. In *Cowan de Groot Properties Ltd* v *Eagle Trust plc* [1992] 4 All ER 700, the first three types of knowledge were again regarded as relevant, and the purchase of property at a vast undervalue was held not to be in itself sufficient notice of a breach of fiduciary duty where there were other possible explanations. Knox J in that case felt that the 'want of probity' required for an agent's liability should also be the criterion for a receiver's.

In *Agip (Africa) Ltd* v *Jackson* [1990] Ch 265, Millett J pointed out that there can be little sense in requiring dishonesty (and actual knowledge) to make a receiver liable, but allowing negligence (and constructive knowledge) to make an agent liable. This has an irrefutable logic in attempting to extract generally applicable principles from this confused area of law. Millett J suggests also that the wider tests of constructive knowledge might be applicable to the knowing receipt of trust property by a person for himself beneficially. He added, however, that Peter Gibson J's categories of knowledge are only helpful in so far as they indicate dishonesty or 'a want of probity', which he felt categories (two) and (three) might do as far as an agent is concerned. Other factors, such as whether the defendant offers a plausible explanation for his conduct, or whether reassurances are given to allay suspicions, should also be relevant. He pointed out that the loss in the 'knowing assistance' cases is caused by the agent's dealing with the property and not by his failure to make enquiries as to the transaction. Moreover, as Knox J pointed out in *Cowan de Groot*, a person who makes the relevant enquiries is unlikely to be told the truth if there is a fraudulent intent. The decision at first instance in *Agip* v *Jackson*, was upheld on the ground that the defendants were dishonest. However, the opinion was expressed by the Court of Appeal, that constructive knowledge would be enough on which to found liability as a constructive trustee, but as was pointed out by Vinelett J in *Eagle Trust plc* v *SBC Securities Ltd* (supra) this was not part of the decision, and Vinelett J himself preferred the view of Millett J.

Although the decisions of *Selangor* and *Karak*, imposing liability as a constructive trustee on an agent fixed with constructive notice of a dishonest design, were accepted by the Court of Appeal in *Agip (Africa) Ltd* v *Jackson* [1991] Ch 547, there has been a trend in some of the recent cases to regard overall evidence of dishonesty, or a want of probity, as the most important factor to be determined. In showing this, the categories of knowledge in *Baden Delvaux* should not be too rigidly applied as tests. The circumstances of the cases will be infinitely variable, and it is only when looked at as a whole that it is posssible to say in any individual case that there is dishonesty or a want of probity.

QUESTION 8

(a)   Wynken and Nod are the two partners in a firm of solicitors, Blynken & Co. Wynken acts for the Fishnet Trust. Wynken, on the instructions of Sleepy, the sole trustee of the Trust, paid out £30,000 to one of the beneficiaries believing her to be entitled to this sum, although had he looked at the trust deed in his office safe he would have realised that she was not.

Consider the liability to the beneficiaries of the Fishnet Trust of (i) Wynken and (ii) Nod. Would your answers differ if it were found that Sleepy's appointment as trustee had not been properly effected?

(b)   Spark was employed as an agent by Watts Ltd to sell the company's electrical goods.

He called on Flex and agreed to sell to him a consignment of refrigerators for £70,000, which was £10,000 below the market price. Flex was aware of this but was told by Spark that they were an end of range consignment.

Spark also said that he wanted an immediate payment by cheque rather than payment by the usual invoice system. Flex therefore gave Spark a cheque for £70,000 payable to Watts Ltd which Spark then endorsed by forging the signature of a director of Watts Ltd. Spark then paid the cheque into a bank account of a company Wire Ltd. Spark, one of two directors of Wire Ltd had floated the company two months previously. There were no other transactions on the company's account. Spark then transferred the money in this account to a personal account of his in Luxembourg.

Spark has now disappeared.

Advise Watts Ltd.

Commentary

This question requires the application of the principles of law outlined in the suggested answer to Question 7 to given circumstances. Because the law itself is uncertain in this area, and because liability will depend upon a detailed analysis of the facts, you cannot be expected to reach any definite conclusions. What you can be expected to do however is to show that you recognise the points of law which the questions raise and to demonstrate a knowledge of the principles applied in the different cases. This is a difficult area and the same observation may be made as regards Question 7 — it is not a topic for the faint hearted!

Suggested Answer

(a)   Wynken may be liable as a constructive trustee to account for the loss to the Trust.

In *Barnes* v *Addy* (1874) 9 Ch App 244, a solicitor who drew up a deed appointing, against his better judgment, the husband of a beneficiary to be the sole trustee of a trust was held not to be liable for the trustee's subsequent default. Lord Selborne LC was at pains to stress that an agent should not be liable for breach of trust unless he has knowledge of the trustee's fraudulent or dishonest design or unless he receives and becomes chargeable with some part of the trust fund. The principle is therefore that an agent should be safe if he acts honestly in carrying out the instructions of his principal.

In *Williams-Ashman* v *Price and Williams* [1942] 1 Ch 219, a firm of solicitors, on a trustee's instructions, paid out money to someone who was not a beneficiary. They were held not liable to account for the loss, even though they could have ascertained the true position from a trust deed in their possession at any time. More recently, in *Re Montagu's Settlement Trusts* [1987] 1 Ch 264, Megarry V-C found that there was no liability even for wrongful (and beneficial) receipt of trust property provided that it was innocent and the result, as in that case, of 'an honest muddle'.

There have been some cases (notably involving banks) which suggest that constructive notice should be sufficient to make an agent liable as a constructive trustee of property which he has dealt with in breach of trust: see particularly *Selangor United Rubber Estates Ltd* v *Cradock (Bankrupt) (No. 3)* [1968] 1 WLR 1555. The general trend of the cases however, suggests that something other than constructive notice is required. The preponderance of authority suggests that an agent will not be liable unless there is a 'want of probity' (see *Carl Zeiss Stiftung* v *Herbert Smith & Co (a firm) (No. 2)* [1969] 2 Ch 276, CA) or a 'Nelsonian shutting of the eyes' on his part. It would not seem logical to make an agent liable where a receiver (as in *Re Montagu's Settlement Trusts*) is not. It is probable therefore that the mere means of knowledge is not sufficient to make the solicitors liable as constructive trustees to account for the money wrongly paid out.

If Wynken is not liable as a constructive trustee, then his partner cannot be liable either. Even if Wynken had been liable, *Re Bell's Indenture* [1980] 1 WLR 1217 suggests that his partner would not have been.

In that case Vinelott J found that the partner of a solicitor who had knowingly assisted in breaches of trust was not liable to account as a constructive trustee, as a partner does not have any implied authority to impose such a burden on his fellow partner.

If the trustee's appointment had not been properly effected, then Wynken could not have been acting as an agent. In *Blyth* v *Fladgate* [1891] 1 Ch 327, Smith, a partner in a firm of solicitors continued to deal with trust funds after the death of the sole trustee. He was held liable for the resulting losses and his co-partners were also held liable as intermeddlers. Similarly, in the problem, Wynken may have realised that he was effectively acting as a principal.

In *Mara* v *Browne* [1896] 1 Ch 199, it was suggested (obiter) in the Court of Appeal that the protection of *Barnes* v *Addy* should still be available to an agent who does not realise that his principal has not been properly appointed. If, therefore, Wynken did not realise that the trustee was not validly appointed, he may escape liability.

In *Re Bell's Indenture*, Vinelott J indicated that the liability of an agent's co-partners depends upon whether the agent was acting for a properly appointed trustee. Another explanation for the earlier cases is, however, possible. Thus in *Blyth* v *Fladgate* the funds, before being invested by Smith, had already been received by the firm in the course of the firm's business. Each partner was therefore liable, under principles of partnership law, for their subsequent misapplication. In *Mara* v *Browne*, by contrast, the solicitor, Brown, paid the trust monies into his own private bank account: there was, therefore, never any receipt by the firm. On this basis, if the trust fund had been received by the firm (perhaps by being paid into the firm's client account) then if Wynken is liable, so is Nod: see Luxton [1981] Conv 310. It should be noted that in *Agip (Africa) Ltd* v *Jackson* [1991] Ch 547, Fox LJ, albeit without any analysis of the earlier cases, assumed that a co-partner of an agent who became liable as a constructive trustee was also liable.

(b)   Spark, as an agent of Watts Ltd, owed a fiduciary duty to his principal, the company. A fiduciary relationship is necessary for the remedy of equitable tracing (*Re Diplock* [1951] AC 251, HL) but Watts Ltd would not be able to trace the property which passed to Flex under a contract for sale unless the contract was voidable (*Cowan de Groot Properties Ltd* v *Eagle Trust plc* [1992] 4 All ER 700).

Watts Ltd may be able to make Flex personally accountable as a constructive trustee, however, if it can be shown that he received the goods knowing that they were sold in breach of a fiduciary relationship. It is uncertain what degree of knowledge would be sufficient. In *Carl Zeiss Stiftung* v *Herbert Smith & Co. (a firm) (No. 2)* [1969] 2 Ch 276, it was held that knowledge of a possible claim to monies in the possession of the solicitors Herbert Smith & Co. did not amount to notice of a breach of trust. In *Re Montagu's Settlement Trusts* [1987] 1 Ch 264, Megarry V-C said that the doctrine of constructive notice applicable to a purchaser of land should not be applied as the test for personal liability as a constructive trustee for receipt of trust property. Such reasoning was, however, obiter as he decided in any event that the breach was the result of 'an honest muddle'.

In *Cowan de Groot Properties Ltd* v *Eagle Trust plc*, real properties were sold by one company to another at a considerable undervalue. The director of the purchasing company had reason to believe from the conditions of sale (payment of a large deposit and a quick completion) that the vendor company needed money too urgently to spend the time marketing the properties normally, and there were in any event conflicting valuations. Knox J came to the conclusion that the director of the purchasing company was 'a moral lightweight' with a cavalier attitude to legal requirements but had not participated knowingly in any fraud on the vendor company. He was prepared to find liability if there was knowledge within the first three categories of knowledge in *Baden Delvaux and Lecuit* v *Societé Generale* [1983] BCLC 325, but said that knowledge should not be readily attributed to someone whose duty was to achieve a good deal for his company. Such a person would not be expected to inquire further into the reasons for a sale at an undervalue when it might seem suspicious but not implausible.

If the first three categories of knowledge in *Baden Delvaux* are to be the standard of knowledge which might indicate a fraud, then it is possible that Flex may be held to be accountable to Watts Ltd as a constructive trustee. If, however, the last two categories are to be included also, then he is likely to be liable. It should be noted that Millett J at first instance in *Agip (Africa) Ltd* v *Jackson* [1990] Ch 265 has warned of 'over refinement' of these tests of knowledge. He said that, although they may be useful guidelines, the overall question to be answered is whether the defendant acted dishonestly or with 'a want of probity'. This was adopted by Vinelott J in *Eagle Trust plc* v *SBC Securities Ltd* [1992] 4 All ER 488, who agreed that generally the first three types of knowledge in *Baden Delvaux* would establish liability but commented that the absence of any explanation by the defendant might assist in inferring this knowledge.

It is possible, but unlikely, that Watts & Co will be able to make the bank liable as a constructive trustee. In order to do so, they would have to show that the bank knowingly assisted in a dishonest design. In the recent case of *Polly Peck International plc* v *Nadir (No. 2)* [1992] 4 All ER 764, the Court of Appeal endorsed the reasoning of Vinelott J in *Eagle Trust plc* v *SBC Securities Ltd* that constructive notice in property law should not be imported into commercial transactions as constructive knowledge. In *Polly Peck*, Millett J held at first instance that the 'sheer scale' of the transfers of money to a Northern Cyprus bank was not sufficient to impute to the bank, in the course of commercial transactions, sufficient knowledge of dishonesty. The bank was not therefore liable as a constructive trustee for knowing assistance. So, although there are some suspicious circumstances in that Wire Ltd was floated recently, there were however, no other transactions in the company's account and the cheque paid in was endorsed over. This would probably not be sufficient knowledge to establish 'a want of probity' by the bank.

10 Administration of Trusts

INTRODUCTION

Administration of trusts involves a study of a number of discrete, but related, topics. You may well find that different topics within administration of trust form separate halves of a single question. Trustee investment, for instance, might form part (a) of a question in which part (b) is variation of trusts. You are therefore advised to revise all aspects of administration of trusts which appear on your course.

QUESTION 1

(a)   'The law requires the same standard of care and skill of all trustees, regardless of whether they are paid or unpaid, professional or amateur.'

Discuss.

(b)   Trevor is the sole trustee of an exhaustive discretionary trust of income, the objects of which are the nephews and nieces of Sally. Sally has two nephews, Benjy and Damian, and one niece, Caroline. Six months ago Trevor lent Benjy the sum of £20,000 out of his (Trevor's) own money. Caroline and Damian have now learned that Trevor has decided to pay the entire income of the trust for the present year, some £15,000, to Benjy. Caroline and Damian claim that Trevor exercised his discretion under the trust in Benjy's favour only in order that Benjy would be in sufficient funds to repay that loan. Caroline and Damian wish to have the proposed exercise of the discretion set aside, and further wish to compel Trevor to distribute the income for the present year amongst all three objects equally.

Advise Caroline and Damian.

Commentary

Part (a) illustrates the point that you cannot necessarily assume that a quotation upon which you are asked to comment is correct.

Suggested Answer

(a)   The quotation is not an accurate statement of the law. Although statute does not itself distinguish between different sorts of trustees, modern case law has come to recognise that different standards of care are appropriate to different sorts of trustees.

The general standard of care is that which was laid down in the nineteenth century in *Speight* v *Gaunt* (1883) 9 App Cas 1, in which the House of Lords affirmed the test indicated by the Court of Appeal: namely, that a trustee must exercise the standard of care of an ordinary prudent man of business acting in his own affairs. This is an objective standard, and it means (as illustrated in *Speight* v *Gaunt* itself), that the trustee is not expected to have knowledge of a specialist or commercial nature. Unlike an ordinary prudent man of business, however, the trustee must not permit commercial ethics to cause financial detriment to the trust: *Buttle* v *Saunders* [1950] 2 All ER 193 (duty to gazump). Furthermore, the standard of the ordinary prudent man of business is not appropriate in the context of trustee investment, since trustees are not permitted to speculate with trust funds: *Learoyd* v *Whiteley* (1887) 12 App Cas 727, HL).

This standard was established in the nineteenth century when many trustees were amateurs. Since that time, however, there has been a growth in the concept of the paid professional trustee. In *Re Waterman's Will Trusts* [1952] 2 All ER 1054, Harman J considered that a paid trustee was subject to a higher standard of diligence, and was expected to have a more extensive knowledge, than an unpaid trustee. This view was supported and further developed in *Bartlett* v *Barclays Bank Trust Co. Ltd (No. 1)* [1980] Ch 515. In that case a trust corporation was held liable for breach of trust under the *Speight* v *Gaunt* test, but Harman J stated obiter that a professional trustee, such as a trust corporation, which holds itself out as having a particular skill, is to be judged by a higher standard. According to Harman J, it will be liable if it neglects to exercise the special care and skill which it professes to have. It would therefore appear that trust corporations, banks, solicitors, accountants, and other professional trustees (who invariably charge for their services) are subject to a higher standard than that laid down in *Speight* v *Gaunt*.

It might be added that where a trustee has committed a breach of trust, the court is in practice far less willing to relieve him under the Trustee Act 1925, s. 61, if he is a paid trustee.

(b)   If Trevor has exercised the discretion vested in him in order to ensure that he is repaid the debt Benjy owes him, this is an improper exercise of the discretion. It is improper because the exercise of the power of selection must be based upon what is in the interests of the objects, not upon what is in the interests of the trustee. If Caroline and Damian can prove that the exercise was so motivated, they can apply to the court to have an improper appointment set aside.

The problem for Caroline and Damian, however, is essentially one of proof. A trustee is not obliged to give reasons for the exercise of his discretions: *Re Beloved Wilkes' Charity* (1851) 3 Mac & G 440 and *Re*

Londonderry's Settlement [1965] Ch 918, CA. If, however, a trustee does give reasons, and these are improper, the objects can have the exercise set aside: *Klug* v *Klug* [1918] 2 Ch 67.

A beneficiary or object has a prima facie right to inspect trust documents: *O'Rourke* v *Darbishire* [1920] AC 581, HL. This right, however, does not extend to documents which detail the trustees' reasons for selecting amongst the objects of a discretionary trust. This principle derives from *Re Londonderry*, where one of the objects of a fiduciary power objected to the small amount of capital allocated to her by the trustees. She asked to see copies of the minutes of trustees' meetings and other correspondence in the hope that these would reveal the basis for the trustees' allocation. The Court of Appeal stated that disclosure of such confidential information could cause infinite trouble in the family out of all proportion to any resulting benefit. Moreover, if the trustees knew that they could be required to make such disclosure, it might interfere with the proper exercise of the discretion.

The Court of Appeal in *Re Londonderry* thought that the position would be entirely different were a case made in *mala fides*. The problem for the objects, however, is that such evidence of *mala fides* may be difficult to obtain without recourse to such documents. Thus, in the absence of a statement by Trevor revealing ban faith, Caroline and Damian may find it difficult to prove that the exercise was improper. It has, however, been suggested that beneficiaries could circumvent this problem by their instituting litigation alleging an improper exercise of the trustees' discretion, and then obtaining discovery of documents in the proceedings: Megarry (1965) 81 LQR 196.

Even if Caroline and Damian succeed in having the exercise set aside, they cannot themselves compel Trevor positively to exercise his discretion as they direct. All three objects together, assuming they are all *sui juris* and form a closed class, could compel the distribution of the income to them under an extension of the rule in *Saunders* v *Vautier* (1841) 4 Beav 115. Caroline and Damian, however, are only two of the three objects of the discretionary trust of income.

It is unclear, however, whether the court would itself be able (or willing) to exercise the trustee's dispositive discretion under a discretionary trust. In *Klug* v *Klug* itself, the court did order the advancement to be made; but it may be that it was merely giving effect to the wishes of the remaining trustee whose decision was not tainted by improper considerations. In *McPhail* v *Doulton* [1971] AC 424, the House of Lords stated that the court would, if called upon to do so, execute a discretionary trust in the manner best calculated to give effect to the settlor's intentions; and, ultimately, where a proper basis for distribution appears, this could be by itself directing the trustees so to distribute. In so holding, it revived the authority of eighteenth century cases where the court had itself executed a discretionary trust: *Warburton* v *Warburton* (1702) 4 Bro PC 1, and *Richardson* v *Chapman* (1760) 7 Bro PC 318. This power may in principle exist, but it will be exercised only in the last resort. Indeed, there is no reported case since *McPhail* v *Doulton* where the court has itself exercised such discretion. In practice, therefore, where a trustee persistently fails properly to exercise his discretion to appoint amongst the objects, the latter might be better advised to seek such trustee's removal and replacement: *Re Gestetner* [1953] Ch 672 admits of such possibility.

QUESTION 2

Six months ago, Topaz, a trustee, wished to sell some jewellery which belonged to the trust. He asked Jade, a jeweller whom he knew to have been fined for smuggling stones into the country a few years earlier, to carry out a valuation. Jade valued the jewellery at £100,000. In reliance upon this, Topaz instructed Jade to sell the jewellery for that amount to Sapphire, which he did. A month later, Sapphire sold the jewellery at an auction for five times that amount.

Three months after the sale, Jade had still not accounted to Topaz for the proceeds. Topaz then began to press Jade for payment, but was met with evasive replies. Last week, Topaz learned that Jade lost the entire £100,000 proceeds whilst gambling, and is now insolvent.

Advise the beneficiaries of the trust as to their rights against Topaz.

Commentary

The need to answer only what is asked and no more is vividly illustrated in this question. You should deal with the rights against Topaz only. It earns no marks whatever to consider any rights the beneficiaries may have against any other parties mentioned. Differently worded, it could easily have become a question on tracing and third party receivers or dealers — but it is not. If you know your stuff, your answer should be a little gem.

Suggested Answer

The sum of at least £100,000 has been lost to the trust as a result of Jade's gambling. It may be that a further £400,000 has been lost through a sale to Sapphire at a considerable undervalue. The beneficiaries have a personal right of action against Topaz to make good this loss if they can establish that it arises from Topaz's own wrongful act or default. There are several different grounds upon which an argument in favour of liability could be founded.

First, it could be argued that the appointment of Jade as agent was wrongful in itself. The Trustee Act 1925, s. 23(1), enables a trustee, instead of acting personally, to employ and pay an agent to transact any business or do any act required to be done in the execution of the trust, including the receipt and payment of money. Section 23(1) states that the trustee shall not be responsible for the default of such agent if employed in good faith. This provision was stated by Maugham J in *Re Vickery* [1931] 1 Ch 572 to have 'revolutionised' the law relating to the employment of agents: a trustee may now employ an agent even if this is not necessary.

It would appear, however, that in other respects the provision has not altered the previous law. Thus, as the judge in *Re Vickery* stated, an agent must still be employed in his proper field. In the problem this requirement appears to be met: a jeweller may properly be employed to value and sell jewellery. Furthermore, as Maugham J also pointed out, the trustee must still use his discretion in appointing the agent. In *Re Vickery* itself, the executor did not know, when he appointed Jennens his agent, that Jennens had previously been suspended from practice by the Law Society. But, even if he had, the result might well have been the same. It would be difficult to argue that an executor is acting wrongfully in employing a solicitor who, regardless of earlier misdeeds, is currently on the roll and issued with a practising certificate. The position may well be different in the case of a jeweller, whose ability to trade does not depend upon the approval of a comparable body. Although the previous wrongful act here was smuggling, not theft, they are both crimes involving dishonesty. A prudent man of business might well prefer not to entrust valuable assets to a person with a conviction for either; in which case Topaz will be personally liable for subsequent losses to the trust.

Secondly, it could be argued that the sale to Sapphire was at an undervalue, and that Topaz is liable for the loss. Whether the sale was at an undervalue is a matter of evidence, but prima facie the price fetched at auction a month later suggests that it might well have been. The phrase 'required to be done' in s. 23(1) indicates that only duties, not discretions, may be delegated, thus the principle of *Fry* v *Tapson* (1884) 28 ChD still applies. If it is found that Topaz simply accepted Jade's valuation without himself considering it, Topaz will be liable for the loss caused by the sale at undervalue. If Topaz had considered the matter, the court might relieve him from liability for the sale at undervalue under the Trustee Act 1925, s. 61.

Thirdly, it might also be argued that Topaz was in breach of his duty as trustee to protect trust assets, in that he left a large sum of money, the sale proceeds, in Jade's hands for an undue length of time. Three months is surely longer than a prudent man of business would allow. Upon one interpretation of s. 23(1), however, so long as the trustee initially appointed the agent in good faith, s. 23(1) relieves him from any subsequent duty to supervise the agent. This point might appear to be supported by *Re Vickery*. In fact, however, the point did not need to be decided in that case because the executor was in any event relieved by the Trustee Act 1925, s. 30(1). Nevertheless, to construe s. 23(1) so broadly would surely go too far in a trustee's favour. Indeed, Gareth Jones has argued that s. 23(1) should not be taken to confer such blanket immunity: Jones (1959) 22 MLR 381. Even assuming this latter view to be correct, however, Topaz might still be able to rely on the Trustee Act 1925, s. 30(1), in order to escape liability.

Section 30(1) states (inter alia) that a trustee is answerable only for his own acts, receipts, neglects or defaults, and not for those of any person with whom any trust money may be deposited, nor for any other loss, unless the same happens through his own wilful default. The expression 'wilful default' occurred in similar provisions in nineteenth century Trustee Acts, and there it was construed objectively, i.e., as not derogating from the principle laid down in *Speight* v *Gaunt* (1883) 9 App Cas 1 that a trustee must act as a prudent man of business would act in his own affairs: *Re Brier* (1884) 26 ChD 238, CA. In *Re Vickery*, however, the judge interpreted the expression in s. 30(1) literally, i.e., as requiring consciousness of wrongdoing. Maugham J reached this construction in reliance upon *Re City Equitable Fire Insurance Co. Ltd* [1925] 1 Ch 407, but that case concerned auditors, not trustees. Furthermore, his view conflicts with earlier cases such as *Re Brier*, and makes the section a fool's charter.

In *Re Lucking's Will Trusts* [1968] 1 WLR 866, Cross J held that s. 30(1) applies only where the trustee has allowed the trust property to come into the agent's hands. This involves construing the words 'nor for any other loss' in s. 30(1) *ejusdem generis* with the preceding words. In *Re Lucking's Will Trusts* no trust property had been deposited with the agent. This was because the agent in that case had been appointed to manage a family company in which the trust had shares. The trust property was therefore not the company but the shares, and these were at no time vested in the agent. The loss to the trust occurred only indirectly through the fall in share values attributable to the agent's misappropriation of the company's funds. In these circumstances, Cross J was able to hold the trustee liable as having failed to meet the 'prudent man of business' test.

The distinction drawn in *Re Lucking's Will Trusts* has the merit of restoring to some extent the 'prudent man of business' test. It does, nevertheless, produce the odd result that the trustee is judged less harshly if he places the trust assets in the agent's hands. In any event, however, this distinction cannot apply to the problem, since the jewellery and the proceeds have come into Jade's hands at Topaz's request and with his approval. Therefore, on the basis of the Trustee Act 1925, s. 30(1), as interpreted by *Re Vickery*, unless he was conscious of his own negligence, Topaz will escape liability on this final ground.

QUESTION 3

Under the terms of an *inter vivos* trust created in 1965, the trustees were authorised to invest any part of the trust fund (then worth £150,000) in the purchase of freehold land as an investment. The trustees used £50,000 to purchase land. In the absence of any other express investment provision, the trustees (in accordance with the Trustee Investments Act 1961), divided the balance of the fund into two parts, each having an initial value of £50,000. The narrower-range part is still worth roughly that amount but the value of the wider-range part is now £170,000.

Advise the trustees:

   (a)   how they should:

      (i)   deal with a bonus issue in respect of shares held by them in the wider-range part;

(ii)   invest £90,000 realised upon the recent sale of the freehold land; and

(iii)   raise and pay out of the trust fund the sum of £20,000, which is to be advanced to a beneficiary under the power contained in the Trustee Act 1925, s. 32.

AND

(b)   how they may seek an extension to the trust's investment powers, and of their chances of obtaining such an extension.

Commentary

Part (a) requires a precise knowledge of particular provisions. Do not therefore waste 'powder and shot' by going beyond this and writing everything you know about trustee investment.

Suggested Answer

(a)(i)   The Trustee Investments Act 1961, s. 2(3), deals with the position where any property accrues to a trust fund after it has been divided in accordance with the Act. If, under s. 2(3)(a), the property accrues to the trustee as owner or former owner of property comprised in either part of the fund, it is treated as belonging to that part of the fund. Since the existing shares are (necessarily) within the wider-range, the bonus shares will be treated as belonging to the wider-range. No compensating transfer of investments from wider- to narrower-range need be made.

(ii)   Since the Trustee Investments Act 1961 does not authorise investment in land, the power contained in the trust instrument to purchase land is a special power, and the land so purchased is a special range investment. If the trustees use the proceeds to purchase other land, this also comprises special range and the other parts of the fund are unaffected. This is not the case where the proceeds are to be invested in investments authorised by the Act. Since the land was purchased before the fund was divided, the proceeds do not accrue to the trustees as former owners of property comprised in either the narrower- or wider-range, so s. 2(3)(a) of the Act does not apply. In this case, the position is governed by s. 2(3)(b), which requires the trustees to secure, by apportionment of the accruing property if necessary or by the transfer of property from one part of the fund to another, or both, that the value of each part of the fund is increased by the same amount. Thus the value of both narrower- and wider-range investments must be increased by £45,000.

(iii)   The Trustee Investments Act 1961, s. 3(1), states that where in the exercise of a power or duty of a trustee property falls to be taken out of the trust fund, nothing in that section shall restrict his discretion as to the choice of property to be taken out. It would not therefore breach s. 3 of the Act if the trustees were, for instance, to draw the entire £20,000 from the narrower-range. Such a withdrawal might nevertheless breach both the trustees' general equitable duty to act fairly as between the beneficiaries, and also the particular duties imposed by s. 6(1). This subsection obliges a trustee to have regard to the need to have appropriate diversification (s. 6(1)(a)) and suitable investments (s. 6(1)(b)). Therefore, although the Act itself requires a trustee to obtain and consider proper advice only when exercising his powers of investment, the trustees would be wise to obtain and consider proper advice in this case. It should be noted that merely following advice unthinkingly is insufficient: the advice must be actively considered.

(b)   The court is empowered, upon an application by the trustees, to authorise investments which are not authorised either by the trust instrument or under the general law. Such power is preserved by the Trustee Investments Act 1961, s. 15, and application can be made under either the Trustee Act 1957 (which enables the court to confer administrative powers upon trustees) or under the Variation of Trusts Act 1958, s. 1. There is, in this regard, no substantive difference between the two methods.

Whether, however, the court will agree to an extension of the trustees' investment powers is another matter. Before the Trustee Investments Act 1961, when investment in company shares was not permissible under the general law, the courts were prepared to allow extensions to the investment powers of trustees. Following the passing of that Act, however, the courts became less willing to accede to requests for such extensions in respect of trusts set up after the statute took effect. The most important of the early authorities was *Re Kolb's Will Trusts* [1962] Ch 531, where the court declined to extend the trustees' investment powers on the ground that those conferred by the Act of 1961 were sufficient.

The principle in *Re Kolb's Will Trusts* could, however, be ousted in special circumstances and, as modern investment circumstances change while the Act remains largely the same, the likelihood of this occurring continues to increase. Indeed, in a report in 1982, the Law Reform Committee concluded that the Act was outmoded and inadequate: 23rd Report, *The Powers and Duties of Trustees*, Cmnd 8733.

There has also been judicial development. In *Mason* v *Farbrother* [1983] 2 All ER 1078, the court authorised the extension of the investment powers of a large pension fund. The special circumstances were the size and nature of the fund, and the impact of inflation.

In *Trustees of the British Museum* v *A-G* [1984] 1 WLR 418, Megarry V-C thought that investment practice had changed so much in the years since the Act was passed that the principle of *Re Kolb's Will Trusts* itself should now be discarded. Megarry V-C pointed (inter alia) to the effect of inflation, the move away from fixed-interest securities to equities, the impact of oil-price rises, and the relatively low rate of economic growth in the United Kingdom as compared with some other countries. In the circumstances, Megarry V-C agreed to a widening of the trustees' investment powers. Factors which he took into account included the vast size of the fund, its objects, the eminence and responsibility of the trustees (there were 24 of them), and the scope of the trust provisions regarding the obtaining of advice.

Similar factors were also crucial in *Steel* v *Wellcome Custodian Trustees Ltd* [1988] 1 WLR 167, where an extension of investment powers was also approved. It should be noted that, in the *British Museum* case, Megarry V-C opined that the wider the power sought the more important it is that that part should be in relatively safe, i.e., narrower-range, investments. By contrast, Harman J in the *Steel* case evidently did not consider such precautions necessary.

Even if, however, the principle of *Re Kolb* is now gone, the court must still be satisfied that the circumstances of the particular case merit an extension of the trustees' powers. The investment opportunities of pension fund trusts and large charitable trusts may be hampered more seriously by the present-day short-comings of the Act than are those of smaller private trusts — even if, like the trust in the problem, they were created in the years immediately after the Act became law. In any event, additional information is needed in the problem before specific advice can be given. Thus it is necessary to know the nature and terms of the trust, the identity of the trustees, the respect in which the trustees' existing powers are considered inadequate, and the details of the desired extensions.

QUESTION 4

Alex died last year. By his will he left his residuary estate to his trustees in trust for his sister, Samantha, for life, remainder to her son, Edwin. The residuary estate comprises the following assets:

    (i)   Rocky, a racehorse;

    (ii)   10,000 shares in Gondwanaland Ltd;

    (iii)   an interest in remainder under a trust which will fall into possession on the death of Lionel, who has a life interest thereunder;

    (iv)   a lease of land which has 40 years unexpired.

Rocky is a two-year old with many wins to her credit. Gondwanaland Ltd has an issued share capital of £500,000.

Advise the trustees:

    (a)   of their duties to the beneficiaries in respect of these assets;

AND

    (b)   whether, and to what extent, the trustees may make advancements to Edwin under the Trustee Act 1925, s. 32.

Commentary

Questions involving the rules in *Howe* v *Dartmouth* and *Re Earl of Chesterfield's Trusts* should appeal to students with an interest in technical details, but wise candidates will not allow the technicalities of the rules to obscure an appreciation of the principles underlying them. The fact that the two parts of the question deal with different areas illustrates the risk that you run if you pick and choose individual topics for revision.

Suggested Answer

(a)   It must be considered whether all or any of the assets comprising residue fall within the rule in *Howe* v *Earl of Dartmouth* (1802) 7 Ves 137, which is designed to promote equality between beneficiaries. The rule applies (subject to a contrary intention) where residuary personalty is settled by will upon persons in succession; it obliges the trustees to convert into authorised investments such parts as are of a wasting, future or reversionary nature, or which consist of unauthorised securities.

The rule is therefore applicable to the racehorse, which for a short time might produce a great deal of income, but whose capital value might eventually be no more than horsemeat. Shares in Gondwanaland Ltd are not authorised by the Trustee Investments Act 1961, since (even if other requirements are met) the company does not have the requisite minimum issued and paid up share capital of £1,000,000. The interest in remainder is also subject to the rule. But for the duty to convert, this property would be of no immediate benefit to the life tenant, Samantha.

Leases with at least 60 years to run are authorised investments (Settled Land Act 1925, s. 73) and are therefore clearly outside the rule. The lease in the problem, however, has only 40 years unexpired. Before 1926, such a lease, being property of a wasting nature, would have been subject to the rule. After 1925, however, this may no longer be the case.

The Law of Property Act 1925, s. 28(2), provides (subject to any direction to the contrary) that the net rents and profits of land held on trust for sale are to be applied in the same way as the income from authorised investments purchased from the sale proceeds if the land had been sold. It was held in *Re Brooker* [1926] WN 93 that s. 28(2) took the leasehold land in question outside the rule, so that the life tenant was thereafter entitled to the actual rents and profit. The will in that case imposed an express trust for sale. In *Re Trollope* [1927] 1 Ch 596, Tomlin J opined that the rule no longer applies to leaseholds held on trust for sale, which suggests that the manner in which such trust arises is irrelevant. It has been argued, however, that the rule continues to apply where, as in the problem, the duty to convert arises not from an express trust for sale but merely from the application of the rule in *Howe* v *Dartmouth* itself: Bailey (1930-32) 4 CLJ 357.

It has also been pointed out that, although the judges in *Re Brooker* and *Re Trollope* referred to the duty to convert, those case in fact concerned the duty to apportion: Hayton and Marshall, *Cases & Commentary on Law of Trusts*, 9th edn, London: Sweet & Maxwell, 1991, p. 674; Hanbury and Martin, *Modern Equity*, 14th edn, London: Sweet & Maxwell, 1993, p. 533. On this basis, a lease with less than 60 years to run remains subject to the rule in *Howe* v *Dartmouth* and so is held upon trust for sale rather than as settled land under the Settled Land Act 1925; but the Law of Property Act 1925, s. 28(2), has nevertheless abolished the duty to apportion the rents and profits. Samantha will therefore be entitled to the actual income the lease produces.

In respect of the other assets, the trustees are under a duty not merely to convert, but also to apportion until conversion takes place.

In the absence of a power to postpone sale, Rocky and the shares must be valued one year after Alex's death. Whatever the actual income these assets produce, Samantha is entitled to interest at the rate (subject to the discretion of the court) of 4 per cent per annum on this sum from the date of Alex's death until the conversion is effected. Any shortfall in the actual income in any year must be made good first out of any surplus in future years, and then (if necessary) out of capital when the asset is sold.

Although an interest in remainder is saleable, the uncertainties surrounding the date it will fall into possession, and the amount of inheritance tax which it may have to bear, considerably discount its market value. Generally, therefore, it is better for trustees to retain such interest until it falls into possession. Apportionment is effected according to the rule in *Re Earl of Chesterfield's Trust* (1883) 24 ChD 643. This requires a reversionary interest to be valued at the date of its sale or (if later) its falling into possession. A proportion of this sum ranks as capital, the balance as income. Let us suppose that the valuation produces a figure of £10,000. The proportion treated as capital is that part of £10,000 which, if invested at 4 per cent interest with yearly rests, would (after deducting income tax at the basic rate) produce £10,000. Edwin receives that part; the balance goes to Samantha.

(b)   The power of advancement under the Trustee Act 1925, s. 32, applies only where the trust property consists of money or securities or of property held upon trust for sale, calling in and conversion, and where the proceeds of such trust are not considered as land or applicable as capital money under the Settled Land Act 1925. It was held in *Re Stimpson* [1931] 2 Ch 77 that s. 32 is applicable to the proceeds of land held upon trust for sale, even though the Law of Property Act 1925 permits such proceeds to be applied as capital money under the Settled Land Act 1925. Therefore, since all the items comprised in Alex's residuary estate are subject to the trust for conversion imposed by *Howe* v *Dartmouth*, the statutory power can be exercised in respect of each of them. The power in s. 32 is one to advance 'money', which means that the trustees would first need to sell one or more of the items comprising the residue. Bearing in mind the discounted market value of an interest in remainder, the trustees might be better advised to sell one or more of the other assets.

The power under s. 32 is to advance up to one half of a beneficiary's vested or presumptive share of capital. Since Edwin has a vested interest in the entire capital, the power could extend to a maximum of one to half the value of the residuary estate. The written consent of any person with a prior interest (i.e., Samantha) is necessary.

The statutory power is exercisable only for the beneficiary's 'advancement or benefit'. 'Advancement' means establishing the beneficiary in life; 'benefit' is broadly interpreted. Together they mean any use of the money which improves the beneficiary's material situation: *Pilkington* v *IRC* [1964] AC 612, HL. Usually a benefit is a financial benefit (e.g., from tax saving); but it can include even a purely moral benefit. In *Re Clore's Settlement Trusts* [1966] 1 WLR 955, an advancement by way of a gift to charity was held to be for the benefit of a wealthy beneficiary: but the court emphasised that the moral compunction must be that of the beneficiary, not that of the trustees. An advancement may take the form of a sub-trust, and beneficiaries of such sub-trust might even include other persons — such as any children Edwin may have in the future: *Pilkington* v *IRC*. It remains unclear whether an advancement under which the beneficiary is merely a discretionary object suffices. The trustees may make the advancement directly to Edwin, or to Edwin's parent or guardian for Edwin's benefit; but if the advancement is for a specified purpose, the trustees should not pay the money directly to Edwin unless they consider that they can trust him to carry out the prescribed purpose: *Re Pauling's Settlement Trusts* [1964] Ch 303, CA.

QUESTION 5

Mole, who died recently, made the following dispositions in his will:

(a) £10,000 to his son Bill, provided he attained the age of 18;

(b)   his shares in Midnight Oil Ltd to his daughter Delia provided she attained the age of 25; and

(c)   his freehold house, Dunromin, to his other daughter Elizabeth.

It was further provided that neither of the dispositions to the daughters should take effect until the death of Mole's widow.

Mole's wife has survived him. Bill is now aged 14, Delia is 16 and Elizabeth is 19.

Advise Mole's executors and trustees whether they may (or must) use income to assist Mole's children; and, if so, to what extent.

Commentary

This is a tricky question: the law is extraordinarily complex, and the things asked are very precise. Some examination papers carry at least one treacherous question like this for those who have worked hard and really enjoy the subject. A cool headed and well prepared student can earn high marks; a persistent waffler, however, will be skating on very thin ice. If you do decide to attempt this sort of question, it is better to leave it until later in the examination, when you already have at least a couple of good answers under your belt. This is definitely not a question for 'writing yourself in'.

Suggested Answer

It is convenient to deal with each child in turn.

(a)   Bill. The Trustee Act 1925, s. 31, provides for the circumstances in which trustees may (or must) pay the trust income to beneficiaries who are not entitled to it under the terms of the trust instrument. In the case of a contingent interest, the section applies only if the limitation carries the intermediate income: s. 31(3).

Since the gift to Bill comprises a sum of money, it is a pecuniary legacy. It is also contingent since it vests only if Bill attains 18. Generally, a contingent pecuniary legacy does not carry the intermediate income: *Re Raine* [1929] 1 Ch 716. However, such a gift does carry this income if (inter alia) it was made to a minor by his father. Two requirements must, however, be met: first, there must be no other fund provided for his maintenance: *Re George* (1877) 5 ChD 837. Secondly, the contingency must not be the attaining of an age greater than the age of majority (presently 18): *Re Abrahams* [1911] 1 Ch 108. This latter requirement is clearly satisfied. Assuming that the former is also met, and that there is no expression of a contrary intention in the will, the gift will carry the intermediate income and so fall within the Trustee Act 1925, s. 31. This exceptional case is indeed expressly recognised by s. 31(3), which states that the section applies to a contingent legacy made (inter alia) by a parent of the legatee if, under the general law, the legacy carries interest for the maintenance of the legatee: s. 31(3). Whether such legacy does carry such interest is determined by reference to the cases, including those mentioned above.

Assuming the gift carries the intermediate income, the Trustee Act 1925 imposes a trust to accumulate the income during Bill's minority, but gives the trustees a power to pay to Bill's (surviving) parent or guardian, or otherwise apply for or towards his maintenance, education or benefit, the whole or such part of the income as may be reasonable, whether or not there is any other fund applicable to the same purpose. The trustees must have regard (inter alia) to the age of the minor, his requirements, and generally to the circumstances of the case: Trustee Act 1925, s. 31(1). Accumulations may be applied for the benefit of the minor as if they were income of the current year: Trustee Act 1925, s. 31(2) proviso.

When Bill attains 18, his gift vests and he is entitled to the capital and accumulations. If Bill dies under 18, the gift does not vest, and (in the absence of a gift over) it will go on a resulting trust to Mole's estate. Any sums previously paid to or for Bill's benefit under s. 31, however, need not be repaid.

(b) Delia. This gift is a contingent and future specific bequest of personalty. Under the Law of Property Act 1925, s. 175, such a bequest carries the intermediate income from the death of the testator, except so far as such income is otherwise expressly disposed of. There being no such express disposal here, Delia will receive the intermediate income eventually if she attains 25.

This does not, however, mean that the income is in the meantime subject to s. 31; for that section gives way to a contrary intention in the will: Trustee Act 1925, s. 69(2). The deferring of the gift suggests that the testator did not intend Delia to have the intermediate income until the widow's death. In *Re McGeorge* [1963] Ch 544, the testator specifically devised land to his daughter but stated that the devise was not to take effect until the death of his widow. Cross J held that by so deferring the enjoyment of the property the testator had shown an intention that the intermediate income should not be subject to s. 31, but should be accumulated for 21 years (the relevant period of accumulation) or until the earlier death of the widow. If Mole's disposition indicates a similar intention, the same result will ensue.

If, however, the court does not find a contrary intention from the postponement of the bequest, the application of the income is governed by the Trustee Act 1925, s. 31(1). Thus it is an accumulation trust during Delia's minority, and the trustees have power to apply income for her maintenance or benefit. The position is the same as that in respect of Bill during his minority. When Delia attains 18, the trustees must pay her the income that arises thereafter: this is indicated by s. 31(1)(ii), which gives a beneficiary who at 18 'has not a vested interest in such income' the right to such income. Since her interest is contingent, however, any accumulations made during her minority are not paid to her at 18, but remain part of the capital of the fund subject to her interest vesting at the age of 25.

(c)   Elizabeth. This gift is a future specific devise of property which carries the intermediate income unless it is otherwise expressly disposed of: Law of Property Act 1925, s. 175. As in the case of Delia, however, the postponement of the gift may evidence an intention to subject such income to an accumulation trust. In support of his decision in *Re McGeorge*, Cross J pointed out that, if such a disposition were to be treated as carrying the intermediate income, an adult devisee with a vested interest would be able to call for an immediate conveyance in disregard of the instruction that the gift be deferred.

There was another, perhaps less convincing, ground for the decision in *Re McGeorge*. The daughter in that case (like Elizabeth in the problem) was over 18 and had an interest which, although future, was vested. Cross J held that she was not entitled to the income under the Trustee Act 1925, since s. 31(1)(ii) confers the right to income at majority only on a beneficiary who does not then have a vested interest in such income. Since Elizabeth does have a vested interest in the income, she cannot therefore rely on s. 31 — which is at least somewhat odd.

On either of these bases, therefore, the result is that the income must be accumulated for 21 years or until the widow's death.

QUESTION 6

(a)   Consider the classes of persons on whose behalf the court is empowered to approve an arrangement under the Variation of Trusts Act 1958.

AND

(b)   In 1988, Mark, a wealthy businessman, settled a large sum of money in trust for such of his two sons, Luke and John, as should attain the age of 30, if both in equal shares, with remainders over in default to their respective issue (if any).

Mark had for several years expressed a desire to retire to the Channel Islands, and last year he went to live on Jersey. His sons, Luke and John, however, who are presently aged 16 and 18 respectively, are at school in Yorkshire and hope to read law at a university in England. Both are presently unmarried and without children. Mark's solicitor has advised him that, on grounds both of administrative convenience and tax-saving, the trust should be transferred to Jersey.

Advise the trustees whether such transfer can be sanctioned by the court under the Variation of Trusts Act 1958; and, if so, of the likelihood that the court's consent will be obtained.

Commentary

The suggested answer to part (b) illustrates the importance of not giving a definite answer to problems likely to turn upon a multiplicity of facts which are not stated. Do not be afraid, in such cases, to indicate what further information you may require. Indeed, sometimes the question will expressly ask you to do this.

Suggested Answer

(a)   The Variation of Trusts Act 1958, s. 1, empowers the High Court to approve an arrangement varying or revoking the trusts on behalf of four classes of persons, these being listed in paras (a) to (d) of s. 1(1).

Paragraph (a) comprises minors and other persons who by reason of incapacity are incapable of assenting; the interest of such person can be either vested or contingent. Paragraph (c) applies to persons unborn. Paragraph (d) refers to persons who have an interest under the discretionary trust which will arise under protective trusts where the interest of the principal beneficiary has not yet failed or determined.

The definition of persons falling within para (b) is, however, the most complex. It includes any person (whether ascertained or not) who may become entitled to an interest under the trusts as being at a future date or on the happening of a future event a person of any specified description or a member of a specified class. The proviso however excludes any person who would be of that description or a member of that class if the said date had fallen or the said event had happened at the date of application to the court.

Case law has indicated the scope of para (b). In *Re Suffert's Settlement* [1961] Ch 1, the settlor's daughter had a life interest under the trust together with a general testamentary power of appointment. In default of appointment, the property was to be held for those persons who would be her statutory next-of-kin if she died intestate and unmarried. The daughter, who was unmarried and aged 61, applied to the court for approval to be given to an arrangement dividing the fund between herself and her statutory next-of-kin. Buckley J held that he was not empowered to give consent on behalf of the daughter's two cousins because they fell within the proviso. If the daughter had died at the date of application to the court, the two cousins would be her statutory next-of-kin: they 'would be' persons of that description. Other potential next-of-kin, however, are not within the proviso, and the court is empowered to give its consent on their behalf. *Re Moncrieff's Settlement Trusts* [1962] 1 WLR 1344 is to similar effect.

In *Knocker* v *Youle* [1986] 1 WLR 934, it was held that para (b) does not enable the court to give its consent on behalf of persons who have contingent (albeit very remote) interests. This is because the paragraph refers only to persons 'who may become entitled', not to those who already are. *Re Suffert* and *Re Moncrieff* were distinguishable because prospective next-of-kin of a living person have no interest in that person's estate, they have merely an expectation (a spes). Riddall, however, has argued that *Knocker* v *Youle* is wrong, and that the word 'interest' in the first part of para (b) refers to a vested interest: Riddall [1987] Conv 144.

This would mean that para (b) would include persons who have merely a contingent interest, provided such contingency is more than one step removed.

It might also be pointed out that s. 1 does not enable the court to give its consent on behalf of persons merely on the ground that they are untraceable. In such cases, however, a *Benjamin* order might be appropriate: *Re Benjamin* [1902] 1 Ch 723.

Finally, it is provided that, except in the case of para (d), the court shall not approve an arrangement unless it is satisfied that it is for the benefit of the persons on whose behalf approval is given.

(b) An arrangement varying or revoking the terms of a trust under the Variation of Trusts Act 1958 has been held to include the sanctioning of the 'export' of a trust to a foreign jurisdiction. The court has power to consent on behalf of beneficiaries who fall within paras (a) to (d) of s. 1(1). As a minor having a contingent interest under the trusts, Luke falls within para (a). Moreover, any issue of either son fall within para (c), since these are persons unborn. Consent cannot be given on behalf of John, however, since he no longer falls within any of the paragraphs: he has already attained majority, and has an interest under the trust, albeit contingent. Under the statute, therefore, John's own consent to the export of the trust is required.

The court is not obliged to sanction an application to the court under the Variation of Trusts Act 1958: the court may give its approval 'if it thinks fit'. Furthermore, the court may not approve an arrangement on behalf of persons within paras (a) to (c) unless it would be for the benefit of those persons. In *Re Seale's Marriage Settlement* [1961] Ch 574, the court approved, on behalf of the children, the export of a marriage settlement to Canada, which was the country to which the family had emigrated many years earlier and in which they were permanently settled. The benefit to the children was one of administrative convenience.

By contrast, in *Re Weston* [1969] 1 Ch 223 the Court of Appeal refused to give its consent, on behalf of minor beneficiaries, to the export of a trust to Jersey. Unlike their counterparts in the aforementioned cases, the family here had only just moved to Jersey and there was no evidence that they intended to stay there any length of time. The judges involved, however, gave different reasons for their refusal. Stamp J at first instance castigated the arrangement as a blatant piece of tax avoidance: yet tax avoidance is lawful, and most applications under the Act have tax saving as a main object. In the Court of Appeal, Lord Denning MR, in Shakespearian vein, considered that the minors' welfare might be imperiled were they to be uprooted from England. This outweighed any benefit from tax-saving. Harman LJ, by contrast, decided on the ground that Jersey law could not administer trusts; but this opinion was evidently made *per incuriam: Re Windeatt's Will Trusts* [1969] 1 WLR 692. Moreover, in the later case of *Re Chamberlain* (1976, unreported) the court approved an export of a trust to Guernsey where the main beneficiaries were resident in France and Indonesia.

It therefore appears that the export of a trust upon the grounds proposed in the problem will be permitted unless the welfare of unborn or minor beneficiaries is endangered. There is probably little likelihood of endangerment as regards the unborn beneficiaries; but more evidence is needed to assess the impact upon Luke's welfare. Such evidence would include whether it is intended that Luke should cease to be educated in England, or whether he is to remain in the country while the rest of his family move to Jersey.

11 Breach of Trust

INTRODUCTION

This chapter includes real and personal remedies against trustees and other persons into whose hands property has passed in breach of trust. Questions are usually predictable. This topic often occurs chronologically at the end of a course and may, therefore, be reasonably fresh in the student's mind — always a bonus.

A question concerning the proprietary remedy of tracing is often popular and an important first step is to read *Re Diplock* [1948] Ch 465, where the Court of Appeal deal thoroughly with the fundamental principles relating to equitable tracing.

Here comes a difficulty. You need to know the extent to which tracing is permitted at law before you can embark on an examination of equitable tracing. So, you have spent the best part of the academic year studying equity and now you are expected to exhibit a familiarity with the common law. That, after all, smacks of real life which is not always conveniently departmentalised. It may be that your course covers the law of obligations and you have dealt with the common law and equity side by side. On the other hand, your lecturer may be an equity lawyer who feels unhappy with common law concepts. You should, therefore, know from the content of your course what is expected of you.

To what extent could you be expected to deal with the personal common law action of conversion or the action for money had and received in a course on equity? The answer is, probably, not at all. It is likely that you will only need to be able to deal with the tracing process at law, and *Taylor v Plumer* (1815) 3 M & S 562 will probably get you through. You should also bear in mind that, although the House of Lord's decision in *Lipkin Gorman* v *Karpnale Ltd* [1991] 2 AC 548 concerned only tracing at common law, their Lordships' observations on the defence of change of position are very broad, and are likely to be held applicable in tracing in equity also.

For additional reading (and you will find numerous articles referred to in the text books), look at Goff and Jones, *The Law of Restitution*, 3rd edn, London: Sweet & Maxwell, 1986.

QUESTION 1

The only restriction on the ability of equity to follow assets is the requirement that there must be some fiduciary relationship which permits the assistance of equity to be invoked. (per Millett J, *Agip (Africa) Ltd* v *Jackson* [1990] Ch 265).

Discuss, in the light of this quotation, the requirement that there must be some fiduciary relationship before tracing in equity is permitted.

Commentary

The central issue in this question is the requirement of a fiduciary relationship. It therefore requires a thorough discussion of the case law on this point. For a contrary view to the general proposition that a fiduciary relationship is required before tracing in equity is permitted see 'A Tracing Paper', Robert A. Pearce (1976) 40 Conv 277. An important case on this requirement is *Re Diplock* [1948] Ch 465, CA, and for a discussion of this see 'The Prerequisites of an Equitable Tracing Claim', A J Oakley (1975) 28 CLP 64.

Suggested Answer

There are certain requirements which must be satisfied before equity is able to follow assets. These are: the property must be traceable; there must be an equity to trace; and the result must not be inequitable.

The reference in the question is to the requirement that, for the remedy of tracing to be available, there must be a fiduciary relationship. The remedy is not available simply because it is possible to show unjust enrichment (*Lister & Co.* v *Stubbs* (1890) 45 ChD 1). It is not necessary, however, for the fiduciary relationship to exist between the parties to the action. An equity to trace is available in circumstances where there is a beneficial owner of property and the property is in the hands of a trustee or other fiduciary. The beneficial owner must show an equitable proprietary interest in the property.

Sinclair v *Brougham* [1914] AC 398, HL, is considered to be authority for the proposition that a fiduciary relationship is necessary for tracing in equity. This interpretation was confirmed in *Re Diplock* [1948] Ch 465, CA. Tracing in equity is sometimes available in circumstances where tracing at common law is not. The most important situation is where the funds are mixed with other property, whether in the hands of a fiduciary or volunteer. It is therefore something of a paradox that tracing into a mixed fund is available to an equitable owner but not to an absolute owner. So, the victim of a theft cannot trace in equity so long as mixing has not occurred. After mixing however, when the legal title passes, it would appear that the thief stands in a fiduciary relationship to the victim: *Lipkin Gorman* v *Karpnale Ltd* [1991] 2 AC 548.

However, the interpretation of the requirement that there be a fiduciary relationship has been generous. In *Sinclair* v *Brougham* the issue was whether the customers could trace their deposits into the general assets of a building society. The House of Lords held that there was a fiduciary relationship between the customers and the directors. The directors had mixed the funds and the customers could therefore trace them. Other cases have accepted the existence of a fiduciary relationship between bailor and bailee, and (in some instances), employer and employee (see *Banque Belque Pour L'Etranger* v *Hambrouck* [1921] 1 KB 321, CA). A fiduciary relationship was held to arise in *Aluminium Industrie Vaassen BV* v *Romalpa Aluminium Ltd* [1976] 1 WLR 676, CA, out of the contract for sale between the plaintiff and the defendant. Under the contract ownership would only pass on payment. The goods, aluminium foil, were sold on to a third party and the proceeds of that sale were received by the defendants. It was held that the plaintiffs could trace into the proceeds of sale on the liquidation of the defendants. In *Chase Manhattan Bank NA* v *Israel-British Bank (London) Ltd* [1981] Ch 105, a fiduciary relationship was held to arise out of the payment of money under a mistake of fact.

The fiduciary relationship is clearly demonstrated in the context of a trust and exists between trustee and beneficiary. It was made clear in *Re Hallett* (1880) 13 ChD 696 by Jessel MR, that, for these purposes, there is no distinction between an express trustee, an agent, a bailee, a collector of rents or anyone else in a fiduciary position.

In *Re Hallett*, Hallett was Mrs Cotterill's solicitor. She gave him money to invest on her behalf, part of which he paid into his personal bank account. On his death there was sufficient money in his account to repay her but not to pay other personal debts. It was held that she could trace this money. It was not necessary to show an express trust.

If the property is sold, then the proceeds of sale can be followed, provided they can be identified. If a bailee sells goods which have been bailed the bailor can in equity follow the proceeds, even into a mixed fund.

It is not necessary to show that the fiduciary relationship exists between the parties to the action. Provided that the action is founded on the existence of a fiduciary relationship, the defendant need not be the person who has mixed the moneys. Equity operates on the conscience of a volunteer provided that some equitable proprietary interest has been created and attaches to the property which is in the hands of the volunteer.

In *Re Diplock*, money was wrongly distributed by the executors to a number of charities. It was held that the next of kin, who were entitled to claim, could trace against the innocent recipients of the money. The next of kin's right to trace in equity arose from their equitable right to see the proper distribution of the estate.

Money paid under a mistake of fact is also traceable in equity. The fiduciary relationship may arise at the moment when the property is transferred. It is not necessary to show that the property was subject to fiduciary obligations before it was transferred into the wrong hands. Where a person pays money to another by mistake the payer retains an equitable property in it. In *Chase Manhattan Bank NA* v *Israel-British Bank (London) Ltd*, the plaintiffs, as a result of a bookkeeping error, wrongly made a double payment of $2 million into the account of the defendant bank. It was held that a constructive trust arose in respect of the second payment, and the plaintiffs were entitled to trace. There was a continuing proprietary interest in the money.

This position was confirmed in *Agip (Africa) Ltd* v *Jackson* [1990] Ch 265, where it was stated that it was sufficient if the payment to the defendant gave rise to the fiduciary relationship. Millett J pointed out that this frequently arises in cases of commercial fraud. Where a company's funds are misapplied by a director, a receipt of trust property occurs. This would apply equally to any situation where a company's funds are misapplied by any person who is in a fiduciary position in relation to those funds.

Thus the existence of a fiduciary relationship, albeit not between the parties to the action, has become a prerequisite to the tracing remedy. It may be the case that *Re Diplock* is not actually authority for this point. However, later cases have accepted it as such. The later cases do demonstrate that the interpretation of what constitutes such a relationship has been widely drawn. The strange result of this, however, is that the legal owner cannot rely on the remedy.

QUESTION 2

Brown is a partner in a firm of solicitors which acts for the Rainbow Trust, and he is also a trustee of the trust. His co-trustee, Grey, is also a beneficiary under the trust, but is content to leave the entire management of the trust to Brown.

(a)   Between 1980 and 1987, Brown made advances of capital sums to one of the beneficiaries of the trust which were in fact in breach of the terms of the trust deed. Brown did not realise that the advances were a breach of trust, although, had he read the trust deed which was kept in the office safe, he would have realised.

(b)   Brown also invests half of the remaining capital in the family firm, Rainbow Ltd, which he understands to be an authorised investment within the terms of the trust deed. In fact, the trust deed only authorises investment of not more than one fifth of the trust fund in Rainbow Ltd. When Rainbow Ltd go into liquidation in 1992, the total investment is lost. However, all the other investments which Brown makes are very successful and during the period when he is administering the trust a healthy capital growth is shown.

Discuss the liability of Brown and Grey to the remaindermen under the trust.

Commentary

This question covers breach of trust by trustees where they fail to comply with the terms of the trust. Distinctions between professional and non-professional trustees need to be considered and, also, between active and non-active trustees.

The question is not difficult but requires a knowledge of the statutory provisions imposing liability and providing defences. Discussion of the case law dealing with the possibility of setting off a profit made from an improper investment is, however, required to achieve a good mark.

There is only one devious point hidden in the question and that relates to the limitation period. The clue to look out for is the careful use of dates. If they are not relevant, the examiner would probably have simply set the events in the previous year.

Suggested Answer

(a)   Brown is in breach of trust as he has failed to comply with the terms of the trust instrument. It makes no difference that the breach is innocent; the trustee is liable to make good the loss to the remaindermen. Brown is personally liable for his own breach: Trustee Act 1925, s. 30.

There are various defences established in *Re Pauling's Settlement Trusts* [1964] Ch 303, CA, which may be raised by Brown. If the remaindermen participated in or consented to the breach, then they cannot later complain about it. If they acquiesced subsequently to the breach, then again they cannot sue.

Brown may seek to rely on the statutory relief contained in the Trustee Act 1925, s. 61. Section 61 permits a trustee who may be personally liable for a breach of trust, but who has acted honestly and reasonably, and ought fairly to be excused, to be relieved from liability.

Brown does not act dishonestly, but his conduct may not be reasonable. The usual standard of care for a trustee, is that of a prudent man of business managing his own affairs. Brown is a professional trustee and the court is less likely to grant relief in his case. In *Bartlett* v *Barclays Bank Trust Co. Ltd* [1980] Ch 515, the court held that a trust corporation which carried on a specialised business of trust management owed a higher duty of care than an ordinary prudent man of business. Brown is not a trust corporation. Nevertheless, he is a professional trustee and his failure to undertake the elementary precaution of acquainting himself with the terms of the trust deed would seem to be inexcusable.

There is a six year limitation period provided in the Limitation Act 1980, s. 21(3). There is a proviso to the section which specifies that time does not run in favour of remaindermen until their interests fall into possession. If the advances made by Brown have been improperly made in favour of any remaindermen, this does not cause the interests to fall into possession for the purposes of the Limitation Act (*Re Pauling's Settlement Trusts*). Therefore, the remaindermen will not be barred by statute from suing Brown provided that their interests have not fallen into possession.

Co-trustees are not liable for any losses caused by another trustee, unless such losses have occurred through their own wilful default: Trustee Act 1925, s. 30. Grey plays no part in the management of the trust. Inaction of this type may constitute wilful default (See *Re Lucking's Will Trusts* [1968] 1 WLR 866). However, in *Re Vickery* [1931] 1 Ch 572, Maugham J held that the words 'wilful default' meant 'a consciousness of negligence or breach of duty, or a recklessness in the performance of duty'. Grey may, therefore, seek to argue that his reliance on the professional trustee was not negligent or reckless. If this argument fails, then Grey may be liable to have his beneficial interest impounded in satisfaction of the loss to the other remaindermen. His property will be taken first, and then the balance will be shared between him and Brown (see *Chillingworth* v *Chambers* [1896] 1 Ch 685, CA).

(b)   In purchasing shares in Rainbow Ltd, Brown is liable for the loss when the firm goes into liquidation. However, the trust deed permits investment up to one fifth of the trust fund. The investment is unauthorised to the extent that Brown exceeds this limit. In the case of a mortgage of realty, the mortgage is treated as an authorised investment for the smaller sum and the trustees are only liable for the excess, with interest: Trustee Act 1925, s. 9. It is arguable, therefore, that Brown's liability will be limited to the excess over one fifth of the investment.

Interest will be payable from the date when the investment took place. The amount, and type, of interest lies in the discretion of the court.

Brown has, however, been successful in his other investments. Normally, a gain made in one transction cannot be set off against a loss made in another transaction. This is the rule established in *Dimes* v *Scott* (1828) 4 Russ 195, where the trustees retained an unauthorised investment for longer than the prescribed period of one year. When the investment was eventually sold, the trustees were able to invest extensively in Consols as the price had dropped. This resulted in a greater gain for the remaindermen. However, the trustees were held liable for the loss caused by the retention of the unauthorised investment without being allowed to set off the gain.

But if the gain and the loss were made as the result of one transaction, then the rule is reversed. In *Fletcher* v *Green* (1864) 33 Beav 426, the proceeds of sale of an unauthorised investment were invested in Consols. The Consols then rose in value. The trustees were allowed to take advantage of the rise in value. In *Bartlett* v *Barclays Bank Trust Co. Ltd (No. 1)*, a sequence of speculative investments in property took place. The Guildford project was successful, but the Old Bailey project was a disaster. The Bank pleaded that they should be permitted to set off the profit from one against the loss from the other. This was permitted by the court, Brightman J considering that it would be unjust to deprive the bank of the element of salvage in assessing the cost of the shipwreck.

The principle seems to be that set off is allowed if the investments are part of one transaction. Brown would, therefore, only be able to plead such a defence if he could show some connection between the transactions.

Grey would be liable on the same basis as discussed above.

QUESTION 3

George was appointed the sole executor of Harriet's will. Harriet died last year leaving her entire estate, worth £130,000 after payment of debts, to her cousin Albert in Australia. George died recently. Albert has only just learned of this and has discovered that George, believing that as executor he was entitled to the estate beneficially and knowing that he was terminally ill, has made the following dispositions of the estate:

(a) £40,000 of the estate was contributed to the purchase of a house by George's daughter, Peggy. The house was purchased for £60,000 and Peggy contributed the remaining £20,000. The house is now worth £80,000.

(b) George settled £40,000 on trust for his son Felix as part of a marriage settlement on the occasion of his marriage to Matilda.

(c) George used £20,000 to buy a valuable antique Grecian urn which he gave to his service club.

(d) George used £20,000 to finance his gambling habits and this has all been lost at the Spend Casino.

(e) George gave the remaining £10,000 to his housekeeper May. May paid this into her current account, in which there was a balance of £5,000, but has since drawn out £10,000.

Advise Albert whether he has any claim against the recipients of Harriet's estate.

Commentary

This problem raises a number of different permutations of the tracing remedy. Most problems raised in this field relate to the issue of tracing in equity. The limitations of the remedy of tracing at common law need to be known.

The issue of the up and coming defence of change of position is also raised and merits some discussion of the important House of Lords decision in *Lipkin Gorman* v *Karpnale* [1991] 2 AC 548, although this case is concerned with tracing at common law.

Suggested Answer

The right to trace is available at common law if the plaintiff retains the legal title to the property. Here, tracing at law is not available because George, the legal owner, has disposed of the property and the legal title has passed. It is necessary, therefore, to consider the availability of the remedy in equity.

(a)   Peggy is presumably an innocent volunteer. The trust funds have been mixed with her money. The mixed funds have been used to purchase a house. The value of the house has now risen.

Albert is the true beneficiary, and therefore has an equitable proprietary interest. £40,000 of the trust property is in the hands of an innocent volunteer and has been used for the acquisition of property. An equitable proprietary remedy may be available which will enable Albert to trace the property.

In equity, where the trust property has been transferred in breach of trust to an innocent volunteer who has mixed it with her own, the trust and the volunteer share *pari passu* in the property purchased with the mixed fund: *Sinclair* v *Brougham* [1914] AC 398, HL, *Re Diplock* [1948] Ch 465, CA. They will share the profits and the capital in the proportions in which they contributed.

The right to trace may be lost where it would produce an inequitable result. In *Re Diplock* it was held that where trust money was spent on altering or improving land then it would be inequitable to force the volunteer to sell the land to satisfy a charge on it. Peggy has used the money to buy land. It might be argued, therefore, that her circumstances have changed as a result of the receipt of the trust money, thus rendering it inequitable for the remedy to be enforced against her. Nevertheless, this defence is not clearly supported by the authorities.

If the action in rem fails, then an equitable claim in personam can be brought for the principal sum of £40,000 without interest. However, Peggy will only be liable to the extent that the money cannot be recovered directly from George. The claim in these circumstances is limited to claims arising out of the administration of estates and is subject to the primary liability of the executor: *Re Diplock*.

(b) £40,000 was settled on trust under a marriage settlement for Felix. He is within the marriage consideration and, therefore, not a volunteer. Where trust property has been transferred to a bona fide purchaser of a legal estate for value and without notice of the equitable interest, the property is taken free from the claims of the beneficiaries. However, Felix has acquired merely an equitable as opposed to a legal interest and does not receive the protection of 'equity's darling'.

Alternatively, and especially if the tracing remedy does not satisfy Albert's loss, he may recover the loss (or the balance) in an action in personam. In this case, Albert should look to the personal remedy against George in the first instance, but may recover the balance from Felix in an action in personam.

(c) The service club is a volunteer as it has given no consideration for the urn. Presumably it is also innocent. Equitable tracing is however, available against an innocent volunteer if the property can be traced into the volunteer's hands. The trust money has been exchanged for the urn with no mixing of other funds. The club have the identifiable proceeds of the trust money. Albert can therefore trace in equity into the urn and obtain an order to restore the urn, being property acquired with the £20,000.

(d) £20,000 of trust property was dissipated by George on gambling at the Spend Casino.

The right to trace is lost where the property has ceased to be identifiable. Where the money has been dissipated, therefore, it can no longer be identified and cannot be traced. However, the money has passed into the hands of the Spend Casino, which is a volunteer, as no valuable consideration is given: *Lipkin Gorman* v *Karpnale Ltd* [1991] 2 AC 548. However, a casino stands the risk of losing or winning when they permit someone to place bets. The defence of change of position was considered in *Lipkin Gorman* v *Karpnale* [1991] 2 AC 548, a case which was concerned with legal tracing only. In *Lipkin Gorman* v *Karpnale*, it was held by the House of Lords that a casino was entitled to set off any winnings made by the gambler on the basis that they had changed their position by allowing him to gamble. Change of position was not a complete defence and the club were held liable in an action for money had and received for the net amount he had lost gambling at the club. It was stated, per curiam, by the House of Lords, that it is right to recognise the defence of change of position in good faith in restitution claims, based on the unjust enrichment of the defendant. The House of Lords, however, left the development of this doctrine to future cases. So, although it is likely that future courts will develop this doctrine, there is presently no direct authority for this defence to be raised by the Spend Casino in an action for tracing in equity.

The Spend Casino will also be subject to an action in personam under *Re Diplock*, as confirmed on appeal in *Ministry of Health* v *Simpson* [1951] AC 251, HL. This will be for the amount which Albert has been unable to claim from George and will be limited to the principal sum without interest.

     (e)   £10,000 of trust money has been mixed in May's current account with £5,000 of her own money. Where trust money is mixed with that of an innocent volunteer, tracing in equity is available. However, May has withdrawn £10,000. As the account is a current account, the rule in *Clayton's case* (1816) 1 Mer 572, applies. So, the rule is first in, first out. As May had £5,000 of her own money in the account, she is presumed to draw that out first, followed by £5,000 of trust money. The remaining money is, therefore, trust money.

If the £10,000 withdrawn has been used to buy an investment, Albert will be able to claim a charge on the investment and rank *pari passu* with May. If, however, the £5,000 trust money cannot be traced (if, for example, it has been dissipated), Albert will be left to pursue an action in personam as discussed previously.

QUESTION 4

On January 1, 1993, Tonto, who was trustee of the Una Charitable Trust, in breach of trust paid into his bank account £10,000 of the charity's money. There was already £6,000 of his own money in his account. One week later he bought shares to the value of £5,000 and withdrew this amount from his account. The next day, he drew out £3,500 which he used to buy a boat. On March 1, 1993, he paid into the account in breach of trust £5,000 belonging to the Duo Trust Fund, of which he was also trustee. The next day he drew out £10,000. He used £5,000 of it to pay debts which he had incurred in his business and he gave the remaining £5,000 to his daughter, Dora, as a deposit on a house she was buying.

The boat has now been destroyed in a hurricane. The shares are now worth £6,000.

Tonto has just been declared bankrupt. Advise the beneficiaries of the two trusts.

Commentary

The sequence of events is important and a rough plan in the form of a flow chart may be useful.

IN	OUT
£6,000 — trustee's money	
£10,000 — charity 1	
	£5,000 — shares (worth £6,000)
	£3,500 — boat (destroyed)
£5,000 — charity 2	
	£10,000 — (£5,000 — Dora's house)
	(£5,000 — debts)

The question deals with tracing where the money has been mixed in a bank account, and raises issues of tracing against an innocent volunteer. Tracing in equity is the central theme. Further discussion on the scope of tracing at common law, however, can be found in Goode (1979) 95 LQR 360 and Millett (1991) 107 LQR.

Suggested Answer

Tonto is in breach of trust. He has mixed money belonging to two trusts of which he is trustee, and has dissipated part of the funds. A trustee is personally liable for a breach of trust. The beneficiaries are entitled to seek compensation for the loss they have sustained. However, Tonto has been declared bankrupt and it will not avail the beneficiaries to sue him directly. The most effective remedy, therefore, is to seek to trace the trust funds in preference to all other creditors of the trustee's estate.

Tracing at common law is not available where, as here, the wrongful disposals are effected by the trustee himself. It is therefore necessary to trace in equity, equitable tracing being available against all except a bona fide purchaser for value of the legal title without notice. Equity operates to create a charge over the fund or over the property acquired with the money.

Tonto mixes £10,000 of the funds of the Una Charitable Trust with £6,000 of his own money. He first draws out £5,000 which he spends on shares, leaving £11,000 in the account. Then he draws out £3,500 which he spends on a boat, leaving £7,500. He then pays in £5,000 from the funds of the Duo Trust Fund which increases the balance to £12,500, and then proceeds to make payments out of £5,000 to Dora, and £5,000 on debts, leaving a final balance of £2,500.

The Two Trusts

Where the funds of two trusts have been mixed together with the trustee's own money, then they are entitled to share rateably in the mixed funds or in any property which has been purchased with the mixed funds. However, there is a special rule which applies in the case where the funds are mixed in a current bank account: the rule in *Clayton's case* (1816) 1 Mer 572. The rule provides that the first payment in is set against the first payment out. Therefore, the trust funds belonging to the Una Charitable Trust, as the funds paid in first, are deemed to be the first paid out. Their money is paid out before the trust funds of the Duo Trust Fund.

The Shares

Where a trustee draws out money from an account where trust money is mixed with the trustee's own money, it is assumed that the trustee's own money is used first. In *Re Hallett's Estate* (1880) 13 ChD 696, a solicitor paid money out of a bank account in which he had deposited client money. It was held that he had drawn out his own money first, as it could be assumed that he had not intended to act improperly in relation to the money held on trust. So, it would be assumed that Tonto draws out his own money first. At that stage there is sufficient money left in the account to cover the funds belonging to the Una Charitable Trust.

However, the next payment out is £3,500 for a boat leaving £7,500 in the account. This leaves inadequate funds in the account to cover the trust money. The right to a charge over the boat would be available to the trust except that the boat has been destroyed. On the other hand, the shares have increased in value. If the principle in *Re Hallett* is to apply, this would operate unfairly against the trust. They are deemed to have a first charge on the fund and the case of *Re Oatway* [1903] 2 Ch 356 demonstrates this point. In this case money had been withdrawn from a mixed account and invested in shares. Further money was withdrawn and dissipated. It was held that the beneficiaries had a right to trace their funds into the shares in advance of any claim by the trustee.

The shares have increased in value. It would seem that the beneficiaries may not be able to claim a proportionate amount of the increase. In *Re Hallett* it was said that the beneficiary only had a charge on the property for the amount of the trust funds. In *Sinclair* v *Brougham* [1914] AC 398, HL, this point was confirmed. In *Re Tilley's Will Trusts* [1967] Ch 1179, where trust money was mixed with the trustee's own money, a proportionate amount of the profit she made on a number of property speculations could not be claimed by the beneficiaries.

However, the decision in *Re Tilley* was reached because it was held that the trust money was used to reduce the trustees' overdraft, not to purchase the properties. Money to purchase the properties came from the overdraft facilities provided by the bank. The judge observed, obiter, that had the purchases been made with trust money, then the beneficiaries would have been entitled to a share of it in proportion to their contribution. This would appear to be consistent with the strict principle that a trustee must not profit from the trust. In that event, it is arguable that the trusts can share in the increase in value of the shares.

The Boat

£3,500 is spent on a boat which is destroyed. It is possible to trace where the fund has been converted into other property. However, where the property has been lost in some way the remedy is lost, as there is nothing against which to trace. If the boat was insured, then the remedy would lie against the proceeds of the insurance.

On March 1, 1993, Tonto pays a further £5,000 of money belonging to the Duo Trust Fund into his account. He then draws out £5,000 which he gives to Dora.

Dora

Dora is presumably an innocent volunteer. Provided she acted in good faith her position will be equal to that of the equitable owners. In other words they will be entitled to share rateably in the house she purchased using the trust money (*Re Diplock* [1948] Ch 465). They are entitled to share in a fund which has been mixed by someone other than the trustee, in this case, the innocent volunteer. However, the beneficiaries' claim does not take precedence over that of the innocent volunteer's. It will not be available where it would be inequitable. For example, in cases where trust money was used by the innocent volunteer in improving property, it was held to be inequitable to impose a charge on the property (*Re Diplock*) because the equitable chargee could thereby compel a sale.

The availability of a defence grounded on the fact that the innocent volunteer had changed his/her position in the light of the receipt of the money is not clearly established. In *Lipkin Gorman* v *Karpnale Ltd* [1991] 2 AC 548, a case on tracing at common law, it was stated, obiter, that such a defence would be available. However, further judicial development of this point is required to establish clearly that such defence is also available in cases of tracing in equity.

If Dora had knowledge of, or assisted in, the breach of trust then her position will be that of a constructive trustee and she will hold the house on trust for the beneficiaries to the extent of the trust's contribution to its purchase. Alternatively, she will be personally liable to account for the money received (see *Baden, Delvaux and Lecuit* v *Societé General* [1983] BCLC 325).

No personal action would be available against Dora, however, if she is an innocent volunteer. Such action appears to be available only where the volunteer receives property wrongly distributed under a will or intestacy: *Ministry of Health* v *Simpson* [1951] AC 251. Such equitable claim in personam is in any event limited to the amount which cannot be recovered from the executor.

The Debts

Once the debts have been paid, then the debt is extinguished (see *Re Diplock*). So, although Tonto has used money which he should not have had, to pay off the debts, it is not recoverable from the creditors (assuming of course that they are bona fide purchasers without notice).

12 Equitable Doctrines

INTRODUCTION

The maxims of equity are the general principles upon which the Chancery Court developed this system of law and reflect the desire to be fair and even-handed among litigants. The maxims underlie the equitable doctrines and remedies. Their origins are to be found in the history of property law but they are sometimes applied to more modern situations and not always very happily. The application of conversion to trusts for sale of land has led to some surprising results (see Question 2) and the Law Commission's Working Paper No. 94, 1985 'Trusts of Land' considered its abolition.

Questions on the doctrines of equity may well be general essay questions which will draw on your overall knowledge of the subject. It would be unwise to attempt these types of questions perhaps, unless you feel you have read generally and widely enough on the background of equity. Problem questions involving the more modern applications of the doctrines are however a possibility.

In deciding how much attention to give to these more general areas of equity, you should look at past examination papers and consider the emphasis given to equity itself by your lecturer. Although all courses on trusts will include some background of equity, some lecturers will not regard it as worthy of examination questions whilst other lecturers may set questions on it. You will only know which type of course your lecturer favours by looking at the past examination questions and listening to your lecturer!

QUESTION 1

Equity looks on that as done which ought to be done.

Discuss critically the applications of this maxim in the equitable doctrine of conversion.

Commentary

The equitable doctrine of conversion is an anachronism which can produce unfortunate results in its present day applications. It probably has more significance in land law than in trusts, although it is still capable of affecting interests on succession. The material for this type of question is more likely to be found in a book on equity rather than a book on trusts, and some reference may well be made to it in books on land law e.g., Maudsley & Burn, *Land Law — Cases & Materials*, 6th edn: London: Butterworth Co., 1992.

It is essentially only something which would be examined on a course which covers equity as well as trusts.

Suggested Answer

Although equity did not have the same rigid rules of precedent as the common law, the Court of Chancery did have certain principles which it applied in administering equity. These became known as the 'maxims' of equity and 'equity looks on that as done which ought to be done' is one of these. Its application is evident in several areas of equity and it underlies the doctrine of conversion.

The doctrine applies wherever there is an obligation to convert property into another form. Equity will then notionally convert the property before the actual conversion takes place. This has the curious result that realty may sometimes be regarded as personalty, and vice versa, in the eyes of equity. This was significant on the passing of property on an intestacy before 1926, when realty devolved upon the heir and personalty to the next of kin, and may still be relevant after 1925 in the case of a will leaving realty to one person and personalty to another.

Jeykll MR gave the reason for the doctrine in *Lechmere* v *Earl of Carlisle* (1733) 3 P Wms 211 as the fact that a *cestui que* trust should not be prejudiced by a trustee's possible delay in dealing with trust property in accordance with his obligations. It has received some unfortunate extensions however, in certain areas, which have produced criticisms from the judges and a suggestion by the Law Commission for its abolition in relation to trusts for sale of land. Indeed, in regard to trusts for sale of land, the courts have not always been consistent in their application of the doctrine.

Wherever there is an immediate binding trust for sale of land, either expressly created or imposed by statute, in the eyes of equity there is a notional sale and the land is regarded as personalty (the proceeds of sale) in the hands of the trustees. Although the legal title to the land is still vested in the trustees, the interest of the beneficiaries is no longer an interest in realty. This can lead to some unexpected results (as to which see Question 2).

The doctrine will not apply however to a mere power of sale. Thus in *Re Goswell's Trusts* [1915] 2 Ch 106, a deed conveying properties to trustees and providing that they should be sold 'on request in writing of the parties hereto' was held to create a power of sale but not a trust to sell, and the properties therefore, remained realty. Also, if a condition upon which a trust for sale is imposed fails, then the trust for sale will not take effect: *Re Grimthorpe* [1908] 2 Ch 675.

The doctrine has not been consistently applied by the courts however, and for certain sections of the Land Registration Act 1925, property held on a trust for sale has been regarded as land. Thus in *Elias* v *Mitchell* [1972] Ch 632, a co-owner under a trust for sale was held to have an interest in land which could be protected by a caution under the Land Registration Act 1925, s. 54(1), and in *Williams & Glyn's Bank Ltd* v *Boland* [1981] AC 487, HL, it was held that a beneficiary's interest under a trust for sale was an interest in land for the purposes of the Land Registration Act 1925, s. 70(1)(g).

Another application of the doctrine of conversion is to a contract for the sale of land. As soon as there is an enforceable contract, equity will impose a constructive trust on the vendor so that he holds the legal title on trusts for the purchaser. The beneficial equitable interest is deemed to have passed to the purchaser as from the date of the contract. The vendor is therefore responsible to the purchaser for the property and the purchaser, who is regarded as having a valuable beneficial interest in the property, is liable to insure it.

In *Re Sweeting (deceased)* [1988] 1 All ER 1016, the doctrine was applied to a conditional contract where the condition was not fulfilled until after the testator's death.

An unfortunate extension of its application is the rule in *Lawes* v *Bennett* (1785) 1 Cox Eq Cas 167, which decided that the doctrine applies retrospectively when an option to purchase is exercised after the grantor's death. Moreover, if the option is granted after a specific devise of the property by will, on exercise of the option, the devise is adeemed and the property, which becomes personalty retrospectively, passes to the residuary legatee: *Weeding* v *Weeding* (1861) 1 J & H 424.

A duty to convert property also arises under the rule in *Howe* v *Earl of Dartmouth* (1802) 7 Ves 137. The rule aims at achieving fairness as to investments between a life tenant and a remainderman. It requires trustees of a residuary personalty fund which is left in succession to convert any wasting assets, or future assets not yielding an income, into authorised investments of a permanent nature which yields an income. The income from any such part of the fund before conversion is apportioned between the life tenant and the remainderman, but the income from short leases of under 60 years which must be sold will go to the person entitled on sale as provided by the Law of Property Act 1925, s. 28(2).

A strict application of the doctrine of conversion can produce some unfortunate results, and it is hardly surprising that the courts have studiously sought to avoid it in some circumstances.

QUESTION 2

James, who died earlier this year, appointed Tina and Tom as executors and trustees of his will and devised all his realty to his son Sam and all his personalty to his daughter Doris. Advise the executors as to who is entitled to the following properties owned by James:

(a) 'The Beeches', held by James and his wife Wynne as tenants in common.

Would your answer differ if James and Wynne had held 'The Beeches' as joint tenants?

(b)   'The Larches', which James contracted to sell to Peter, subject to Peter obtaining planning consent for an extension, shortly before he died. Peter has now obtained planning consent.

(c)   'The Firs', upon which he had granted an option to purchase to Frank. Since James died, Frank has given notice to Tina and Tom of his intention to exercise the option.

Would your answer differ if the will had included a specific devise of 'The Firs' to Sam?

(d)   'The Cedars', which James and his mother owned as joint tenants until James' mother died last year.

Commentary

This question requires a knowledge of some of the circumstances where the doctrine of conversion applies.

Like all questions in parts, it is probably unwise to attempt it unless you know the answer to at least three parts of it! If you have revised this topic however, it is a fairly straightforward question, with almost arithmetical answers. You should achieve at least a pass if you can apply the principles, although a more detailed knowledge of the cases would be required to pass well.

Suggested Answer

(a)   Wherever there is co-ownership of land, the Law of Property Act 1925, s. 34, imposes a trust for sale. Because a trust imposes a binding obligation on the trustees and 'equity looks on that as done which ought to be done', the equitable doctrine of conversion operates to convert property held on a trust for sale to personalty. In the eyes of equity, there is a notional sale and the property is regarded as money.

Because 'The Beeches' is held by James and Wynne as co-owners, s. 34 imposes a trust for sale and the property is regarded as personalty, and James' share of it will therefore go to Doris.

If James and Wynne had held 'The Beeches' as joint tenants, although there would still have been a trust for sale under the Law of Property Act

1925, s. 34, as there is still co-ownership, the right of survivorship applies to a joint tenancy and the property will not pass under a will at all. James' interest in 'The Beeches' therefore, passes under the right of survivorship to Wynne.

(b) As soon as a binding and enforceable contract to sell property exists, equity regards the equitable beneficial interest as having passed to the purchaser, and the vendor holds the legal title as a constructive trustee for the purchaser. Because the contract is enforceable by equity, equity regards the transaction as a notional sale. The interest of the vendor is therefore in the proceeds of sale, which are personalty.

In *Re Sweeting (deceased)* [1988] 1 All ER 1016, conversion applied to property subject to a conditional contract for sale when the condition was fulfilled after the testator's death.

The proceeds of sale of 'The Larches' will therefore go to Doris also.

(c) The application of the doctrine of conversion to contracts for the sale of property was extended by the rule in *Lawes* v *Bennett* (1785) 1 Cox 167 to options to purchase. As soon as an option to purchase property is exercised, the property becomes personalty in the hands of the vendor because there is a binding obligation to sell it. This is still the case, even if the option is made exercisable after the death of the grantor (*Re Isaacs* [1894] 3 Ch 506). Therefore, as soon as Frank gives notice to Tina and Tom of his intention to exercise the option, it is regarded as personalty in their hands and will again go to Doris.

However, if the will makes it clear that the devisee of property is to take all the testator's interest in it, then the devise may operate to override the rule in *Lawes* v *Bennett*. Moreover, it is relevant whether the option was granted before or after the devise in the will. If it was granted before the devise, then there may be a presumption that the testator intended to give the whole of his interest in the property to the devisee, including any rights under the option. In *Calow* v *Calow* [1928] Ch 710, a devise of land or 'the proceeds of sale of the land' was held to survive a subsequent contract to sell the land completed after the testator's death. Conversely, if the option was granted after the devise, then the option is regarded as overriding the devise: *Re Carrington* [1932] 1 Ch 1.

If James' will was made before the option to purchase was granted, then the effect of Frank's notice to Tina and Tom to exercise the option is to operate the doctrine of conversion retrospectively. 'The Firs' becomes personalty in their hands and will go to Doris.

If James's will was made after the option was granted however, then it is likely that the option will be regarded as a right attaching to the property, and 'The Firs' will pass, together with the right, to Sam as realty.

(d) There would be a statutory trust for sale under the Law of Property Act 1925, s. 34, when 'The Cedars' was owned jointly by James and his mother and the property would therefore be regarded as personalty, owing to the operation of the doctrine of conversion. When James' mother died however, the right of survivorship would apply and the property would then vest in James alone. This operates to reconvert the property to realty: *Re Cook* [1948] Ch 212.

'The Cedars' would therefore pass under James' will to Sam.

QUESTION 3

(a) Two sisters, Amy and Bertha, were joint tenants of a house. Amy, who died recently, by her will purported to leave the house to Bertha and their brother Cyril in equal shares. There was also a bequest in the will of valuable jewellery worth at least half of the value of the house to Bertha. Advise Bertha and Cyril.

(b) John, who died recently, made a will in which he gave a legacy of £5,000 to Bill. Bill had lent John £5,000 secured by a charge on John's house. There is a sum of £3,000 outstanding on this debt. Advise Bill as to whether the debt will be satisfied by the legacy.

Commentary

The first part of this question is on the application of the doctrine of election, and the second part on a possible application of the doctrine of satisfaction.

Both of these doctrines have their origins in equity's desire to be fair to the children of a family in the distribution of family wealth. The doctrines were extended, however, beyond the family circumstances and the doctrine of satisfaction particularly, in its application to creditors to whom a legacy was left. There are few recent cases on the doctrines although they are still occasionally applicable today.

This is not a subject to cover unless your lecturer directs you to do so or deals with it in your lectures.

Suggested Answer

(a) The doctrine of election means that a person who receives a benefit from a transaction from which he also suffers a loss must elect to take with the transaction or against it; that is, he may elect to take the benefit and suffer the loss, or not to accept the benefit at all. It usually applies to a will and arises where property is left to A and some of A's property is left by the same will to B. A cannot accept the gift under the will unless he compensates B from his own property. It is irrelevant that the testator has made a mistake as to the ownership of A's property which he has purported to leave to B.

Because Amy and Bertha were joint tenants of the house and the right of survivorship applies to a joint tenancy, the house automatically passes to Bertha on Amy's death. Amy is therefore leaving to Cyril property which is not hers to dispose of. In *Re Gordon's Will Trusts* [1978] Ch 145, where a mother and son owned a house as joint tenants and the mother devised it to her trustee upon trust for sale and left other property to her son, Buckley LJ accepted that the doctrine of election would apply to the son.

In this case, the property devised to the son was not freely alienable by him, which in fact prevented the application of the doctrine. The jewellery in this case would appear to have been given outright to Bertha however, so it would seem that the doctrine would apply.

Bertha will therefore, have to elect to take with the will, in which case she may keep the jewellery but must convey half of the house to Cyril, or against it, in which case she may keep the whole of the house but must compensate Cyril by letting him have the jewellery. She will be obliged to let him have the whole of the jewellery however, and not just jewellery to the value of half of the house.

Hanbury and Martin's *Modern Equity*, 14th edn, London: Sweet & Maxwell, 1993, criticises the doctrine of election as too uncertain an instrument of equity', pointing out that the ultimate donee of the elector's property will always benefit, whereas the person put to their election may not benefit at all. This would seem to be the position here.

(b)   The doctrine of satisfaction evolved in order to ensure, as far as possible, an equal distribution of family wealth among the children of a family. It was applied in certain circumstances to adeem a legacy left to a child who had previously received a portion (a sum of money to set him up in life).

It also applies where a legacy is left to a creditor, the underlying maxim for this being that 'equity imputes an intent to fulfil an obligation'. It must be possible to presume from the circumstances that the testator did intend to pay the debt with the legacy and, like all presumptions, it is rebuttable. Certain technical rules have developed to rebut the presumption.

Firstly, the legacy must be as beneficial to the creditor as the debt (see *Re Van den Bergh's Will Trusts* [1948] 1 All ER 935). As Bill's loan was secured by a charge on John's house, this would not be the case.

Secondly, the doctrine only applies if the will was made after the debt was incurred. We are not told the dates of the will or the debt.

Thirdly, it will not apply if the will includes a clause (which is frequently included in wills) directing the testator's executors to pay the testator's debts and funeral and testamentary expenses. In these circumstances, both the debt and the legacy will be payable.

For all these reasons, it is possible that the doctrine of satisfaction will not apply to the legacy in John's will and Bill will be able to recover his debt from the estate and also take his legacy of £3,000.

13 Equitable Remedies

INTRODUCTION

Equitable remedies are available in all fields of law, so do not assume that you will be confined to discussing cases involving trusts. Contract and commercial law, labour law, tort and breach of confidence are all areas which may be used to consider the application of an equitable remedy. Although you are not being examined on your knowledge in these fields, you will clearly need to have some background knowledge. Since equity and trusts is normally taught towards the end of a course this should not present too much of a problem. If it happens to occur earlier in your course then do not panic, your examiner will probably take this into account.

During your course of study some controversial or notorious case may arise where equitable remedies are sought. A bitter industrial relations dispute may be fought out in the courts; a breach of confidence action may be brought in a case involving national security such as the *Spycatcher* case. It is likely that your examiner will frame a question round such a case. So, keep abreast of current case law, particularly if it features on the national news. If your lecturer starts referring you to newspaper reports as an example of the topicality of the subject, then take the hint and read up the material. It is very gratifying for your lecturers when they can prove to you how relevant to the modern world their subject is. If they can, they will try to reflect it in the examination.

The most likely remedies to be examined are specific performance and injunctions. They can occur as either essay or problem questions. The question might deal more narrowly with types of injunctions, such as *Anton Piller* or *Mareva* orders, where there have been a number of recent developments. Rescission and rectification are less commonly examined but listen to your examiner for pointers on this one. For that reason the sample questions in the chapter concentrate on specific performance and injunctions.

As equitable remedies are discretionary you will need to bear in mind general equitable principles, for example, the maxims of equity, when answering the questions. As usual, the area is mainly case law except for the provisions of the Supreme Court Act 1981. If there is a question involving labour law, you will need to refer to the Trade Union and Labour Relations Act 1974.

QUESTION 1

The draconian and essentially unfair nature of *Anton Piller* orders
from the point of view of respondents against whom they are made
requires, in my view, that they be so drawn as to extend no further than
the minimum extent necessary to achieve the purpose for which they
are granted, namely the preservation of documents or articles which
might otherwise be destroyed or concealed (per Scott J in *Columbia
Picture Industries Inc.* v *Robinson* [1987] Ch 38).

Discuss critically.

Commentary

A quotation of this sort can be followed by various commands:
'comment', or 'examine', or, as in this question, 'discuss'. Sometimes you
are required to perform the test 'critically'.

Whatever the form adopted by your examiner you are required to do two
things for a degree-level answer to this question. First, you must show you
know what the procedure entails. So, in this question you must explain
what the *Anton Piller* order is all about. You will be expected to cite the
relevant authorities.

Secondly, you must be critical. The key is to read the quotation. This may
seem obvious, but there is a great temptation in the exam room to read
and digest only key words. In this question the key words are '*Anton
Piller*'. An answer which simply describes the *Anton Piller* procedure will
achieve a pass, but little more. What is required is a critical analysis of the
current use of the procedure.

The quotation gives the lead. You should explain in what respects the
procedure is considered by the judge to be 'draconian'. The quotation is
provocative so your answer can be argumentative, even bullish. Give
both sides of the argument, then come down on one side and give reasons
for your decision. Provided you have argued your case well, you will not
lose marks if your examiner happens to disagree with your verdict.

As with all discussion questions, beware of losing your way. Plan your
arguments in advance. Prepare a checklist of the points to be made, then
tick them off as you make them. A question of this sort gives you the

opportunity to show off your skills in arguing a case, providing you have a sound knowledge of the law involved.

This type of question may also occur as an assessment which would require a deeper analysis of the literature. For example, more should be made of the article by Dockray and Laddie (1990) 106 LQR 601 and the judgment of Nicholls V-C in the latest judicial authority on this point, *Universal Thermosensors Ltd* v *Hibben* [1992] 3 All ER 257. The application to the European Court of Human Rights in *Lock* v *Beswick* [1989] 1 WLR 1268, noted in the article by Dockray and Laddie, should also be considered.

Suggested Answer

Anton Piller orders have sometimes been described as civil search warrants, enabling the applicant to enter on the respondent's premises, search and take relevant evidence.

Since their initial use, originally in *EMI Ltd* v *Pandit* [1975] 1 WLR 302, and subsequently in *Anton Piller KG* v *Manufacturing Processes Ltd* [1976] Ch 55, from which the name is derived, these orders have been extensively used.

Their popularity has ensured that the injustice which they were created to remedy has been ameliorated. However, applicants have not always been entirely honest when seeking this remedy; they have not always come to equity with clean hands. Concern has been expressed, both on the Bench, and by academic writers, that such orders are being abused. In *Universal Thermosensors Ltd* v *Hibben* [1992] 3 All ER 257, Nicholls V-C laid out a series of guidelines for the use of these orders. He recognised that they can be both a virtue in eliciting evidence which would otherwise not have seen the light of day, and a vice in that the procedure is open to abuse.

Anton Piller injunctions are sought where there is a risk that vital evidence may be lost or destroyed. Their use has been particularly appropriate in cases where the defendant is suspected of infringing the plaintiff's intellectual property rights or of breaching trade secrets. They have also been used in one reported case within the field of family law (*Emanuel* v *Emanuel* [1982] 1 WLR 669), to enable the wife's solicitors to enter the husband's home and inspect documents relating to his financial means.

In order to bring such a case, a plaintiff needs evidence which might be in the hands of the defendant. It might consist of confidential documents or material such as videotapes. In the *Anton Piller* case the defendants were the plaintiff's selling agents. The plaintiffs believed that the defendants were selling confidential information about their electrical equipment and plans to their competitors. However, to prove this they needed access to documents kept at the defendants' premises. The Court of Appeal granted an order which permitted them to enter the defendants' premises and inspect the documents.

It is crucial that the application is made *ex parte*. If the other side knew of the application the risk is that the evidence would be destroyed forthwith. Surprise is a key element of the procedure. Herein lies the danger. The judge, at the *ex parte* hearing, must rely exclusively on the word of the applicant.

In the first place, the judge may be required to determine to what extent any particular scientific or technical knowledge is the subject of patent or copyright, or is merely legitimately accepted scientific research. As Hoffmann J said in *Lock International plc v Beswick* [1989] 1 WLR 1268, 'It may look like magic but turn out merely to embody a principle discovered by Faraday or Ampère'.

Secondly, an unscrupulous applicant might abuse the power in a commercial situation by seeking to crush a competitor by the use of oppressive tactics. In *Lock International plc v Beswick*, the *Anton Piller* order was carried out by five representatives of the applicant. These were solicitors or employees of the applicant. They were, however, accompanied by 11 or 12 police officers who were armed with a search warrant in respect of alleged criminal activities of the respondent.

On appeal (noted (1990) 106 LQR 173), it was said that what had happened was regrettable, and it was unfortunate that the judge had not been informed of the involvement of the police.

Three conditions for the grant of the order were laid down in *Anton Piller KG v Manufacturing Processes Ltd* by Ormrod LJ:

(1)   There must be a very strong prima facie case.
(2)   There must be actual or potential damage of a very serious nature.

(3)   There must be clear evidence that the defendant has the requisite evidence and a real risk that it might be destroyed before an *inter partes* application can be heard.

These conditions are more onerous than the conditions laid down in *American Cyanamid Co.* v *Ethicon Ltd* [1975] AC 396 for the issue of interlocutory injunctions. This reflects the concern of the courts to protect the respondent from an abuse of process. The procedure should not be used as a means of finding out what proceedings can be brought (*Hytrac Conveyors Ltd* v *Conveyors International Ltd* [1983] 1 WLR 44). In other words, the material sought should be specific and should support the cause of action proposed by the plaintiff for the trial of the main action. Fishing expeditions are not permitted. The orders are not, in fact, search warrants. They are precisely limited.

When applying for the order, the applicant must make a full disclosure to the court. There is clearly a potential weakness in a procedure which only hears one side of the case. Therefore, there is a particularly strict duty for a full and frank disclosure of all relevant facts. As Scott J pointed out in *Columbia Picture Industries Inc.* v *Robinson* [1987] Ch 38, the procedure constitutes an apparent breach of the rule of natural justice that citizens should not be deprived of their property without a fair hearing.

In carrying out the order the applicant should be accompanied by a solicitor. Documents or other evidence may be inspected and removed according to the terms of the order. They may not be used for any other purpose unless the respondent has consented or the court has so ordered. If damage is caused to the respondent then the applicant may be obliged to pay damages which could be exemplary in nature.

Two cases have sought to limit the scope of Anton Piller orders: *Tate Access Floors Inc.* v *Boswell* [1991] Ch 512 and *Rank Film Distributors Ltd* v *Video Information Centre* [1982] AC 380. The former case emphasises a requirement for the plaintiff to make a full disclosure. In the latter case it was held that the privilege against self-incrimination could be raised by a defendant. This decision was abrogated by the Supreme Court Act 1981, s. 72, in cases relating to intellectual property.

In *Universal Thermosensors Ltd* v *Hibben*, Nicholls V-C set out seven points of procedure. The defendant must have the opportunity to get legal advice so the order should be served at a time that enables this to happen. If the defendant is a woman alone in a private house, the plaintiff's solicitor must be a woman, or accompanied by a woman. A detailed list of items removed should be prepared at the premises and checked by the defendant. The defendant should only be restrained from communicating with others, apart from a lawyer, for a limited period of time; a week is too long. Orders at business premises should be executed in the presence of an officer or employee. The plaintiff should not use the opportunity for a general search of the defendant's papers. The order should be served and supervised by an experienced solicitor independent from the plaintiff, who should submit a written report to the defendant and to the court at a subsequent *inter partes* hearing.

The courts are clearly concerned to ensure that the procedure is not abused. As an equitable remedy, the *Anton Piller* order has shown the willingness of the courts to adapt well established remedies to new situations. The maxim that equity will not allow a wrong to be without a remedy is still valid today, yet the dangers of the procedure are acknowledged by the courts that developed it. Concern over abuse of *Anton Piller* orders has been expressed both by the judges and the legal profession as a whole. While providing a valuable remedy, the balance must be maintained between the potential parties to an action. Although it is unlikely that this remedy will disappear, it is likely that, in future, judges will need very cogent evidence before granting *Anton Piller* orders.

QUESTION 2

Lex Ltd produces videos and tapes of lectures and accompanying notes for the purpose of teaching law to overseas students by distance learning. Ten staff are employed on a full-time basis. Portia, a senior member of staff, and author of a leading textbook on European law, is employed on a five-year contract to develop new materials within her field. Her contract requires her not to work for any other firm of law tutors during the period of her contract and for one year thereafter. Portia is a member of the National Union of Law Teachers (NULT).

Negotiations over conditions of service between Lex Ltd and its staff have now broken down. The following circumstances have occurred:

(a) Portia, who has three years left to run on her contract, has written a letter of resignation to Lex Ltd. She has accepted an offer of employment at the Cambridge base of the tutorial firm, Law sans Larmes, which has its headquarters in Brussels.

(b) All the materials that Portia had been working on have disappeared from the office, and Lex Ltd fears that they may now be in the possession of Law sans Larmes. The company has also discovered that its current students have received advertisement material from Law sans Larmes, and believes that Portia took a list of clients with her. It also believes that Law sans Larmes have bank accounts in Cambridge and Brussels, and that fees received are transferred on a regular basis to the Brussels account.

(c) NULT has called a strike at Lex Ltd's premises as a result of the breakdown in negotiations. Picketing is taking place on a daily basis.

Advise Lex Ltd of any equitable remedies it may have in these circumstances.

Commentary

This problem question has a variety of points in it and mixes both specific performance and injunctions. They are, however, quite straightforward and not too difficult to spot. You should be able to score a good 2(i) if you work methodically through the various remedies, explaining their availability in each instance. For a first-class answer, some critical analysis of their usage would be necessary.

Suggested Answer

(a) Portia is in breach of her contract of employment with Lex Ltd. An employment contract, that is, a contract *of* service, cannot be enforced specifically against an employee (Trade Union and Labour Relations Act 1974, s. 16). This statutory provision stems from the equitable principle that such contracts should not be turned into 'contracts of slavery' (per Fry LJ in *De Francesco* v *Barnum* (1890) 45 ChD 430 at p. 438). An action for damages would provide an adequate remedy since, although Portia is a leading author and a senior member of staff, it is likely that she could be replaced.

Lex Ltd may, however, wish to enforce the term in her contract restraining her from working for anyone else during the remaining period of her contract. Earlier case law indicates that an action for an injunction to this effect would be successful. In *Lumley* v *Wagner* (1852) 1 De G M & G 604, an opera singer broke her contract which required her to sing at the plaintiff's theatre for three months. The remedy of specific performance was refused but an injunction preventing her singing at any other theatre during the contractual period was granted. This was followed in *Warner Bros Pictures Inc.* v *Nelson* [1937] 1 KB 209 where the actress, Bette Davis, was prevented from working for a rival film company in breach of a no-competition clause.

However, these cases have been modified where it appears that to grant the remedy would mean that the defendant was prevented from working in any capacity (*Whitwood Chemical Co.* v *Hardman* [1891] 2 Ch 416). In effect, the defendant would be required to work for the plaintiff or starve. It is considered unrealistic to expect an individual with a particular talent to work in an entirely different capacity. *Warner Bros Pictures Inc.* v *Nelson* was disapproved in *Warren* v *Mendy* [1989] 1 WLR 853, a case where an injunction preventing a boxer from seeking financial services from anyone other than his manager was refused. The principle was stated that an injunction will not be granted if its effect is to prevent a person from working for anyone other than the plaintiff.

Portia has expressly agreed not to work for any other firm of law tutors in the UK during the contractual period. If an injunction is granted, then, in effect, she will be obliged to resume employment with Lex Ltd. Such a result is contrary to the principles expressed in the later cases and is, therefore, likely to be refused.

The principle would be the same if Law sans Larmes or Portia were sued.

(b)   Lex Ltd may seek an injunction to prevent Portia taking its latest teaching materials. There is a right in equity to restrain an abuse of confidential information. This does not necessarily rely on an employment relationship.

Knowledge of the list of customers is critical to Lex Ltd's commercial enterprise and would also amount to confidential information. An interlocutory injunction could have been sought to prevent the information being released. However, the information has already been acted upon, and equity will not act in vain. In *A-G* v *Guardian Newspapers Ltd (No. 2)* [1990] 1 AC 109, the final injunction in the

Spycatcher case was refused. The information had already been published worldwide and the injunction would have been futile. An action for damages against Law sans Larmes might be appropriate if a profit has been made (*Seager* v *Copydex Ltd (No. 2)* [1969] 1 WLR 809).

If Lex Ltd fear that the teaching materials have also been taken, it may seek an *Anton Piller* order against both parties (named after the case of *Anton Piller KG* v *Manufacturing Processes Ltd* [1976] Ch 55). This would permit the company's agents to inspect the evidence at the premises of Law sans Larmes and at Portia's home. The application is made *ex parte* where there is a risk that the evidence might be destroyed before an action could be brought. The application must be made, and the order served, in accordance with the procedures established in *Universal Thermosensors Ltd* v *Hibben* [1992] 1 WLR 840. In particular, as the defendant is a woman, the order must be served by, or in the presence of, a woman.

Lex Ltd must show a very strong prima facie case and actual or potential damage of a very serious nature. It already has evidence that the information is in the hands of Law sans Larmes and the damage to its business could be irreparable.

(c)   Lex Ltd is clearly concerned that if it sues Law sans Larmes for damages they may be unable to satisfy the claim if assets are transferred abroad. It may, therefore, consider seeking a *Mareva* injunction under the procedure established in *Mareva Compañía Naviera SA* v *International Bulkcarriers SA* [1975] 2 Lloyd's Rep 509. This is an order which prevents the defendant from transferring assets abroad. It is usually obtained *ex parte* and could be sought at the same time as the *Anton Piller* order.

The principles in *American Cyanamid Co.* v *Ethicon Ltd* [1975] AC 396 must be satisfied. Further to the Supreme Court Act 1981, s. 37(3), the injunction may be granted to prevent the defendant removing the assets from the jurisdiction of the court or dissipating them in some way.

Lex Ltd must show that it has a good arguable case and will be required to give an undertaking in damages in the event that it is unsuccessful at trial.

Some of the assets of Law sans Larmes appear to be in Brussels. Lex Ltd may consider the possibility of seeking a *Mareva* injunction which covers not only the English bank account, but also the Brussels account. It was held in *Babanaft International Co. SA v Bassatne* [1990] Ch 13 that there is no geographical limit to the jurisdiction of the court. However, it would not be available where it may adversely affect third parties and where its effect may be oppressive to the defendant.

(d)   In order to obtain an interlocutory injunction against the union to prevent picketing, Lex Ltd must first show that there is a serious question to be tried according to the principles in *American Cyanamid Co. v Ethicon Ltd* [1975] AC 396. Secondly, it must show that it would suffer irreparable damage if the injunction is not granted and the dispute continues. Lex Ltd may decide to seek an *ex parte* injunction. This is permitted under the Trade Union and Labour Relations Act 1974, s. 17(1), provided that all reasonable steps have been taken for the defendant to be notified and heard.

The Trade Union and Labour Relations Act 1974, s. 17(2), provides that the court shall have regard to the possibility of the defendant establishing a defence of immunity to tortious liability under the 1974 Act. This modifies the *American Cyanamid* principles to the extent that Lex Ltd may have to show a *prima facie* case. This is particularly important in cases of this type where the outcome of the interlocutory proceedings may be decisive. In *NWL Ltd v Woods* [1979] 1 WLR 1294, where an interlocutory injunction was sought restraining industrial action, the merits of the case were considered at the interlocutory stage.

QUESTION 3

To what extent have the requirements for interlocutory injunctions decided by the House of Lords in *American Cynamid Co. v Ethicon Ltd* [1975] AC 396 been followed by subsequent cases?

Commentary

This essay question requires a discussion of the way in which the leading case, *American Cyanamid Co. v Ethicon Ltd*, changed the rules relating to interlocutory injunctions, and the further development of those rules in subsequent cases. It is one of those colourful areas where Lord Denning MR has robustly defended a certain position, and where other developments have occurred in particular fields.

As with all essay questions, the way to a high mark is to launch into a critical analysis of the case law. You would not be asked a question of this sort if the case law were straightforward.

One of the difficulties in dealing with a question of this sort in an exam is what to put in and what to leave out. You could spend all the allotted time dealing with *Anton Piller* and *Mareva* orders. It is preferable, however, to deal with the central issue, that is, should the defendant be required to establish a prima facie case? Then show, by example, the extent to which this point has moved from the position established in the leading case.

This also is a question which could be encountered as an assessed essay. in that case, you will have much more scope to expand the examples and refer to the literature, for example, Christine Gray, 'Interlocutory Injunctions since *Cyanamid*' [1981] CLJ 307.

Suggested Answer

The House of Lords in *American Cyanamid Co.* v *Ethicon Ltd* [1975] AC 396 established new criteria for the granting of an interlocutory injunction.

Prior to *American Cyanamid* it had been necessary for the plaintiff to show a prima facie case before the injunction would be granted. See, for example, *J. T. Stratford & Son Ltd* v *Lindley* [1965] AC 269. In addition, it had to be shown that the balance of convenience supported the grant. So, if the plaintiff could show that damage would be suffered which could not be compensated by an award of damages at the trial, then, once a prima facie case was made out, the injunction would be granted. This meant that frequently the issues which were to be heard at the trial of the action were rehearsed at the hearing of the motion for the injunction.

In *American Cyanamid* the House of Lords disapproved of the court conducting a trial on affidavit evidence, when the essential purpose of an injunction is to preserve a party's position until trial. They decided that it was no longer necessary to establish a prima facie case at the interim proceedings. Provided tht it could be shown that there was a serious question to be tried, then the remedy would be granted. Subject to this, the main test was the balance of convenience between the parties. The balance of convenience would be tested primarily by the adequacy of damages. If the balance of convenience was not clearly established then the *status quo* would be maintained. There is only one qualification made, which is that in individual cases special factors might have to be considered. The House of Lords did not classify these special factors.

One of the difficulties encountered with this approach is that frequently the action never comes to trial. Litigation is expensive, and a party against whom an injunction was been made may feel sufficiently discouraged to settle or drop the case. So, the decision to grant the injunction at the interlocutory hearing may dispose of the action and the issues may never be fully aired. Under the former position, this did not matter. If a prima facie case had to be made out, then the evidence would be presented and cross-examined.

An example of this occurs in trade disputes. The strength of the workers' case often lies in their ability to withdraw their labour. If an injunction is sought barring them from strike action, then on the *American Cyanamid* principles, the balance of convenience will invariably be in favour of the employer. This was recognised in the Trade Union and Labour Relations Act 1974, s. 17(2), which was inserted by the Employment Protection Act 1975 and the court is to have regard to the likelihood of the defendant establishing the defence of immunity to tortious liability.

However, this statutory modification to the *American Cyanamid* principle is an exception. Criticism of the application of the principle has been left to the judges in later cases.

In *Fellowes & Son* v *Fisher* [1976] QB 122, the Court of Appeal had differing views on the application of the *American Cyanamid* principles. The majority of the court refused an injunction to prevent a breach of a restrictive covenant in an employment contract, on the ground of the balance of convenience. Lord Denning MR, however, refused the injunction on the ground that no prima facie case had been made out. He stated that *American Cyanamid* did not apply because the facts of *Fellowes & Son* v *Fisher* fell within one of the exceptional cases outlined by Lord Diplock where special factors could be considered.

In *Hubbard* v *Pitt* [1976] QB 142, Lord Denning MR again took a different approach to the rest of the Court of Appeal. An injunction was granted by the majority of the court to restrain protesters obstructing access to the premises of an estate agent. The majority took the view that there was a serious question to be tried and the balance of convenience supported the grant. They did not require that a prima facie case should be made out. Lord Denning MR, dissenting, argued that a prima facie case was required and that the case fell outside *American Cyanamid* because 'special factors' applied. These 'special factors' related to freedom of speech and the right to demonstrate.

Thus Lord Denning MR has relied on the reference to 'Special factors' to take cases outside *American Cyanamid* and rely on the former rule that a prima facie case must be established.

Other cases where special factors have prevailed include *Smith* v *Inner London Education Authority* [1978] 1 All ER 411. Here the defendant was a public body and it was held that in such cases the interests of the general public must be considered. In libel cases where the defendant intends to plead justification, an interlocutory injunction is unlikely to be granted on *American Cyanamid* principles.

Trade disputes are dealt with by statute. The Trade Union and Labour Relations Act 1974, s. 17(2), provides that the defendant in an application for an interlocutory injunction may prove a prima facie defence under the statute. In *NWL Ltd* v *Woods* [1979] 1 WLR 1294 Lord Diplock observed that *American Cyanamid* was not dealing with a case where the grant or refusal of the injunction would dispose of the action. He stated that in such a case the consideration of the balance of convenience should take into account the likelihood of success had the case gone to trial.

There are two areas in which there have been important developments in the field of interlocutory injunctions. These are the *Anton Piller* and *Mareva* orders (named respectively after *Anton Piller KG* v *Manufacturing Processes Ltd* [1976] Ch 55 and *Mareva Compañía Naviera SA* v *International Bulk Carriers SA* [1975] 2 Lloyd's Rep 509).

Anton Piller orders have been described as being of a 'draconian nature' permitting a plaintiff to enter the defendant's premises and inspect evidence which it is believed may be removed or destroyed. They are available *ex parte* so that the defendant is not forewarned. Ormrod LJ laid down three conditions, the first of which was that the plaintiff must have an extremely strong prima facie case. This is an exception to the *American Cyanamid* principles. *Anton Piller* orders are mandatory in nature. The courts are less willing to grant a mandatory order without an indication of the strength of the plaintiff's case.

Mareva injunctions are available to prevent a defendant moving assets or otherwise disposing of them in order to make the pursuit of the main action fruitless. The plaintiff must have a legal or equitable right to protect and have a good arguable case.

The jurisdiction to grant *Anton Piller* and Mareva orders is now contained in the Supreme Court Act 1981, s. 37.

Thus, there are various situations where the principles in *American Cyanamid* have been refined or distinguished to meet the particular case.

QUESTION 4

(a) Amelia, a sculptress, agrees with Belinda to make a bust of Belinda, a world renowned child actress, for £500. When the bust is completed, Cindy, a film buff and fan of Belinda's, offers Amelia £1,000 for it. Amelia, who is in severe financial difficulties accepts Cindy's offer.

Advise Belinda on the availability of any equitable remedies for breach of contract in these circumstances.

(b) Delia took a long lease of the top flat on the 14th floor of a tower block being built two years ago. The service contract requires Easimoney Ltd, the freeholder, to undertake external building repairs, to have the outside of the windows cleaned once a month, and to install a lift within a reasonable period of time.

A recent gale has dislodged some tiles from the roof, and rain now leaks into Delia's flat. Despite repeated requests, this has not been repaired. The windows are never cleaned and the lift has not been installed.

Advise Delia of any equitable remedies that might be available to her.

Commentary

This is a straightforward question requiring a knowledge of the rules relating to specific performance. It is a good illustration of the need to read the question. For example, the plaintiff in part (a) is a child. This is not simply to add local colour to the question but is designed to raise the issue of mutuality. If you miss this point, your marks go down.

The second part of the question requires you to know the application of specific performance to contracts requiring supervision and construction contracts. You have to know the case law. If you can answer the first part, but know nothing about the construction cases, then it is too risky to tackle this question. A superb answer to the first part but zero on the second will barely earn you a pass.

However, if you have specific performance at your fingertips, then this question is fairly uncomplicated if you pick up all the points.

Suggested answer

The equitable remedy of specific performance is discretionary. It will not be available where damages provide an adequate remedy nor where the plaintiff has acted in an inequitable manner. Nor will the court grant the remedy unless it can be enforced; equity will not act in vain. If it is unjust to the defendant to grant the remedy, then it will not be awarded.

Normally, contracts for the transfer of personal property will not be specifically enforced. They can usually be compensated for by an award of damages. However, if the item of property has some particular rarity or beauty or uniqueness, such as King Canute's hunting horn (*Pussey* v *Pussey* (1684) 1 Vern 273) then specific performance may be granted.

There is statutory authority for the remedy contained in the Sale of Goods Act 1979, s. 52. This enables the court to grant specific performance of a contract to deliver specific or ascertained goods where it is just to do so.

The contract between Amelia and Belinda is for personal property, a bust of Belinda. In order for the remedy of specific performance to be granted there must be something unique about the property. In *Cohen* v *Roche* [1927] 1 KB 169, a contract for the sale of eight Hepplewhite chairs was not specifically enforceable. The chairs were not considered to be of any special value or interest. On the other hand, a contract for the sale of a ship was enforced in *Behnke* v *Bede Shipping Co. Ltd* [1927] 1 KB 649, where the ship was of 'peculiar and practically unique value to the plaintiff'.

The bust of Belinda is unique, there is only one in existence. It is a case which falls within the ancient jurisdiction of cases such as *Pussey* v *Pussey* where the goods are distinguishable because of their rarity rather than *Cohen* v *Roche*, where the goods, though rare and valuable, are still no more than ordinary commercial articles.

However, Amelia is in severe financial difficulties, and, for that reason, accepts the offer from Cindy. Since the remedy is discretionary, the court would consider whether it is equitable in the circumstances to enforce the contract against Amelia. Where a hardship would amount to an injustice (if Amelia could show that it would put her out of business) then the court may be reluctant to enforce the contract (*Patel* v *Ali* [1984] Ch 283).

Nor will the court act in vain. An equitable remedy will only be granted if it can be complied with by the defendant. In *Jones* v *Lipman* [1962] 1 WLR 832 the defendant attempted to defeat a contract for the sale of land by transferring the land to a company he had set up for this express purpose. The court awarded specific performance because the company was a sham. Normally specific performance would not be granted against a defendant who no longer owned the property. If Amelia has already sold the property to Cindy and it is irrecoverable, then the court will rely on the remedy of damages.

For specific performance to be awarded, it must be available to either party. If there is a lack of mutuality, there is a discretion to refuse the remedy. In *Flight* v *Bolland* (1824) 4 Russ 298, a minor was refused specific performance as it would not have been available against him. There is judicial authority for the viewpoint that the time to determine mutuality is at the time of the trial, not the contract. In *Clayton* v *Ashdown* (1714) 2 Eq Ab 516, it was held that where a minor attained majority at the time of the trial the remedy would be available. This principle was confirmed by the Court of Appeal in *Price* v *Strange* [1978] Ch 337.

There are, therefore, various grounds on which the court may refuse to exercise its discretion to award specific performance in favour of Belinda.

(b) Delia is seeking specific performance of her landlord's covenants. The general principle is that the court will not grant specific performance of a contract where constant supervision would be required. Equity will not act in vain and the court is unable to supervise the performance of a contract. It will not, therefore, enforce a contract where such supervision would be necessary.

There are, however, exceptions to this principle and the courts, in some of the modern cases, are more willing to grant specific performance even where there are potential problems relating to supervision.

The earlier case of *Ryan* v *Mutual Tontine Westminster Chambers Association* [1893] 1 Ch 116 shows the application of the general principle. The lessor of a flat covenanted to appoint a caretaker who would be in constant attendance and would undertake cleaning and general portering duties. A caretaker was appointed but he was frequently absent. The Court of Appeal refused to grant specific performance as it would be unable to supervise the performance of the covenant. It awarded damages instead.

However, in *Posner* v *Scott-Lewis* [1987] Ch 25, specific performance of a similar covenant to employ a resident porter was awarded. The court held that if the obligation was sufficiently defined and the degree of supervision was not unacceptable, then, if the plaintiff would suffer greater hardship, the equitable remedy would be awarded.

So, there is a modern trend to order the specific performance of contracts even where there is some degree of supervision involved.

The terms in Delia's lease are threefold. The first is to install a lift. Contracts to build or repair are not normally enforceable in equity. Again, however, there are exceptions. In *Wolverhampton Corporation* v *Emmons* [1901] 1 KB 515, the Court of Appeal established three requirements: the building work must be clearly defined; damages would be an inadequate remedy; and the defendant has possession of the land. It would seem that these requirements are satisfied. The building work is clearly defined except that the time-limit is vague. However, the court is unlikely to be unwilling to specify what would constitute a reasonable time. Since the work would have to be undertaken on part of the block of flats which is in the landlord's possession, it would be impossible for Delia to carry out the work herself. Damages would, therefore, be an inadequate remedy.

This exception was extended to landlords' covenants to repair in *Jeune* v *Queens Cross Properties Ltd* [1974] Ch 97. The Landlord and Tenant Act

1985, s. 17, now provides that specific performance of a landlord's repairing covenant may be granted. This overrides any equitable principles restricting the remedy. Delia would therefore be able to seek specific performance of the covenant to repair in respect of the damage to the roof caused by the gale.

The covenant to have the windows cleaned highlights the problem of supervision. Clearly, such a contractual obligation is ongoing and would require constant superintendence. However, applying *Posner* v *Scott-Lewis*, the work is clearly defined. If an order is issued requiring the landlord to appoint a firm of window-cleaners to carry out the work, then the supervision required is no more than the appointment of the porter in *Posner* v *Scott-Lewis*. Damages might be an adequate remedy in that they would enable Delia to employ a window-cleaner herself. However, to employ a window-cleaner to clean the exterior of the windows on the 14th floor is not practicable and the court would no doubt take the view that it would cause greater hardship to Delia than to the landlord. Therefore, Delia has a reasonable prospect of success in enforcing this covenant.

14 Pick 'n' Mix Questions

INTRODUCTION

Your examination paper may contain one question which mixes a number of different topics. This may be upsetting at first sight. You may have carefully revised several topics which are covered in the question only to discover that it includes one topic which you thought safe to leave out. Assuming that each section in the question bears equal marks (and that is a reasonable assumption unless there is any contrary indication), then it is probably unsafe to tackle it in these circumstances. Most (if not all) questions in the paper will be discrete and you will find the question on charities or administration of trusts or whatever your favourite topic may be, without any difficulty. Once you have identified it, then you are away.

However, the possibility of a mixed topic question is another reason why you should read the questions carefully before starting to write. A question might include two sections on charities, then a section on a private purpose trust with a question mark over its validity, and a concluding section on a gift to an unincorporated association. One question spotted in a university exam paper contained four problems: a secret trust; certainty of objects; certainty of intention; and wound up with the doctrine of election — not a pretty sight. If you glance at the question, think 'charities', and plough into it, only to discover 20 valuable minutes later that you have to deal with a subject about which you know nothing, you have wasted a great deal of effort and lost, probably, a class or worse.

Needless to say, if you know each of the topics, then you do not have a problem. In fact, if your luck holds and you are thoroughly familiar with the case law for each point this question may be a dream ticket.

Three questions have been selected to illustrate these points. Question 1 mixes charitable trusts, discretionary trusts, covenants to settle and liability for breach of trust. Question 2 mixes constitution of trusts, *donationes mortis causa* and certainty of objects. Question 3 mixes the doctrine of conversion, secret trusts and trusts of imperfect obligation.

The main advice is: do not be taken by surprise by a pick 'n' mix question. Suspend disbelief, just because section (a) is on secret trusts does not mean the other sections must also be on the same theme. READ THE QUESTIONS CAREFULLY.

QUESTION 1

Four years ago Alpha transferred £100,000 to Beta 'upon trust to provide, at his discretion, grants for law students in the United Kingdom, absolute preference to be given to my relatives'. Shortly after, Alpha covenanted with Beta to transfer to Beta, upon the same trusts, any property he (Alpha) might subsequently acquire under the will of Gamma. Three years ago Gamma died, and in his will he bequeathed 10,000 shares in Delta Ltd to Alpha. Two years ago, Beta entrusted the £100,000 to Epsilon, a stockbroker, for investment.

Alpha died last month, without having taken steps to transfer the shares in Delta Ltd to Beta. In his will Alpha gave all his property to his niece, Omega. It is now discovered that Epsilon has vanished with the £100,000.

Discuss.

Commentary

The separate parts of the question are not intrinsically difficult, but the higher marks will be obtained by a student who can show how the different areas interact.

Suggested Answer

It is first necessary to consider who is entitled to the shares in Delta Ltd. As sole beneficiary of Alpha's will, Omega is entitled to the shares if they formed part of his estate at his death. They will not comprise part of such estate if they are the subject-matter of a fully constituted charitable trust. Alpha, however, never transferred the legal title to the shares to the trustee, Beta, as he had covenanted to do. Furthermore, there is no evidence that he did everything necessary to be done by him in order to perfect the transfer in equity: see *Milroy* v *Lord* (1862) 4 De GF & J 264 and *Re Rose* [1952] Ch 499, CA. The trust therefore, remains incompletely constituted in respect of the shares. There is no evidence that valuable consideration has been supplied for the creation of the trust. As regards the shares, therefore, the trust is an incompletely constituted voluntary settlement. Equity will not compel Alpha's estate to transfer the shares to Beta, since equity will not assist a volunteer: *Re Plumptre* [1910] 1 Ch 609. The person entitled to the shares is, therefore, Omega.

Nevertheless, even though the shares are not themselves bound by the trust, it is still necessary to consider whether Beta can sue Alpha's estate for damages for breach of covenant. It has been argued that a covenantee of a voluntary covenant should be able to sue for damages for its breach and hold such damages in trust for the volunteers: see Elliott (1960) 76 LQR 100. The courts, nevertheless, are opposed to such an action. In *Re Pryce* [1917] 1 Ch 234, the court would not direct the covenantees to sue, and in *Re Kay* [1939] Ch 329 it positively directed them not to sue. There is no objection to such an action if the covenantee is suing in respect of her own loss as beneficiary, as in *Cannon* v *Hartley* [1949] Ch 213; but this is not the situation in the problem. By contrast, in *Fletcher* v *Fletcher* (1844) 4 Hare 67, the court held that there was already a perfect trust of a chose in action: viz, the benefit of the covenant itself. This suggests that if Alpha intended the benefit of the covenant to comprise trust property, Beta will be obliged to sue Alpha's estate for damages for breach of covenant and to hold the substantial damages which he will recover upon the trusts declared. There is, however, no evidence that this was Alpha's intention.

An alternative explanation was proffered in *Re Cook's Settlement Trusts* [1965] Ch 902 by Buckley J. He considered that, whilst it might be possible to create a valid trust of the benefit of a covenant concerning property in existence and owned by the settlor at the date of the covenant, it is not possible to create a trust of the benefit of a covenant which relates to after-acquired property. If this view is followed, there can be no trust of the covenant in the problem.

However, even if a trust of a chose in action has been created, Beta will not hold it upon the trusts declared unless these are valid trusts. A trust to provide grants for law students is itself a valid charitable purpose within the second head of Lord Macnaghten's classification in *Pemsel's Case* [1891] AC 531: namely, for the advancement of education. The problem is whether the expression of an 'absolute preference' for Alpha's family denies it charitable status. For a trust to be charitable it must be for the public benefit. This means (inter alia) that a sufficient section of the community must be capable of benefiting. Where the beneficiaries are defined by reference to a personal nexus, which includes a family relationship, the trust is not charitable: *Re Compton* [1945] Ch 123, CA. Furthermore, in the context of the advancement of education, an indirect benefit to the public is insufficient: *Re Compton*.

Nevertheless, it was held in *Re Koettgen's Will Trusts* [1954] Ch 252, that provided the primary class is a sufficient section of the community, a preference for a private class will not destroy the trust's charitable nature. This case has not, however, met with general approval (see *IRC* v *Educational Grants Association Ltd* [1967] Ch 993, CA). Thus, the trust will not be charitable if the preference is not limited (as in *Re Koettgen*) to 75 per cent of the trust income. Secondly, it will not be charitable if the preferred class has priority: *Caffoor* v *ITC* [1961] AC 584, PC. In the problem the words used are 'absolute preference', which may suggest a priority. If so, the trust will fail to achieve charitable status on both grounds.

If it is not charitable, can the trust be valid as a private discretionary trust? It would probably satisfy the test for certainty of objects, since it would appear to be possible to say of any given person whether or not they are a law student in the United Kingdom: *McPhail* v *Doulton* [1971] AC 424, HL. It would probably also not fail for administrative unworkability, since the description of objects probably does form something like a class: *McPhail* v *Doulton*. Nevertheless, unless (which is unlikely) it can be construed as a trust for immediate distribution of capital, it would be void for perpetuity. Assuming this to be so, the benefit of any chose in action would be held by Beta on a resulting trust for the benefit of Alpha's estate. In practice, this means that the covenant is simply unenforceable.

If the purported trust is void, the money which Alpha transferred to Beta is also held on a resulting trust for Alpha's estate. Omega is, therefore, entitled to it. Since, however, the money has been lost, has Omega any action against Beta for breach of trust? A trustee may employ and pay an agent to transact any business or do any act required to be done in the execution of the trust: Trustee Act 1925, s. 23(1). The section would appear to apply to a trustee of a resulting trust. Under the section, a trustee is not responsible for the default of such agent if employed in good faith. Any agent must still be employed in his proper field (*Re Vickery* [1931] 1 Ch 572). This requirement would appear to be satisfied in Epsilon's case, as investment is the proper business of a stockbroker. Furthermore, there is nothing to indicate anything other than good faith on Alpha's part when he appointed Epsilon. Beta will not, therefore, be liable for the loss merely because he appointed Epsilon.

Nevertheless, Beta may be liable for any failure to supervise Epsilon subsequently. In particular, he may be liable for leaving such a large sum in his agent's hands for a long period without requiring him to account. A trustee may, however, have a defence under the Trustee Act 1925, s. 30, which provides that a trustee is liable only for his own acts and defaults and not for those of any person with whom trust moneys have been deposited, unless the loss happens through his own wilful default. In earlier cases, notably *Re Brier* (1884) 26 ChD 238, 'wilful default' had been interpreted objectively, i.e., as not displacing the standard of care laid down in *Speight* v *Gaunt* (1883) 9 App Cas 1 (viz, that of the prudent man of business acting in his own affairs). In *Re Vickery*, however, Maugham J construed the words subjectively, i.e., as requiring a consciousness of wrongdoing. Where the trust property is not placed under the agent's control, it has been held that s. 30 does not apply: *Re Lucking's Will Trusts* [1968] 1 WLR 866. But, in the problem, Beta did place the funds under Epsilon's control. If, therefore, Beta was not aware of his own wrongdoing in leaving the funds for a lengthy period in Epsilon's hands, he will escape liability to Alpha's estate.

QUESTION 2

Discuss, with reference to decided cases, whether any of the following words create a valid trust. Indicate any problems which may have to be overcome before a trust can be imposed in these cases.

(a)   Look, I am giving this cheque to our baby.

(b)   The money in my deposit account is as much yours as mine.

(c)   I hereby give to my executors and trustees £500,000 on trust to apply the said sum at their absolute discretion for the maintenance and support of red haired women in London.

(d)   It is my dying wish, Marjorie, that you should have my London flat. Here are the deeds and the keys, put them in your bag. My solicitor will sort out the details when I am dead.

Commentary

This question contains a mixed bag of problems relating to the constitution of a trust. It draws heavily on particular cases, which can make it very unattractive if you are not familiar with the exact case. In that sense, it is not a very sporting question. Many examiners try to avoid questions which rely on the student's knowledge of a particular case, preferring to test the understanding of general principles. However, if you are faced with a question of this type, and you know the relevant cases, then it can be a gift. Avoid the temptation of starting your answer with an immediate reference to the case. For example, do not start with: 'This is a *Jones* v *Lock* problem . . .'. Instead, state the issue raised by the question, then the general rule with exceptions, and then illustrate your answer with cases. Some questions of this sort can subtly vary the facts of the case. Watch out for those!

Suggested Answer

(a)   In order for a trust to be created there must be a clear manifestation of an intention to create a trust. The statement made implies a gift not a trust. For an effective transfer of a cheque, an indorsement is required. If this has not occurred, then the gift will fail. In *Jones* v *Lock* (1865) 1 Ch App 25, an attempt was made to argue that, in effect, the donor had made a declaration that he was a trustee of the cheque for the beneficiary. It was held that a failed gift will not be construed in equity as evidence of an intention to declare a trust. Although there is present an intention to benefit the donee, there is no intention present to hold the property as trustee. This was confirmed in *Richards* v *Delbridge* (1874) LR 18 Eq 11, where words written on a lease which indicated an intention to give the lease to the grandson of the leaseholder were held ineffective at common law to effect the transfer. Since they were words indicating a gift, they were ineffective in equity to operate as a declaration of trust.

Therefore, if the cheque has not been validly transferred, the words will not operate as a declaration by the donor of himself as trustee.

(b)   This statement again raises the issue of certainty of intention to create a trust. In this situation the holder of the deposit account has not made an attempt to transfer the account into joint names. It may be arguable, according to the circumstances of the case, that the account holder has manifested an intention to hold the account on trust by conduct. The words are not sufficient in themselves, but, coupled with the conduct of the parties, they may be. For example, in *Paul* v *Constance* [1977] 1 WLR 527, where money was put into an account in the sole name of Mr Constance, his assurances to Mrs Paul that the money in the account was owned jointly were held sufficient to indicate an intention by him to hold the account on trust for them jointly. In *Re Vandervell's Trusts (No. 2)* [1974] Ch 269, where money from a settlement was used to purchase shares in exercise of an option, it was held, that the conduct of the trustees in using this money and paying dividends into the settlement, constituted sufficient evidence of an intention to create a trust even though no specific words had been used.

Therefore, although it is difficult to state that the words are sufficient on their own to create a trust, coupled with other conduct there may be sufficient certainty of the requisite intention.

(c)   In this gift there is a clear intention to create a trust. However, the issue is whether a gift to red haired women in London is sufficiently certain to be carried out by the trustees. The trust appears to be discretionary. The test for certainty of objects in a discretionary trust was outlined in *McPhail* v *Doulton* [1971] AC 424, HL, where it was held that the test was the same as that established for powers in *Re Gulbenkian's Settlements* [1970] AC 508, HL. The test is 'can it be said with certainty that any given individual is or is not a member of the class?'

The problem of definition arises, therefore, in respect of red haired women. Can it be said whether any given person is or is not a member of the class? The problem is not, in this case, in proving whether a person is or is not within the class. Instead, the difficulty lies in defining the term red haired. Whereas all people may agree whether certain individuals are red haired, there may be some borderline cases where the trustees could not decide. The concept of what constitutes red hair may, therefore, be so unclear that it is impossible to carry out the trust.

Another problem might arise in relation to the width of the class. If a discretionary trust is so wide that it is administratively unworkable, this may invalidate it. In *McPhail* v *Doulton*, Lord Wilberforce suggested that a gift to the residents of Greater London might be so wide that it was unworkable. This was followed in *R* v *District Auditor, ex parte West Yorkshire Metropolitan County Council* (1986) 26 RVR 24 (QBD), where a discretionary trust was purportedly created for the inhabitants of the county of West Yorkshire. The description of objects was considered to be so large that the trust was invalidated for administrative unworkability. This would be different if the gift was construed as a mere power (see *Re Manisty's Settlement* [1974] Ch 17).

The difficulties inherent in validating this gift to red haired women indicate a capriciousness in the mind of the donor. While there is no general principle that a donor may not act capriciously, where the gift involves the exercise by a trustee of a fiduciary obligation, the position is different. The difficulties, in the first instance, of defining red hair, and secondly, in the potential width of the class, indicate an element of caprice which may cause a court to invalidate a gift on that ground alone (see *Re Hay's Settlement Trusts* [1982] 1 WLR 202).

(d)   It appears from the wording that this is a death bed gift. In order to effect a transfer of land at common law there should be a deed: Law of Property Act 1925, s. 52. There would appear to be no deed transferring legal ownership in this case. Nor does there appear to be any consideration given. Marjorie is, therefore, a volunteer. The normal principle is that equity will not assist a volunteer in enforcing an incompletely constituted gift.

However, there are some exceptions to this and one in particular, the principle of *donatio mortis causa*, may assist Marjorie. There are three conditions which must be satisfied before this exception will be allowed. The gift must be conditional on death, it must be made in contemplation of death and the donor must give the donee control over the gift (see *Cain v Moon* [1896] 2 QB 283).

Here, the question indicates that the gift is made in contemplation of death and it is not difficult to raise the presumption that it is, therefore, conditional on death. The donor states that the formalities will be dealt with after death. The subject matter of the gift is land. Until recently, it was thought that it was not possible for land to be the subject of a *donatio mortis causa*. However, this was changed by the Court of Appeal decision in *Sen v Hedley* [1991] Ch 425. In that case, someone who already had the keys of a house was given a bunch of keys including one to a steel box in the house containing the title deeds. It was held that the donor had parted with dominion over the house and the title deeds in circumstances otherwise satisfying the conditions for a *donatio mortis causa* and the gift was completed. It would, therefore, seem that as Marjorie has the keys, giving her physical control, and the deeds, this would be sufficient to give rise to the application of the rule that gifts made in contemplation of death are enforceable despite a lack of the appropriate formalities.

QUESTION 3

Sam, who died recently, appointed Tick and Tack as the executors and trustees of his will and made the following dispositions:

(a) £50,000 to my sister Doris feeling sure that she will give her son a reasonable amount.

(b) £30,000 to Tick and Tack for purposes of which I will inform them.

(c) My freehold property 'Dunroamin' to Tick and Tack upon trust to sell and to hold the net proceeds of sale for such worthy causes as they shall think fit.

(d) He left his residuary realty to his son Percy and his residuary personalty to his daughter Mavis.

Advise Tick and Tack as to the validity of these dispositions, and as to who should benefit if any of them fail.

Commentary

This is a question which requires a fairly detailed knowledge of different parts of an equity and trusts syllabus. You may be lucky and find that you remember the relevant law and cases, but unless you feel fairly confident of doing well on two of the four parts, you might be wise to leave it alone. It is a question on which you might scrape a pass if you know some law, but would find it difficult to score well.

Hard-pressed examiners like to be able to see clearly which part of a question they are marking. It will help the examiner, therefore, if you number each part of your answer and leave a space between the different parts.

Suggested Answer

(a) It is unlikely that the words in the disposition to Doris are sufficiently obligatory to attach a trust to the property in the hands of Doris. Such words are precatory words and since *Lambe* v *Eames* (1871) 6 Ch 597 and the Executors Act 1830, the courts will not lean in favour of a trust: they simply construe the words in the context of the instrument to ascertain if the trust obligation is imposed. In *Mussoorie Bank* v *Raynor* (1882) 7 App Cas 321, the words 'feeling confident' were held to be precatory and failed to impose a trust, and the words 'feeling sure' used here would probably similarly fail. Doris would therefore, take the gift beneficially.

Even if the words were sufficiently certain to impose a trust, a 'reasonable amount' would be too uncertain as regards subject matter. Although the court held in *Re Golay* [1965] 1 WLR 969, that a 'reasonable income' was capable of objective determination by reference to a person's life style, a reasonable amount in this case would not seem to have any objective criteria by which it could be assessed, and it would therefore fail.

(b)   This disposition could create a half secret trust if it is found to have the necessary element of obligation. Although the words 'upon trust' are not used, it seems fairly clear from the face of the will that Tick and Tack are not intended to take the disposition beneficially.

In the case of a half secret trust, the half secret trustees must accept the trust before the execution of the will. This does not appear to have happened, as Sam refers to a future communication. Although communication of the beneficiary at any time before death would be sufficient for a fully secret trust, there are dicta in *Blackwell* v *Blackwell* [1929] AC 318, HL, and it was accepted in *Re Bateman's Will Trusts* [1970] 1 WLR 1463, that this must be before the execution of the will in the case of a half secret trust. The reason given for this is that a communication after the will would allow the testator to change his mind and effectively make testamentary dispositions without complying with the Wills Act 1837. This is criticised as failing to take account of the fact that the secret trust arises from its acceptance by the trustees quite independently of the will.

Even if there has already been a communication of the purposes which Tick and Tack have accepted, it will still be invalid as there would then be an inconsistency on the face of the will, which is fatal to a half secret trust: *Re Keen* [1937] Ch 236. The will clearly refers to a future communication and evidence of a prior communication would be inconsistent with it.

(c)   This will impose a trust for sale as regards the property Dunroamin. There would appear to be a discretionary trust as regards the proceeds of sale, but the trust is a purpose trust. There are no objects of the trust who can, if necessary, enforce it against Tick and Tack. Moreover, a trust must be sufficiently certain for a court to enforce it if necessary and 'worthy objects' would be too vague. In *Re Atkinson's Will Trusts* [1978] 1 WLR 586, it was held that it would be impossible to confine worthy objects to charitable objects, so there is no possibility of this taking effect as a charitable trust. Although charitable trusts are purpose trusts, they are valid as they are enforceable by the Attorney-General. A non-charitable purpose trust fails, however, for certainty of objects, and also because it will infringe the rule against perpetual trusts. This trust will therefore fail.

The disposition in (a) will go to Doris beneficially as the gift itself is effective, and it is only the trust grafted onto it which fails. The disposition in (b) and (c) fail completely however, and will result back to the testator's residuary estate on failure.

The pecuniary legacy in (b) is personalty and will go as residuary personalty to Mavis. The effect of the trust for sale in (c) is to impose upon Tick and Tack a binding obligation to sell, so that the doctrine of conversion will apply. The property is regarded as personalty even before it is sold. It will, therefore, go to Mavis also.

Index

Advancement
  presumption of   107
  trustees power of   52-5, 144-5
Agent
  declaration of interest of   122
  liability of
    co-partners   128
    constructive notice   123-30
  liability of trustee for defaults of
    135-8, 202-3
Animals, trust for maintenance of
    81, 82, 86
Ante-nuptial agreements   33
Anton Piller order   10, 181-5, 188, 192-3
  carrying out of   184
  conditions for grant of   183-4
  ex parte application, necessity for   183
  full disclosure, requirement of   184
  mandatory nature of   192-3
  procedure   184-5
Assets, duty to convert   15, 173

Bankruptcy   54, 55
Breach of trust   34, 133, 153-69
  action in personam   163, 164
  agent, liability of trustee for defaults of
    135-8, 202-3
  constructive trusts and   103, 105, 122-6
  disposition of property in   103
  failure to comply with terms of trust
    158-61
  remaindermen, liability to   159-61
  set-off plea   160-1
  strangers liability for   100
  tracing *see* Tracing

Capriciousness   48, 205-6
Certainties, the three   20-31
  certainty of objects   23, 27, 31, 49-52,
    81-7, 202, 205
    indirect objects   86-7
    McPhail v *Doulton* test for
      31, 49-52, 57
  certainty of subject matter   23, 24-5, 27,
    30-1
  certainty of words/intention   23-5, 26-8,
    94-5, 208-9
    oral statements   27
    commercial cases   26-8
Chancery Division   18-19
Charitable trust   60-78, 200-3, 208-9
  Attorney General and   64, 69, 85
  charitable purpose requirement   62
  collecting boxes   78
  cy-près doctrine *see* Cy-près
  deserving purposes and   71
  disaster funds   69
  education, advancement of
    62, 63, 66, 201
  environment, preservation of   64
  failure of charitable purpose   74, 77-8
  fiscal exemptions and reliefs   71
  gun clubs   62,72
  insufficiency of estate   74, 77-8
  investment of funds   75-8
    ethical considerations   75-8
  lotteries   78
  perpetuities, rule against   70, 81
  personal nexus test   67, 201
  political purposes   64-5, 66
  poverty, relief of   66, 67-8, 74

Charitable trust — *continued*
  private class, preference for   201-2
  private trust distinguished   68-71
  public benefit requirement   62, 65-8,
    69, 201
  raffles   78
  recreational charities   63
  religion, advancement of   63-4, 66, 68
  remoteness of vesting, rule against   70
  sport   61, 62-3
  street collections   78
  tax exemptions   71
  trustees   70
  unidentifiable donors   77-8
Cheque
  charitable donations by   77-8
  donatio mortis causa of   46
Chose in action
  donatio mortis causa of   35, 45-6
  equitable assignment of   42
  trust of   39-40, 201
Common law   7
  equity distinguished   7-8, 16-19
Confidence, breach of   8-9
Confidential information   8-9
  injunction protecting   187-8
Constructive notice   123-30
Constructive trust   14, 100-30
  agent, liability of, constructive
    knowledge   122-30
  breach of trust, where   103, 105
  categories of   103
  co-ownership of property   103-4
  common intention   92, 107-8
  definition   102
  fiduciary relationship, profit from
    103, 104, 118-22
  fraudulent behaviour, where
    102, 103, 104
  implied trust distinguished   89-92
  incomplete transfer of legal title,
    where   103
  licence giving rise to   12
  mutual wills *see* Wills
  nature of   102-5
  new model   9, 10, 11-12, 100
  party's interest under, calculation of
    105-9
  proprietary estoppel   112-13
  resulting trust distinguished   89-92, 106
  secret trust *see* Secret trust
  specifically enforceable contract for
    sale, where   103
  stranger receiving trust property   122-6

Constructive trust — *continued*
  unconscionable behaviour, where
    100, 102, 103
  unjust enrichment, where   100, 102
Contract
  breach of, anticipatory, injunction
    against   8
  conditional   15
    doctrine of conversion, application
      of   173
  estate   14
  for lease   14
  oral, enforcement of   112
  privity of   11
  for sale of land   14, 112
    doctrine of conversion, application
      of   172, 175
  of service   186-7
  stipulations as to time in   6
  surplus funds, entitlement to   97-8
Contractual licence   10, 11-12
Conversion   13, 14-15, 171-6
  assets, hazardous, wasting or
    reversionary, duty to convert   15, 173
  co-ownership of land, where   173-6
  conditional contracts   173
  contract for sale of land   172
  contracts for the sale of property   175
  definition   14
  Howe v *Earl of Dartmouth*, rule in
    15, 173
  joint-tenancy where   173-16
  Lawes v *Bennet*, rule in   13, 15
  retrospective operation of   173, 176
Copyright, breach of   10
Court of Appeal   7
Court of Chancery   7
Courts, fusion of   7-8
Covenant
  breach of
    damages for   34, 38, 39
    statute-barring   36
  not a consideration in equity   39
  voluntary   34
Cy-près doctrine   71-4
  failure of charitable purpose   77-8
  insufficiency of estate   74, 77-8
  unidentifiable donors   78

Damages
  at common law   8
  breach of covenant   34, 38, 39
  'clean hands', necessity for   8
  in equity   8

Damages — *continued*
  substituted for specific performance
    196
Deeds of covenant   75
Dependants, meaning of, *McPhail* v
    Doulton test   50
Discretionary trust   1, 24, 47-59
  certainty of objects   31, 49-52
  conceptual certainty   31
  duty of trustees under   57
  position of beneficiaries under   58
  power distinguished   47, 56-9
    construction of document   58-9
  private   202
Donatio mortis causa   35, 43-6, 206
  of chose in action   35, 45-6
  delivery of donor's own cheque   46
  dominion, parting with   45-6
  key
    delivery of   45
    duplicate, retaining of   45, 46
  of land   46
  suicide, made in contemplation of   45

Easements, equitable   8
Election
  doctrine of   176, 177
  will under   177
Employment contract   186-7
Equity
  'clean hands', necessity for   8, 13
  common law distinguished   7-8, 16-19
  development of   16-17
  doctrines of   170-8
  fusion of administration of law and   6-9
  maxims of   13, 17, 22, 170
  meaning   16-19
  nature of   4-19
  new developments in   9-12
  rules of precedent and   10
  volunteer, will not assist   33-5
Estate contract   14

Gift
  conditional, certainty of objects   31
  *donatio mortis causa see Donatio mortis
    causa*
  imperfect, equity will not perfect   33
  inter vivos, rule in *Strong* v *Bird*
    34-5, 42
  perfection of where donee becomes
    executor   34-5, 42-3
  trust distinguished   30, 204
  validity of   48

High Court   7
  divisions of   18-19

Implied trust   88-99
  constructive trust distinguished   89-91
  meaning   89
  resulting trust distinguished   89-92
In loco parentis   92-5
Injunction   10, 185-6
  anticipatory breach of contract   8
  confidential information, protecting
    187-8
  ex parte   189
  interlocutory   189
    American Cyanamid   189-93
    Anton Piller order *see Anton Piller*
      order
    balance of convenience, test of   190-2
    irreparable damage must follow
      refusal   189
    Mareva injunction *see Mareva*
      injunction
    prima facie case   190, 191, 192
    requirements for   189-93
    in trade disputes   191, 192
  nuisance, stopping   8
  restrictive covenant, breach of   191
Intention, certainty of *see* Certainties,
  the three

Land
  co-ownership of, conversion and   173-6
  contract for sale of   14, 112, 195
    application of doctrine of conversion
      172
  donatio mortis causa of   46
  investment in   139-40
  registration of   8
  trust of, creation of   29
  trust for sale of   14-15, 143, 172, 208
Law of Property Act 1925   20-31
Lawes v *Bennet*, rule in   13, 15
Lease
  contract for   14
  investment in   143-4
  trustee of   120-1
  as wasting asset   15
Licence
  constructive trust, giving rise to   12
  contractual   11-12

McPhail v *Doulton* test
    31, 49-52, 57
Maintenance orders   54, 55

Mareva injunction   11, 188-9, 192, 193
  assets, removal of   188-9
  ex parte application for   188
Marriage
  as consideration for trust   33, 38
  settlement   33, 35-40
Membership subscriptions   75
Monuments, trust for maintenance of
  80, 81, 86

Non-charitable purpose trust
  81, 83-4, 85-7
  surplus funds, entitlement to   95-9
Notice, equitable doctrine of   8
Nuisance, injunction preventing   8

Object, certainty of *see* Certainties, the
  three
Option, exercise of   15

Part performance, doctrine of   8
Perpetuities, rule against   70, 81, 83-4
Powers
  discretionary trust distinguished   56-9
    construction of document   58-9
  donees of, duty of   57-8
  exercise of   58
  fiduciary   47-8, 57
  mere   47-8, 50, 57
  position of objects of   58
  of sale   172
  trust distinguished   47-8
Proprietary estoppel   10, 11, 12, 35, 112-3

Queen's Bench Division   19

Rectification   10
Registration of equitable interests   8
Relatives
  meaning of   31
  McPhail v *Doulton* test   50
Remaindermen
  conversion and   15
  liability of trustees to   159-61
  limitation period and   159-60
Rent review clauses   6
Rescission   10
Restrictive covenants   8, 10, 191
Resulting trust   28, 34, 70, 88-99
  automatic   90
  construction, questions of   92-5
  constructive trust distinguished
    89-92, 106
  implied trust distinguished   89-92

Resulting trust — *continued*
  in loco parentis   92-5
  meaning   89
  non-charitable unincorporated
    associations, surplus funds of   95-9
  party's interest under, calculation of
    106
  presumed   90, 93
  strangers, transfers to   93, 94

Satisfaction, doctrine of   176, 178
Secret trust   43, 103, 104, 113-18
  communication must be in testator's
    lifetime   116
  disclaimer by trustee   117
  half-secret trust   114, 116, 117, 208
  joint tenants   117-18
  operates outside will   115-18
  sealed envelope, details handed over in
    113-15
  secret trustee predeceasing testator   117
  tenants in common   117-18
Shares
  held in trust   40-3
  transfer of   38, 200-3
Specific performance   10, 185-9, 193-7
  construction cases   194, 196
  contracts to build or repair   196-7
  damages substituted for   196
  discretionary character of   194, 195
  mutuality, lack of   195
  personal property, contracts relating to
    194-5
  refusal of   195-7
  supervision of   194, 196
    constant, requirement of   195-6, 197
  volunteers and   33, 34
Stranger, liability for breach of trust   100
Strike action, interlocutory injunctions
  and   191
Subject matter, certainty of *see*
  Certainties, the three
Suicide, *donatio mortis causa* made in
  contemplation of   45
Superior courts, amalgamation of   7
Supreme Court of Judicature, creation of
  7

Tombs, trust for maintenance of   81, 86
Tracing   153-69
  at common law   162, 166
  in equity   161-4, 166
  fiduciary relationship, requirement of
    8, 155-8

Tracing — *continued*
  identification of property   163-4
  innocent volunteer, position of
    162-3, 168
  mixed funds   156, 157, 162, 166-9
  money paid under mistake of fact   157
Trade disputes, interlocutory injunctions
  in   191, 192
Trade secrets, breach of   182
Trade union, dissolution of, surplus funds
  97
Trust
  administration of   131-52
  administrative workability
    48, 51, 202, 205
  animals, maintenance of   81, 82, 86
  ante-nuptial agreeements   33
  breach of *see* Breach of trust
  certainties, the three *see* Certainties,
    the three
  cestui que   171-2
  charitable *see* Charitable trust
  of choses in action   39-40, 201
  constitution of   32-46, 203-6
  constructive *see* Constructive trust
  declaration of   29
  discretionary *see* Discretionary trust
  documents, right of beneficiaries to
    inspect   134
  evidenced in writing   29
  fixed   48, 50
    position of beneficiaries under   58
  gift distinguished   30, 204
  of imperfect obligation   79-87
  implied *see* Implied trust
  intention, certainty of *see* Certainties,
    the three
  intention to create   30, 204-5
  of land *see* Land
  law of, nature of   4-19
  limited   14
  marriage as consideration for   33
  monuments, maintenance of   80, 81, 86
  non-charitable purpose   81, 83-4, 85-7
  objects, certainty of *see* Certainties,
    the three
  perpetual, rules against   70, 81,
    83-4, 202
  power distinguished   47-8
  power of sale, with   15
  private, charitable trust distinguished
    68-71
  protective   48, 52-5
  purpose   83, 84-7, 208-9

Trust — *continued*
  remoteness of vesting, rule against   70
  resulting *see* Resulting trust
  revoking   149-52
  for sale   172
  secret *see* secret trust
  shares held in   40-3
  subject matter, certainty of *see*
    Certainties, the three
  tombs, maintenance of   81, 86
  transfer of   149-52
  variation of   149-52
  will, creation by   58-9
  words, certainty of *see* Certainties,
    the three
Trustee
  advancement, power of   144-5
  agent, responsibility for defaults of
    135-8, 202-3
  assets, conversion of   143-4
  in bankruptcy   54, 55
  breach of duty   137
  breach of trust *see* Breach of trust
  charitable trusts   70
  co-trustees, liability of   160
  default, wilful   160
  discretionary powers   57, 132-5
    see also Discretionary trust
    exercie of   133-5
  duties of   57
  ex parte Lacey, rule in   121
  investments   138-42
    advice in relation to   140
    ethical considerations   75-8
    extension of powers   140-2
    in land   139-40
    leases   143-4
    narrower-range   139-40, 141
    rule in *Howe* v *Earl of Dartmouth*
      143
    wider-range   139-40
  land held on trust for sale   143-5
  of lease   120-1
  minors, maintenance of   145-9
  misuse of position   120
  paid   133
  private trusts   70
  professional   133, 158, 159
  purchase of trust property prohibited
    121
  remaindermen, liability to   159-61
  standard of care   132-5, 159
    of prudent man   132-3, 138, 159
  wilful default   160

Unconscionable behaviour   100, 102, 103
Unincorporated associations
  gifts to   80, 83-4, 86-7
  surplus funds, entitlement to   95-9
Unjust enrichment   100, 102

Volunteer
  equity will not assist   33-40
    exceptions   34-5
  marriage settlement   35-40
  specific performance and   33, 34

Wills
  election under   177
  mutual   100, 103, 114-15
    enforceability   109-13
    trust established under   111
  trusts created by   58-9
Words, certainty of *see* Certainties,
    the three
Writing, trust evidenced in   29